An Introduction
To The Philosophy
Of Religion

WILLIAM J. ABRAHAM

Seattle Pacific University

PRENTICE-HALL, INC., Englewood Cliffs, New Jersey 07632

Library of Congress Cataloging in Publication Data
Abraham, William J. (William James), 1947–
    An introduction to the philosophy of religion.
    Bibliography: p. 252
    Includes index.
    1. Religion—Philosophy.   I. Title.
BL53.A24   1985   200'.1   84-13446
ISBN 0-13-491887-8

Editorial/production supervision and
    interior design: Kate Kelly
Cover design: Lundgren Graphics, Ltd.
Manufacturing buyer: Harry P. Baisley

To Basil Mitchell

Printed in the United States of America

10 9 8 7 6 5 4 3 2 1

ISBN 0-13-491887-8   01

Prentice-Hall International, Inc., *London*
Prentice-Hall of Australia Pty. Limited, *Sydney*
Editora Prentice-Hall do Brasil, Ltda., *Rio de Janeiro*
Prentice-Hall Canada Inc., *Toronto*
Prentice-Hall of India Private Limited, *New Delhi*
Prentice-Hall of Japan, Inc., *Tokyo*
Prentice-Hall of Southeast Asia Pte. Ltd., *Singapore*
Whitehall Books Limited, *Wellington, New Zealand*

Contents

v   *Contents*

Chapter Twenty
PHILOSOPHY AND COMMITMENT   239

FOR FURTHER READING   252

INDEX   254

Preface

The demands laid upon an author of an introductory textbook in philosophy of religion are enormous. Decisions have to be made on several levels, and no matter how carefully they are pondered, different philosophers will disagree vehemently about their merits. This is true generally in philosophy but especially so in philosophy of religion.

THE NEED FOR A COMPREHENSIVE INTRODUCTION

Ideally students need a comprehensive introduction, which will give a sense of the wealth of material to be covered without losing out on careful analysis and rigor. The former tends to be sacrificed for the sake of the latter. Some teachers prefer detailed and even technical treatment of a few issues rather than a general introduction to a broader set of questions. Clearly it is essential that beginning students explore some central philosophical questions in depth. Yet this can be done without sacrificing the need for students to develop adequate horizons about the boundaries of the discipline.

In this text I have sought to meet both conditions in this fashion. On the one hand, I have covered a very wide range of topics. This means that the treatment cannot but be cursory in places. I am content if the student gets a good idea of some of the questions which arise on the topic and comes to realize that there is a vast terrain which has yet to be discovered. On the other hand, in certain areas I have not only given a broad treatment of the issues in hand but provided detailed exposition and evaluation of important positions currently held. For example, much of the first half of the book is devoted to the justification of religious belief. In this part I have provided summaries and evaluations of the classical arguments for and against theism and yet also focused specifically on the argument from religious experience and the problem of evil. Within that I have also examined in some detail the arguments propounded of late by Alvin Plantinga, Basil Mitchell, and Richard Swinburne.

No matter what one does, some subjects have to be left out. For example, there is no developed treatment of theological predication. It is omitted because I deal with the cognitive status of religious language and because on balance I think other topics relatively more important. Even with the topics which remain one could easily devote a whole book to each of them and still not exhaust them. In the last analysis different teachers will prefer very different topics, and one cannot please everyone.

THE SCOPE AND CHARACTER OF THIS INTRODUCTION

Crucially relevant to the choice of topics which one makes is one's conception of the scope and nature of the discipline of philosophy of religion. It is not sufficiently recognized that philosophy of religion belongs both in philosophy departments and in religion and theology departments. At a time when it is common in educated circles to dismiss opponents by construing their proposals as "theology," it is not surprising that some philosophers reject such arrangements with scorn. Occasionally one finds a fascinating alliance between philosophers and theologians to keep philosophy of religion out of religion and theology entirely. I do not share this approach to the philosophy of religion. On the contrary, philosophy of religion has a vital role to play in departments of religion and theology. It can play this role without at all sacrificing its integrity as a discipline within philosophy. Indeed, philosophers of religion need to keep in contact with the material they seek to explore and examine, and this is guaranteed when philosophy of religion is given a proper place within religion and theology.

The main reason for this policy stems from the fact that crucial philosophical questions arise not just about the foundations of religious belief but about the internal content of the various religious traditions of the world. It is agreed on all sides that philosophical questions arise about the concept of God and about the justification of the central tenets of theism. But philosophical considerations also impinge on such theological issues as the relation between free will and divine sovereignty or the nature of divine revelation. It is wholly artificial to limit philosophical investigation to the former matters. The latter deserve attention in their own right; they deserve far more analysis than the current orthodoxy about the limits of the discipline will allow. This is a serious weakness in most introductory texts, which I have sought to avoid.

To be sure, when this policy is pursued in detail it means that students must become acquainted with the content of the religious tradition under review. Moreover, it also means that it is quite impossible sometimes to avoid straying over into theology proper. The former can easily be supplied by making the relevant religious material available, while the latter is a fact of life which has to be accepted. It is unspoken testimony to this fact that the set of essays most responsible for the revival of philosophy of religion in Britain and now justly famous worldwide was called *New Essays in Philosophical Theology.*[1]

Perhaps it is paradoxical that the editors of that volume are atheists, but the paradox highlights another dilemma for the author of introductory textbooks in philosophy of religion. Should the author express an opinion on the specific religious or theological topics being treated? Some modern philosophers, following Wittgenstein, have held that philosophy leaves everything as it is and that philosophers have no right to pronounce on the disputes about first-order religious discourse. On this view philosophers should confine themselves to an examination of the grammar of religious language without committing themselves either way to its actual usage. This stricture depends on assumptions about language which have now been abandoned. In any case many philosophers have happily pronounced in the past on the merits of various religious proposals. In this they were correct. It is restrictive and artificial to cast the philosopher as a neutral observer of the religious scene. Philosophy of religion deals with perennial issues which are inordinately controversial because of their self-involving relevance to life generally. It is inevitable that the author's personal convictions will sooner or later become manifest or intrude.

Yet *intrude* is surely the wrong word in this context. It suggests that those convictions get in the way and should be eliminated if at all possible. But suppose a philosopher holds, with Hume, that theology and religion seem to be intellectually bankrupt. Or, to go further, suppose a philosopher shares, with Nietzsche, the view that religious beliefs are not only false but intellectually corrupt and dangerous. Suppose, on the other side, he or she holds, with Locke, that religious belief can be justified, or agrees with Aquinas and Berkeley that religious beliefs and practices are essential to the proper fulfillment of human destiny. In such circumstances it is question begging to seek to prevent that philosopher from coming to such conclusions. To be sure, most of the arguments deployed must be recognizably philosophical in nature, but there must be freedom to follow the argument where it leads, and hasty judgments must not be made about what is to count as a recognizably philosophical argument. Moreover, retreating to some kind of neutrality on the issues tends to be illusory, and it takes the life and blood out of the discipline. One wonders what Locke, Berkeley, or Hume would have written in philosophy of religion should they have had to abide by such a convention.

[1] Antony Flew and Alasdair MacIntyre, eds., *New Essays in Philosophical Theology* (London: SCM Press, 1955).

These remarks provide a brief explanation for two features of this book. It explains first why I have included examination of particular religious doctrines rather than confined my attention to the standard topics associated with theism. Specific religious issues invite philosophical analysis and scrutiny in their own right, and beginning students should be made aware of this. So in the second half I have included material on such topics as freedom and grace, divine revelation, and the relation between religion and science.

Secondly, it explains why I have decided to articulate and develop a particular position on the issues addressed. As it happens, I share the minority opinion among contemporary philosophers that religious belief is capable of rational assessment and can be rationally justified. The broad outlines of the case for these claims are presented here; it is not my intention to offer a full-dress defense of them, as this would exclude the presentation and assessment of contrary positions. Furthermore, in the examination of particular doctrines I have not hesitated to pronounce a verdict at times. Students will quickly discover that my conclusions are contested within both philosophy and religion. Their own thoughtful reactions will be the best evidence for this. Sometimes they will have no difficulty pointing out the error of my ways; sometimes, I hope, they will have great difficulty. I have only one aim: I want them to seek and find the truth.

THE FOCUS ON CHRISTIANITY

A further feature of my approach needs mention at this point. For the most part I have concentrated in the discussions on the religious traditions of the West, more particularly on Christianity. This should not be interpreted as a parochial prejudice motivated by partisan ends. It rests on three considerations. First, philosophy of religion should concern itself not with the religion in the abstract but with actual, living religious traditions. Necessarily this in the end involves focusing on some particular religious tradition. To cover more than one leads either to superficiality or to an excess of religious exposition. This policy is in line with the way in which the classical philosophers have worked. Secondly, focusing on Christianity is appropriate because it is this religion with which most students are likely to be familiar. Should they be fortunate enough to be acquainted with other religious traditions, working through the present text will still be worthwhile. They will be able to identify issues which confront almost every religious tradition, and they will be shown in detail how philosophy impinges on one major religious tradition. I hope that this will encourage them to explore their chosen religious tradition with thoroughness. Lastly, I have focused on Christianity because detailed attention to it shows up the need for philosophical examination of the internal content of religion. This emphasis has led in places to the exposition of particular doctrines and of the views of particular theologians. Again the choice at this level can be contested, but I have tried to gravitate towards those issues which can be found in the classical Christian heritage. Be it noted that despite the concentration on the Christian tradition, I have included a chapter on the relationship among world religions.

A COMMENT ON STYLE

I have varied my approach to the topics covered. Sometimes I have provided a survey of the issues and arguments; sometimes I have concentrated on one issue and examined it in some detail. Occasionally I have expounded and evaluated the arguments of the great philosophers, ancient and modern; occasionally I have set out options in my own terms, relating them only marginally to actual positions. In certain places I move rather quickly through a quicksand of philosophical problems, providing footnotes to be followed up; in other places I provide very basic, elementary exposition, giving everyday illustrations to explain a point. Here I bring an issue to closure; elsewhere I outline a tentative suggestion for new directions.

This will not suit the needs of most advanced students, but it will kindle and retain the interest of the many students who unfortunately give up philosophy of religion prematurely. Too many have abandoned the subject because it has become excessively technical and far removed from religion and from life. By meeting them halfway at times I hope to attract them into the discipline, and they can then go to the more technical work as required. Besides, I agree with Hume that philosophy is a more regular and methodical operation of the kind of reasoning we use in common life.[2] An introductory text should reflect this judgment not just in its content but in its style.

ACKNOWLEDGMENTS

The author gladly acknowledges the generous help that was given to him in the preparation of this book. Robert Davis was a great source of encouragement at the outset. Jerry Wall and Patrick Roche gave invaluable assistance by courteously giving their evaluation of much of the argument. Frank Gourley helped enormously by discussing at length the content of chapter 10. David Livingstone did the same for chapter 8. My wife, Muriel, cheerfully and patiently supported me through it all. Lastly, Marbeth Reid came as near to perfection as is possible in the typing. The mistakes that remain despite all this precious help are entirely my own.

[2] David Hume, *Dialogues Concerning Natural Religion* (New York: Hafner, 1948), p. 9.

Chapter One
Philosophy Of Religion

Philosophy understands naught of divine matters. I do not say that men may not teach and learn philosophy; I approve thereof, so that it may be within reason and moderation. Let philosophy remain within her bounds, as God has appointed, and let us make use of her as of a character in a comedy; but to mix her up with divinity may not be endured.[1]

This caustic comment of Martin Luther is very revealing. Luther would not have been very worried if philosophers had agreed to embark on an eternal strike. Life might in such circumstances be somewhat more boring than usual, but nothing essential would be lost. In this judgment he is typical of the majority of mankind. Much as people may admire the existence of philosophers from a distance, it is difficult to imagine many mourning their removal from the world. At best the reaction would be one of indifference.

If their removal would be a matter of indifference to the general run of mankind, it would almost certainly be a matter of joy to many students. Many do not flock to lectures on philosophy of religion with manifest enthusiasm; there is often a tendency to treat it as a cross that has to be borne if the resurrection to a diploma or a degree is to be reached.

[1] Hugh T. Kerr, ed., *A Compend of Luther's Theology* (Philadelphia: Westminster Press, 1956), p. 4.

SUSPICIONS OF PHILOSOPHY IN RELIGION

Philosophers are not apt to pay too much attention to Luther's comment. His view reflects a classical Protestant reaction to philosophy and thus constitutes a minority report rather than an agreed opinion. Religions vary enormously in their response to philosophy. The great Eastern religious traditions, for example, embody at times an explicitly philosophical approach to reality. Yet it is worth pausing to look at the suspicion of Luther more closely. His remarks reflect a longstanding attitude to philosophy from within the Christian religion, an attitude which also crops up in Judaism and Islam.

It is easy for philosophers to ignore this suspicion. In a very critical mood, they might dismiss it as caused by laziness. After all, they might say, the vast majority of people are content to live in a world of self-inflicted prejudice and opinion. Religious believers in their varied complexities are no exception at this point. To think long and hard on fundamental matters demands discipline and hard work; the lazy and indolent will necessarily object to this and cast around philosophy a halo of suspicion. In a more expansive mood philosophers might be more charitable and say that this ingrained suspicion is due less to laziness than to fear. The fear in question is the fear of losing one's faith. If one asks too many questions then doubts may arise, and if doubts arise who is to say where it might end? Who is to say that one may not become an agnostic or even an atheist? So no wonder religious believers are suspicious of philosophy, they want to protect their beliefs from criticism.

Undoubtedly these considerations help explain why religious believers are often hostile to philosophy and why some philosophers are hostile to religion. But as they stand, they are incomplete. Such suspicion as does exist reaches far deeper than these explanations will allow. No doubt some are lazy and others afraid, but theologians and believers who are neither of these have been deeply suspicious of philosophy. The reasons for this suspicion are understandable. Two of the more significant as revealed by the Christian tradition deserve mention at this point.

To begin with, the theologian might understandably protest that his or her religious faith has always involved a stumbling block to the world. As Paul, one of the first Christian theologians, expressed it:

> For the Word of the cross is folly to those who are perishing, but to us who are being saved it is the power of God. For it is written, "I will destroy the wisdom of the wise, and the cleverness of the clever I will thwart." Where is the wise man? Where is the scribe? Where is the debater of this age? Has not God made foolish the wisdom of the world? For since in the wisdom of God, the world did not know God through wisdom, it pleased God through the folly of what we preach to save those who believe.[2]

Much as some may like, one cannot dismiss this material as insignificant. This is no Pauline aberration; it is central to his theology, and his theme if not his exact words has been revived again and again in the history of theological ideas.

[2] 1 Cor. 1:18–21. (All biblical quotations are taken from the Revised Standard Version. Used by permission.)

The surface implications of his claim, even when we make allowances for hyperbole and dramatic rhetoric, are obvious. On this view the content of the Christian message is not something that is readily acceptable to the wise and the reasonable. It is far from obvious and sensible; indeed at first sight it is foolishness and madness. At best, therefore, reason, if it is not a positive hindrance to faith, may be of limited value. So religious believers must be aware of the limitations of philosophy. At the very least, there is no guarantee that philosophy is a blessing; it may be a snare and a distraction.

Here surely is a much more obvious cause for the latent hostility there has always been directed to philosophy by the believer. There is a self-confessed foolishness about faith that one cannot ignore. Philosophy, with its emphasis on reason, clarity, and logic, will forever tempt one to ignore this foolishness. It should not surprise us therefore if believers are uneasy about taking a course in the philosophy of religion. This unease is reinforced by their initial impressions, if not their own experience, of philosophy itself. Here we come to a second reason for suspicion on the part of religious believers.

As far as first impressions go, the image of the philosopher is that of a sceptic. But the scepticism is not of the ordinary sort. Most of us are sceptical—we are sceptical of what we read in the paper; we are sceptical of politicians; we are sceptical of astrologers; we are sceptical of reports about UFO's. The philosopher's scepticism is disturbing in at least two ways when we compare it with these examples.

First, his or her scepticism is deliberate and studied. Thus modern philosophy began with the doubts of Descartes, who proceeded to make doubt the cornerstone of his approach to philosophical problems.

> Because I wish to give myself entirely to search after truth, I thought it was necessary for me to adopt an apparently opposite course and to reject as absolutely false everything concerning which I could imagine the least ground of doubt, in order to see whether afterwards there remained anything in my beliefs which was entirely certain.[3]

Here is the philosopher's mandate to disbelieve; he or she has a professional duty to disbelieve. The religious person by contrast is a believer. He or she has a duty to do the opposite and believe. So no wonder there will be a clash between the two, or so it would seem.

There is a further reason why the philosopher's scepticism is disturbing. It is not just deliberate and studied, it is directed against beliefs that most people of common sense take for granted. Freddie the fireman will be naturally sceptical about the report of a fire that has come to him from dubious sources. But Freddie the philosopher might be sceptical of the existence of the fire that stands before his very eyes. Bertie the butcher might wonder whether Abraham Lincoln was born in Kentucky rather than, say, Washington. But Bertie the philosopher might worry whether any event has taken place in the past. Annabel the accountant might query

---

[3] René Descartes, *A Discourse on Method*, pt. 4.

whether in certain circumstances she might not cheat the internal revenue service. But Annabel the philosopher might query whether she should not cheat the internal revenue service in every conceivable circumstance. Harriet the hairdresser might be driven to wonder whether the president had a wise turn of mind at all, especially given his fumbling attempts to increase the rights and status of women. But Harriet the philosopher might be driven to question whether anyone has a mind at all, even herself.

In other words, the scepticism of philosophers is of a very general sort. They ask themselves strange, difficult, and abstract questions about the external world, about the existence of other minds, about the foundations of our knowledge of the past and the foundations of morality, and so on. No wonder beginning students are both perplexed and puzzled. They instinctively feel the cold draft of scepticism eroding their most cherished convictions. If they cannot believe that the external world exists or that the past exists or that other minds exist, they can believe nothing. In such straights it were better to crush one's doubts and let philosophy be forgotten.

It should surely not take us by surprise therefore if we find that theologians have from time to time declared war on philosophy. Dim awareness of the foolishness of faith confirmed by one's general image of the philosopher is enough to explain this declaration of war. Nor can we deny the theologian the theoretical right to declare such a war, for we cannot guarantee in advance that the philosopher must always be allowed to say the last word; the matter has to be argued through to that conclusion.

OUTRIGHT HOSTILITY AND ITS INADEQUACY

There is in fact a reputable tradition that sees philosophy as intrinsically irreligious. One of the best examples of this tradition is Tertullian of Carthage. Tertullian was born around 150 A.D., was trained as a lawyer, and was converted to Christianity in his thirties. In reaction against the encroachments of Gnostic rationalism, Tertullian branded philosophy as heretical. Heresies, as he saw them, were nothing less than the ancient errors of the philosophers transposed to the level of faith. To confuse revelation and philosophy, as the heretics do, is to be unfaithful to revelation, for "What indeed has Athens to do with Jerusalem? What concord is there between the Academy and the Church? What between heretics and Christians?"[4] This text of itself would suggest that Tertullian was anti-intellectual. There is worse to come.

> The son of man was crucified; I am not ashamed of it. And the Son of God died; it is by all means to be believed, because it is absurd. And he was buried and rose again; the fact is certain, because it is impossible.[5]

[4]Quoted in Justo L. Gonzalez, *A History of Christian Thought* (Nashville: Abingdon, 1970), vol. I, p. 179.
[5]Ibid.

What is anyone committed to the life of the mind to make of such claims? It would be easy to dismiss it all as an outburst of irrationalism which should be ignored. What is called for however, is historical and intellectual sensitivity. Tertullian is far from being a blind irrationalist. He is registering a protest against unrestrained speculation in religious matters. As he sees it, philosophy is a speculative enterprise, which tends to ignore or destroy the riches of divine revelation. Such a claim demands to be carefully examined rather than quickly dismissed, not least because it finds an echo in such later figures as Pascal, Kierkegaard, and Barth. Moreover, it has been attractive to generations of orthodox theologians over the centuries. Later, therefore, we shall take time to examine the concept of revelation and see why it is such an important idea.

Taken as a whole, this tradition of hostility to philosophy has its merits. It rightly highlights how crucial revelation is in claims to discern the intentions of a transcendent God, as I shall argue later. Furthermore, it awakens us to the danger of hyperintellectualism in religion by showing the importance of the personal and inward character of actual faith in God. Yet again, this tradition safeguards the mystery and transcendence of God insisting that those who study religion must grapple with the possible limitations of all thought about the divine. All this is important. But we can take note of all this without branding philosophy as intrinsically antireligious. The issue requires greater dexterity than this tradition allows. Overall, it merits the following comments on its inadequacy.

First, this tradition itself tends to rely heavily on philosophical argument, sometimes without realizing it. Thus Tertullian was much indebted to Stoicism. More significantly, it is clear that both Kierkegaard and Barth, who shared much of Tertullian's hostility to philosophy, were heavily dependent on the philosophy of Kant and his claims about the limits of reason in theology. To put it at its simplest: both Barth and Kierkegaard say that philosophy can neither prove nor disprove the objects of religious faith. But this view itself depends upon philosophical argument and cannot merely be taken for granted just because it harmonizes conveniently with a certain view of religion. If one is dependent on philosophical argument, it is surely much better that one admit it and satisfy oneself that one is not led astray at this juncture.

Secondly, this tradition fails to see that philosophy is too rich and too complex to be dismissed in a sweeping fashion. Philosophy, like everything else that is human, is subject to change. What Paul, for example, said against the Athens of the first century may not at all fit the Oxford or Harvard of the twentieth century. Changes are too deep to allow this kind of brutal application of Paul's teaching to go unchallenged.

The richness and diversity of philosophical conclusions and methods are in fact well illustrated by the history of the relation between philosophy and theology. As an academic subject, philosophy of religion is a relative newcomer. It stems from the eighteenth century when Kant, Hume, and others began to consider religion as a distinct phenomenon susceptible to investigation in its own right in a critical and systematic way. But philosophers have always found time to comment on religion. We can isolate four variant attitudes that take a more positive approach.

Philosophy has seen itself as a religion. Thus it has attempted to lead people to a quasi-religious view of the world and a quasi-religious view of life. This position makes a religion out of philosophy. Plato, Platonists, and Neoplatonism are good examples. In modern philosophy Spinoza and Hegel provide illustrations.

Philosophy has seen itself as an essential complement to religion. On this view philosophy supplies an underlying world view or a metaphysical program which will furnish an intellectual foundation for religion. It provides a conceptual backbone without which a religion will necessarily be incomplete. Idealism in the nineteenth century and Process Philosophy in the twentieth have attempted to play such a role.

Philosophy has seen itself as the positive handmaid of religion. On this view its task is defensive or apologetic. It justifies the foundational beliefs of faith and defends the details of faith in a negative way by showing their negative possibility, i.e., they are not self-contradictory. We might call this the classical position: it develops a synthesis of faith and reason. Undoubtedly its most brilliant exponent was Thomas Aquinas, but he is one of a long line of thinkers which includes Origen, Augustine, Abelard, Locke, John Wesley, Bishop Butler, Basil Mitchell, and Richard Swinburne.

Philosophy has seen itself as the negative servant of religion. This position differs from the previous in that philosophy has no justificatory role with regard to religion. There is no grand synthesis of faith and reason; the aim is more modest, for philosophy's role is to make room for faith. It establishes that religion is a possibility. Philosophy demonstrates its own limitations with respect to the object of religious faith, but it leaves open the possibility of religion. Perhaps the best example is Kant, but this position was shared by Al Ghazzali, the great Muslin philosopher, and in our own day is capably represented by Alvin Plantinga. This was probably the position of Luther and Calvin, though there is considerable debate about the latter.

Philosophy has seen itself as an analytic tool in the clarifying of religious language. Philosophy of religion, on this reading, is the analysis of the function of religious language. Is religious language descriptive of the way things are, or is it really moral or poetic or emotive or unique? The key inspiration here is the modern philosopher Wittgenstein, who has influenced such scholars as I. T. Ramsey, D. Z. Phillips, Paul Van Buren, and R. B. Braithwaite as well as a host of others.

The variant attitudes sketched above highlight the richness and complexity there is in the history of philosophy. It is too facile to dismiss it all as nonsense or as intrinsically irreligious. However, there is a more fundamental objection to be made against the position of Tertullian; this objection constitutes the third main criticism.

Put curtly, it is this: philosophers inevitably ask important questions about religious faith, and it is quite hopeless to pretend that these questions can be shrugged aside or dismissed as sinful. The questions here are legion. The following is a typical sample. Are there good grounds for belief in God? Does the existence of evil count decisively against theism? What is revelation? How is it related to faith? What are miracles? Do science and critical history rule out their taking place? What is the soul? Is there a life after death? What form could that life conceivably take? Is religious language peculiar and special? What concepts most adequately do justice to the objects of religious belief? Can we synthesize the great world religions into one superreligion? Such questions as these are some of the central questions which have occupied philosophers who have reflected on religion. They are perfectly genuine and proper. To cast them aside is to create the suspicion that truth does not matter. Of course, not everyone need attempt to answer them, but they occur with sufficient regularity for us to attend to them with diligence and enthusiasm.

Here is the ultimate justification for approaching philosophy of religion in a positive spirit. Here is why the Athenians should be allowed into Jerusalem. The pervasiveness and relevance of its questions demand a space no less welcome than that of church history or biblical studies or even systematic theology within theology and religious studies. It is entirely proper, therefore, that philosophy of religion should have an honored position within the study of religion. Indeed philosophy of religion is an essential part of a sound education in religion. Without it theologians and students of religion will ignore crucial dimensions of the areas they explore. Moreover, it is vital for the welfare of philosophy of religion as an academic discipline that there be those within it who bring to it the riches of their training in other areas of religious studies, such as church history, comparative religions, and biblical studies. Otherwise there is a danger that philosophy of religion will lose touch with its subject matter and become insensitive. It is to be hoped that philosophy of religion will get within theology and religion departments all the support it richly deserves.

Within philosophy the case is equally strong. Religion precipitates philosophical questions which are important in their own right. Besides, philosophy of religion can be an exciting point of entry into philosophy for it touches on questions which are of intrinsic and universal interest. It is small wonder that all the great philosophers of the past from Plato to Wittgenstein have found time to reflect on philosophical aspects of religion. By so doing they have secured an honorable position for the philosophy of religion within philosophy itself.

CENTRAL TASKS OF PHILOSOPHY OF RELIGION

How are we to define philosophy of religion? Definitions of philosophy in general and philosophy of religion in particular are notoriously difficult to formulate. The reason for lack of consensus at this point is simple. Part of the task of philosophy is to determine what philosophy is; therefore any account of that task calls for extended discussion in its own right. As the task of philosophy is a matter of some dispute, this essentially contested issue will be reflected in any definition one might offer. This does not mean that there is no room for definitions, but their place is perhaps at the end rather than at the beginning. At this point all one need say is that philosophy has been interested in at least three kinds of questions, broadly speaking. There has been an interest in the analysis of key concepts in everyday language, e.g., What is justice, being, causality? There has been an interest in argument, e.g., What constitutes a good as opposed to a bad argument? There has been the articulation of a world view, e.g., What can we believe about life as a whole? What is the place of human beings in the scheme of things? What is the good life?

All three of these interests are reflected in the central constructive tasks of philosophy of religion. We can identify at least five of these tasks. To begin, philosophers can help clarify some of the pivotal concepts of a religious tradition. For example, it is difficult to get very far in religion without coming to terms with such words as meaning, action, myth, causality, revelation, and necessary being. Secondly, philosophers can scrutinize the internal consistency of a particular religious tradition. A good example of this is the discussion as to whether divine fore-knowledge is compatible with human freedom. Thirdly, the philosopher can help explicate and examine the philosophical presuppositions which inevitably find their way into theology and religion. For example, it is widely held at present that certain Marxist presuppositions and categories are the most useful tools theologians can draw on in their analysis of contemporary society. Philosophers are not in an exclusive position to examine this proposal, but they are in a privileged position, and it is important that they exercise their critical skills to determine whether this alliance is really feasible. Fourthly, philosophers can aid in mapping the relation between a particular religious tradition and other areas of life. Thus they can help clarify the relation between religion and morality or between religion and historical inquiry. Finally, philosophers can scrutinize the intellectual foundations of religion by examining those arguments which have been deployed to defend or attack religious belief. No better example for this can be found than the long debate about the existence of God. These tasks should not be viewed in isolation, for they overlap and interrelate in ways which constantly surprise, but taken together they capture the primary dimensions of the philosophy of religion. By drawing attention to these broad concerns we can see reasonably clearly what philosophy of religion is without begging too many questions about its nature.

We can also see what philosophy is by noting how it differs from three other fields of inquiry that are closely related to it, namely, phenomenology of religion, apologetics, and systematic theology. Philosophy of religion differs from phenomenology of religion by asking questions about the truth of religious claims. Thus it goes beyond the attempt to understand what religion is or says; it does not bracket out critical questions about the truth or falsehood of religion but pursues these with patience and care. As for apologetics and systematic theology, philosophy of religion differs from these in two ways. First, it does not presuppose the truth of a particular religion. Apologetics and systematic theology both do. Applied to Christianity, apologetics is concerned exclusively with the defense of the Christian faith against attack; while systematic theology is concerned with the articulation of the Christian faith and its application to the life of the Christian in the church and the world. In both cases it is either assumed or shown that Christianity is true. Philosophers of religion do not assume nor need they show that Christianity is true. Certainly they may do so, but there is no necessity for it. Certainly they will be concerned about the truth-claims of religion but not exclusively so. For this reason there is no inherent necessity that they be religious believers; they could be, and often are, agnostics or atheists. It is best that this be so. Religious issues are far too important to be the concern of one exclusive group of believers or unbelievers. Disagreement at this fundamental level can be the necessary enemy of shallow analysis, invalid argument, and windy rhetoric.

Secondly, philosophy of religion is much broader in scope than either apologetics or systematic theology. Its questions, as we have seen, are very general, even abstract, and there is no limit to their number. By contrast, apologetics is concerned with the truth, say, of Christianity, and systematic theology is concerned with the details of Christian doctrine. Philosophy of religion is not necessarily in tension with either of these disciplines and their aims. It has just got different aims. Inevitably it will overlap with these areas at times, but overall it is much more general in scope.

THE WAY AHEAD

How then are we to proceed? That is the next question. The standard introductory textbooks provide the classical model for the ordering of the material. They begin with some general comments on the nature of philosophy and the necessity of philosophy of religion. They then begin in earnest. They outline the classical arguments of theism and proceed to summarize the arguments against theism. This forms the core of the subject; classically this material has been called natural theology and natural atheology. Here the relation between faith and reason is usually decided. That done, the standard textbooks take up enduring problems such as the problem of evil, miracles, immortality, free will, and the relation of the world religions to each other.

On the whole, this approach to the philosophy of religion has been very satisfactory. The order in which it takes up the issues reflects on a small scale the historical development of the discipline, for questions about the rationality of belief in God were some of the first to be raised. Moreover it has, at least in the past, suited the interests of the student, for many students were interested in the rationality of belief in God.

As we all know, however, there are many ways to attain the same goal. I am unhappy with this model for various reasons. For one thing, it overemphasizes the place of natural theology (and natural atheology) in philosophy of religion. Philosophers have a wider role than that of examining arguments for and against belief in God. Moreover, this model is in great danger of lacking internal coherence. This danger arises when the model either ignores or leaves to the end the crucial question of the nature of religious language. Let me explain more fully what I mean.

When philosophers inquire into the meaning of religious language, what they ask is something like this: How are we to construe the central sentences of the Judaic-Christian tradition? Are these sentences factual, or are they poetic, or are they moral, or do they have some other function? For example, let us take the simple sentence "God is good." Is this an attempt to describe the character of a transcendent being? Or is it a piece of poetry intended to describe the natural world in a special way or perhaps to induce certain religious sentiments? Or is it a disguised way of expressing a commitment to a certain policy of action? All of these have been offered as an account of the meaning of the sentence "God is good." It is surely clear that the answer we give to this question will radically affect the answers we give to some other questions. There is a logical, as opposed to temporal, priority involved. Thus the central question of the rationality of belief in God will automatically assume a different form when we construe the meaning of religious discourse in different ways. Thus if we say the sentence "God exists" is a piece of poetry, it is unlikely that we will look for arguments of the traditional sort to establish that it is true. We will appeal to the imagination or to intuition with the eighteenth-century Romantics. Likewise, if we see it as disguised moral discourse, we will simply ignore or dismiss natural theology as utterly misguided. Classical and contemporary natural theology would, on this view, involve a radical misunderstanding of the nature of theological discourse. Natural theology of necessity presupposes that religious language, or key parts of it, intends to make claims about the way things are, for example, that there is a transcendent agent who is responsible for the existence of the universe. This claim would be rejected by those who argue that the language of faith is moral language.

It is abundantly clear that the contemporary philosopher of religion, if he or she is to be coherent overall, cannot begin with natural theology and then take up the question of the meaning of religious language. The two are intimately connected, and the latter has logical priority. As this applies to other matters as well, e.g., miracles, revelation, immortality, it is obvious that this issue should be taken first. To treat it at the end is to misconstrue its importance and to leave the inevitable feeling that the cart has come before the horse.

In this book I propose, therefore, to take the question of the meaning of religious language much earlier than is customary. In doing so I recognize that I am taking a calculated risk. This issue demands determined attention if it is to be understood. Moreover, it requires extended excursion into recent developments in philosophy for adequate appreciation of its nature and significance. The danger, therefore, is that beginning students will be put off or discouraged by initial complexity. On the other hand, if they can keep their heads and stay the course, they will be in a much better position to appreciate the nature and continued relevance of the classical issues that will be taken up in the later phases of our inquiry.

The reader should be aware that in taking up the question of the meaning of religious language I am entering a field which involves controversy on two separate levels. First, I shall be providing an interpretation of recent developments in philosophy. The interpretation I shall offer is not necessarily original, but even with this concession, we are too close to the events for it to be as accurate as future study and developments would allow. It must of necessity be provisional. Secondly, I intend to argue a case as to how the meaning of religious language is to be construed. This is a highly contested matter even yet; therefore the reader should realize that I am not merely reporting. I am also arguing for a particular philosophical proposal regarding the meaning of religious discourse. To be warned at this point is to be forearmed against taking that conclusion uncritically.

After resolving the issue of religious language, we shall then proceed to explore the rationality of religious belief. This shall preoccupy us from chapters 3 to 10. The remaining chapters will be devoted to enduring questions in philosophy of religion. As already indicated, I shall concentrate on philosophical issues generated by the internal content of the Christian religion and look at questions which arise when religion comes into contact with other areas of thought and action.

Chapter Two
Religious Language

When modern philosophers enquire into the meaning of religious language, it is not easy to discern what they are doing or to understand why they make such a fuss. Their fundamental question does not fit the routine expectations we have when we raise questions about the meaning of a piece of discourse. None of our typical concerns match the peculiar interest of the modern philosopher.

PHILOSOPHERS AND MEANING

For example, religious teachers in church or synagogue are deeply interested in questions about the meaning of religious language as found, say, in their classic religious texts. These questions vary enormously in their nature and scope. On one level the quest for meaning involves the search for an adequate translation of the text in hand. On another level the quest for meaning involves the resolution of ambiguity or vagueness in certain key religious concepts. Consider, for example, the elaborate discussion within Christianity about such terms as salvation, covenant, justification, sanctification, and sin. On still another level the quest for meaning involves the description of the varied forms of speech and communication found in the text, all the way from a humble metaphor to an elaborate allegory, parable, myth, legend, saga, or apocalypse. Classical textbooks on hermeneutics attend in part to such issues. On yet another level the quest for meaning involves the exploration of the ramifications and significance of the religious text for everyday life. Philosophers pass beyond such issues to yet another dimension of meaning. In doing so, they restrict themselves in at least two ways.

First, they concentrate on the very basic assertions of theism. Thus they focus on those sentences which speak of the existence, nature, and acts of God. Secondly, they fix their attention on whether these sentences can be construed as factual or informative. In other words, they want to know if theistic discourse in its most basic forms has the right to be considered true or false, that is, they desire to know if religious language is cognitive. Can one really use it to express a claim to know something about the way things are? This is the issue which absorbs them.

This question is a radical question, but one can be forgiven for wondering why so much time has been spent on it in recent years. After all, it seems obvious that central religious assertions should be construed as cognitive. Believers naturally construe such a sentence as "God exists" as true, for if they did not, why would they bother to adopt the religious practices, attitudes, and policies of action which are central to their faith? To raise the question is to answer implicitly that religious language in its core is factual. It is intended to say something crucial about the nature of ultimate reality. It may, of course, turn out to be false, and arguments as to whether it is false may go on forever, but that it purports to be true or false would seem to be so obvious as not to demand further investigation.

THE POSITIVIST POSITION

It is precisely this argument that a whole school of modern philosophy, known as logical positivism, has called in question. The logical positivists argued with passion and precision that religious language, although it appeared cognitive, failed to meet the requirements which were essential to cognitive discourse in general. The development of this position, the response it evoked, and the general significance of both will detain us in this chapter. Because many theologians and their students tend to dismiss much too insensitively the hostility of logical positivism to religious language, it is important to pause and place the positivist tradition in its historical setting. Much is to be gained by attending to the reasons which lie behind the positivist position.

By the time logical positivism emerged in the 1930s there had been in Anglo-American philosophy something of a revolution. The changes can be mapped in terms of both content and method of philosophy. As to content, philosophers had come to reject the prevailing idealist position of the late nineteenth century. Idealists, like any school of thought, differed considerably within their ranks but shared the common convictions that the real world lay beyond this world and that the present world of shifting, impermanent appearances found its ultimate and rational unity in that absolute world beyond the senses. Access to that real world came only through the exercise of a special kind of thinking commonly called reason or intuition, which was contrasted with the kind of understanding deployed by scientists, historians, and ordinary people. All of this conflicted sharply with the outlook and intellectual canons of common sense.

Initially the revolt concentrated on the content of the idealist position. G. E. Moore argued extensively that it was so much at variance with the convictions of common sense that it was incredible. In time, however, the criticism cut much deeper when it was claimed that the problem with idealism was not so much its content but the very conception of philosophy, which undergirded it. Idealists held that the philosophical task was essentially constructive; one aimed to provide an overall view of ultimate reality. A new generation of philosophers looked to science to provide this view and construed philosophy as critical and analytical in intention; one aimed to give an analysis of meaning and truth. With this shift there developed a deep interest in the nature and limits of language, especially of that segment of language which expressed claims to knowledge. Logical positivism represents the zenith of this interest. When its claims were applied to religious discourse, the effect was thought to be devastating. Put bluntly, religious language was construed as nonsense. A very particular theory of meaning generated this intriguing conclusion.

Drawing on what they believed were true instances of cognitive discourse, positivists argued that one made a genuinely factual assertion only where one could in principle conceive of some way in which one could show by empirical observation that what one said was true or false. They enshrined this doctrine in the principle of verification. A. J. Ayer, one of the most famous positivists, expressed this principle as follows:

> The criterion which we use to test the genuineness of apparent statements of fact is the criterion of verifiability. We say that a sentence is factually significant to any given person, if, and only if, he knows how to verify the proposition which it purports to express—that is, if he knows what observations would lead him, under certain conditions, to accept the proposition as being true, or reject it as being false. If, on the other hand, the putative proposition is of such a character that the assumption of its truth, or falsehood, is consistent with any assumption whatsoever concerning the nature of his future experience, then, as far as he is concerned, it is, if not a tautology, a mere pseudo-proposition. The sentence expressing it may be emotionally significant to him; but it is not literally significant.[1]

The implications of positivist doctrine for religion seemed obvious. Ayer drew them with characteristic precision. Talk about God was clearly not verifiable by sense experience. Moreover, religious language was radically different from the propositions of logic and mathematics, for they were not tautologies, i.e., true in virtue of the meaning of the concepts involved. Hence sentences about God could be neither true nor false. They were literally nonsense. They might be emotionally significant to a person, but they were not saying anything about the way things are. Necessarily, therefore, attempts to defend or attack theism as traditionally con-

---

[1] A. J. Ayer, *Language Truth and Logic* (New York: Dover, 1952), p. 35.

ceived were out of order in principle. Hume, Kant, Aquinas, and Paley—these and others had worked with wrong assumptions because sentences about God were not even candidates in the election of truth and falsehood. An analysis of their surface grammar might suggest they were, but an analysis of their depth grammar revealed they were not. Thus did Ayer dispose of religion and most traditional philosophy of religion. Not surprisingly his views often met with hostility and anger, and it was tempting to dismiss his position by believing that he had no deep acquaintance with a living religious tradition.[2] It was more difficult to dismiss the positivist tradition when it was given a fresh expression by Antony Flew, the son of a respected British theologian.[3]

Flew set out his positivist views by focusing on falsifiability rather than verifiability. He borrowed and adapted a parable of John Wisdom.

> Once upon a time two explorers came upon a clearing in the jungle. In the clearing were growing many flowers and many weeds. One explorer says, "Some gardener must tend this plot." The other disagrees, "There is no gardener." So they pitch their tents and set a watch. No gardener is ever seen. "But perhaps he is an invisible gardener." So they set up a barbed-wire fence. They electrify it. They patrol with bloodhounds. (For they remember how H. G. Wells's *The Invisible Man* could be both smelt and touched though he could not be seen.) But no shrieks ever suggest that some intruder has received a shock. No movements of the wire ever betray an invisible climber. The bloodhounds never give cry. Yet still the Believer is not convinced. "But there is a gardener, invisible, intangible, insensible to electric shocks, a gardener who has no scent and makes no sound, a gardener who comes secretly to look after the garden which he loves." At last the Sceptic despairs, "But what remains of your original assertion? Just how does what you call an invisible, intangible, eternally elusive gardener differ from an imaginary gardener or even from no gardener at all?"[4]

Flew argues that religious believers kill their assertions by qualification. In the end they will allow nothing to count against their proposals. No matter what happens the believer will not abandon his or her original assertion. Flew drives home his point with a concrete illustration.

> Someone tells us that God loves us as a father loves his children. We are reassured. But then we see a child dying of inoperable cancer of the throat. His earthly father is driven frantic in his efforts to help, but his Heavenly Father reveals no obvious sign of concern. Some qualification is made—God's love is "not a merely human love" or it is "an inscrutable love," perhaps—and we realise that such sufferings are quite compatible with the truth of the asser-

[2] Ayer in his autobiography explains that he abandoned such religion as he had when a prayer for a place on a sports team went unanswered.

[3] Flew's father was R. Newton Flew, who taught at Cambridge and was a leading Methodist theologian.

[4] Antony Flew, "Theology and Falsification," in *New Essays in Philosophical Theology*, eds. Antony Flew and Alasdair MacIntyre (New York: Macmillan, 1955), p. 96. Reprinted with permission of Macmillan Publishing Company.

tion of "God loves us as a father (but, of course . . .)." We are reassured again. But then perhaps we ask: what is this assurance of God's (appropriately qualified) love worth, what is this apparent guarantee really a guarantee against? Just what would have to happen not merely (morally and wrongly) to tempt but also (logically and rightly) to entitle us to say "God does not love us" or even "God does not exist"? I therefore put to the succeeding symposiasts the simple central questions, "What would have to occur or to have occurred to constitute for you a disproof of the love of, or of the existence of, God?"[5]

INADEQUATE REBUTTALS

The positivist critique of religious language has evoked an almost endless discussion. The crucial divide has been between those who continued to hold that religious discourse was cognitive and those who claimed that it was not. The latter offered a bewildering array of options as to how religious language was to be positively interpreted; the former disagreed on how seriously to take the positivist challenge and on how to meet its requirements. The debate has now grown somewhat stale, so we are in a good position to take stock of the rival alternatives. We shall concentrate here on some of the more significant samples to be found on either side of the cognitive-noncognitive divide. Within this we shall need to sketch an important shift in the discussion of meaning initiated by the most famous of all modern philosophers, Ludwig Wittgenstein.[6]

One way to respond to the positivist argument was to accept the positivist position on verification as a condition of cognitive discourse, to concede that religious language did not meet this condition but to argue that religious discourse did not have to meet it. Two philosophers who took this route were R. B. Braithwaite and Paul Van Buren. Both accepted that sentences about God were not true or false. Such a sentence as "God created the world" could no longer be taken to refer to the activity of a transcendent, personal agent, for this was impossible as a matter of principle. However, language about God still had a significant function. For Braithwaite theological discourse was really moral discourse.[7] To speak of believing in God was another way of saying that one declared one's intention to follow an agapeistic way of life and thus love one's neighbor as oneself. What made one a Christian was the coupling of this with the additional commitment to draw inspiration from the stories which have been central to Christianity down through the ages. On that basis Braithwaite was baptized as an Anglican.

Van Buren was already a trained theologian when he expounded his position, having studied with Barth. He attempted a more thorough analysis, which would

[5]Ibid., pp. 98–99.

[6]In what follows I draw on my "Some Trends in Recent Philosophy of Religion," *The Theological Educator* IX (1979), 93–102.

[7]See R. B. Braithwaite, *An Empiricist's View of the Nature of Religious Belief* (Cambridge: Cambridge University Press, 1955).

address itself to the traditional claims of Christianity as expressed, for example, in its Christology, but his strategy was similar to that of Braithwaite. He construed statements about God as really statements about human beings. Statements of faith are statements which express, describe, or commend a particular way of seeing the world, other people, and oneself and the way of life appropriate to such a perspective. All of traditional discourse about God, Christ, sin, predestination, and so on, was to be interpreted after this fashion.

Many have found it difficult to take these proposals seriously. Instinctively they feel that they are elaborate rearguard actions to sustain what has already been surrendered. Their sophistication, their subtlety, their genuine learning, their trumpet call to secularism in the name of religion—all these were resisted by both believer and unbeliever. To some unbelievers they employed an expensive, if not archaic, theological vocabulary where a sane and sensible humanism would suffice. To some believers they appeared like naked atheism masquerading as the faith of the church and part of a wider failure of nerve among mid-twentieth-century theologians and religious thinkers. Philosophically, the most serious problem was that such a position was vastly removed from what religious believers mean when they speak of God. Moreover, insufficient attention was paid to the distinction between an interpretation of the way religious language is commonly understood and a reinterpretation of how it should be understood. Either one equivocated on this issue or failed to provide warrants for the move from interpretation to reinterpretation. Philosophers who are in the business of offering an account of the meaning of religious language cannot isolate themselves so conveniently from the linguistic intentions of historic, religious communities.

Another way to meet the challenge of positivism is to cut deeper into its position and argue that not only does it misconstrue the logic of religious discourse but it rests on a totally inadequate theory of meaning. To understand this strategy we need to return to developments in modern philosophy. The crucial work at this juncture is the later work of Ludwig Wittgenstein.[8]

In his earlier career Wittgenstein had espoused a theory of meaning which was not substantially far removed from that of the logical positivists. Believing that he had solved the main problems of philosophy, he gave it up for other pursuits. Later he reversed this decision and returned to Cambridge to pursue fresh ideas about meaning. What he proposed was that there was much more to meaning than verification. Meaning was to be found in the use of an expression rather than in its verification by sense experience. Moreover, when one looked closely at ordinary language, one found that it was rich in variety of use. One did more than just make claims about the way things are when one used a language. One used language to tell a joke, to pray, to give orders, to thank, to curse, to greet, and to do countless other things. Language was a tool or rather a set of tools, and philosophers had overlooked the great multiplicity of these tools in ordinary discourse. To change the analogy, to speak a language was to have mastered a whole series of different

---

[8] Especially his *Philosophical Investigations* (Oxford: Basil Blackwell, 1958).

games, each with different rules as to how they were to be played, so to reduce all language to one game, the game of saying how things are in the world, was narrow and restrictive in the extreme. The meaning of an expression was to be found, therefore, not in its verification by sense experience but in its standard, correct employment. The job of the philosopher was to map and make known the variety of usage in our discourse and to explore its implications for traditional philosophical puzzles. The shift to this position was aptly marked by a shift in label: philosophers abandoned logical positivism and embraced linguistic analysis.

It took time for these ideas to filter through to the grass roots of philosophy. When they did, many quickly recognized their importance for the philosophy of religion. The immediate reaction was sometimes one of profound relief and liberation. Here was a philosopher of genius who in one simple shift in the theory of meaning had rehabilitated religious discourse. After all, religious discourse was there as a solid piece of the linguistic landscape. All that was needed was to map its use and lay bare its standard correct employment. The details at this point did not matter overmuch, for the issue of principle had been established: religious discourse was not nonsense, it was perfectly respectable. It had its own use and therefore was as meaningful as any other language game one can care to mention. All that was left to be done was to work out the details.

Not everyone has agreed that even this had to be done. One of the more articulate philosophers who does not is D. Z. Phillips.[9] For Phillips religious discourse is sui generis; it is unique, and it can be understood only from the inside. The religious believer does not need to be told the meaning of religious discourse, for he is the one who uses it. To provide an analysis for the outsider is impossible because attempts to use nonreligious discourse to explain the use of religious discourse will involve an unacceptable reductionism. It will involve the reducing of religious language to some other language use, a serious mistake once one grasps the unique character of religious language. A similar view has been developed with much clarity and skill by W. D. Hudson, who has written a number of books to argue for the crucial significance of the later Wittgenstein for religion and ably defended his claims in the journals.[10] The general position of Phillips and Hudson is sometimes known as Wittgensteinian Fideism.

The key controversy in contemporary analytical philosophy of religion centers on the viability of this approach to philosophy of religion. Philosophy conferences have split down the middle on this matter with each side passing the other like the proverbial ships in the night. My own view is that the liberation supposedly made possible by linguistic analysis is an illusion. At its heart it involves a surrender of the claim that the religious have always made, namely, their claim to say something substantial about the world. Christians, for example, have always maintained that the world is created and sustained by a transcendent God and that this God has intervened decisively in Jesus of Nazareth to bring forgiveness and salvation. If the

[9] See D. Z. Phillips, *The Concept of Prayer* (London: Macmillan, 1966).
[10] See W. D. Hudson, *A Philosophical Approach to Religion* (London: Macmillan, 1974).

sentences which express this are not taken to be true or false, if their depth-grammar is not seen as a matter of their being assertions, then theism has been abandoned, and all the philosopical sophistication one can muster will not make up for it. In claiming that religion has a logic of its own, linguistic analysis has asserted indirectly that religion does not make claims about the way things are. Therefore its much vaunted liberation means the end of religion as generally understood.

It matters little at this point how one expounds the manifold logic of religion. Indeed one of the first signs of weakness in the new approach was the failure to reach agreement on the nature of the logic of religious discourse. The variety here is enormous. Even claims that make no pretence to be connected with analytical philosophy were interpreted to throw light on the peculiar logic of religious language. Thus Frederick Ferré can take the work of the Barthian T. F. Torrance and press it into service as a live option in discussions about the logic of religion.[11] John Macquarrie can write as if the claims of Heidegger can be interpreted in a similar fashion.[12] Perhaps they can. But the general impression one gets on reading the literature is that Wittgenstein's slogan, "The meaning is the use," is being employed to legitimize one's own favored theological tradition while the crucial challenge to theology about the nature of its fundamental doctrinal discourse is passed over in silence. Either one has abandoned theism in favor of some kind of religious humanism or one keeps intact one's theism and fails to see the inconsistency of also maintaining that religious discourse has a logic all of its own. To be sure, there is more to religious discourse than making assertions about the way things are, but undisciplined analysis of this extra dimension does not help us uncover what it is, nor does such analysis salvage enough of the content of religion to make what remains worth believing.

Needless to say, this interpretation of our recent past is much disputed. It would not be the key controversy of recent years if it were not. However, I am convinced that it will stand the test of time. Thus it is being increasingly seen that linguistic analysis is paradoxically dependent in an indirect way upon its forerunner, logical positivism. Both were in agreement that the test of factual discourse was to be found in something not unlike the principle of verification. Where they differed was in the significance they attributed to discourse that did not satisfy this criterion. Logical positivism rather crudely dismissed such language as nonsense, albeit useful nonsense in that it gave expression to one's emotions. Linguistic analysis offered a much more sophisticated account of this language, brought it into prominence, and roundly proclaimed its full citizenship in the kingdom of meaning. Nevertheless, underlying both is the metaphysical thesis that only science with its extended dependence on sense observation can give us information on how things are. Religion can have no stake in the occupation of this crucial territory and must be analyzed in some other way. It should be added at this point that any single-story analysis of

---

[11] See Frederick Ferré, *Language, Logic and God* (New York: Harper and Row, 1961), chap. 4.

[12] See John Macquarrie, *God-Talk* (London: SCM, 1967).

religious language is doomed to failure. There is no such thing as a religious use of language. Rather, within religion language is used to perform a whole range of jobs, for example, to pray, to praise, to exhort, to comfort, to awaken, to declare the truth about God. Therefore it is futile to search for one use which would somehow analyze the meaning of religious discourse.

RELIGIOUS LANGUAGE VINDICATED

From the outset of the positivist challenge there were many philosophers who did not accept that the positivists had established that religious language was not cognitive. They agreed that it certainly purported to be cognitive, but they argued that either the positivist position was too erroneous in its theory of meaning to be taken seriously or else it could be met on its own terms. The former position was adopted by Alvin Plantinga and Anthony Kenny; the latter by John Hick and Basil Mitchell.

Plantinga's response drew heavily on the inability of the positivists to rescue the verifiability criterion from criticism. "If the notion of verifiability cannot so much as be explained, if we cannot so much as say what it is for a statement to be empirically verifiable, then we scarcely need worry about whether religious statements are or are not verifiable."[13] Kenny's position echoed this when he wrote: "Verificationism itself is too much in need of qualification to be a useful tool against theism."[14] This line of argument is technically impeccable. It is now generally agreed that the central doctrines of logical positivism are indefensible. Even A. J. Ayer has publicly confessed that "most of the defects were that nearly all of it was false."[15]

It is somewhat insensitive, however, to drop the issue as if positivism has made no difference in the present climate of opinion or in recent debates about religion. Put at its lowest, positivism has raised doubts about the cognitive character of religious language which deserve attention in their own right. Such doubts are reflective of a widespread, implicit commitment to secularism, which the modern philosopher of religion should explore in some detail. Moreover, it is generally agreed that verification or falsification, while possibly failing as necessary conditions of cognitive discourse, can serve as sufficient conditions of cognitive discourse. Thus were the believer to meet the positivist on his or her own terms, the doubts raised by the positivist challenge would be relieved. It was this route which was taken by Hick and Mitchell.

Hick focused on the issue of verification. He suggested that religious claims were cognitive because they could be verified eschatologically in the world to come. This general suggestion is delightfully expressed by means of a parable.

---

[13] Alvin Plantinga, *God and Other Minds* (Ithaca, N.Y.: Cornell University Press, 1967), p. 168.

[14] Anthony Kenny, *The Five Ways* (London: Routledge and Kegan Paul, 1969), p. 2.

[15] *The Listener*, March 2, 1978, p. 270.

Two men are travelling together along a road. One of them believes that it leads to a Celestial City, the other that it leads nowhere; but since this is the only road there is, both must travel it. Neither has been this way before, and therefore neither is able to say what they will find around each next corner. During their journey they meet both with moments of refreshment and delight, and with moments of hardship and danger. All the time one of them thinks of his journey as a pilgrimage to the Celestial City and interprets the pleasant parts as encouragements and the obstacles as trials of his purpose and lessons in endurance, prepared by the king of that city and designed to make of him a worthy citizen of the place when at last he arrives there. The other, however, believes none of this and sees their journey as an unavoidable and aimless ramble. Since he has no choice in the matter, he enjoys the good and endures the bad. But for him there is no Celestial City to be reached, no all-encompassing purpose ordaining their journey—only the road itself and the luck of the road in good weather and in bad.

During the course of the journey the issue between them is not an experimental one. They do not entertain different expectations about the coming details of the road, but only about its ultimate destination. And yet when they do turn the last corner it will be apparent that one of them has been right all the time and the other wrong. Thus, although the issue between them has not been experimental, it has nevertheless from the start been a real issue. They have not merely felt differently about the road; for one was feeling appropriately and the other inappropriately in relation to the actual state of affairs. Their opposed interpretations of the road constituted genuinely rival assertions, though assertions whose status has the peculiar characteristic of being guaranteed retrospectively by a future crux.[16]

A life after death would not in itself of course verify theism. What is required is greater precision in the kind of life after death which would do this. Hick found this precision in the classical Christian view that the life after death involved an experience of the fulfillment of God's purpose for ourselves, as this purpose has been disclosed in the Christian revelation, and an experience of communion with God, as he has revealed himself in the person of Christ. Unfortunately, this solution does not succeed. It fails not because it postpones verification until after death but because it resorts to religious rather than empirical categories in order to describe the kind of life which would verify religious language. In other words, it appeals to inescapably religious language about the activity of God in revelation and in Christ to establish the cognitive character of that very same language. It is unsatisfactory to salvage this proposal by arguing that the religious language invoked was not intended to exhaust the divine nature.[17] This is another matter which is beside the point at issue.

Mitchell, in his response to the positivist challenge, approached it on the level of falsification. He simply drew attention to the fact that believer and unbeliever alike are fully aware that certain states of affairs very definitely count against theism. All agree that theists must grant that the existence of evil counts against

---

[16] John Hick, *Faith and Knowledge* (Glasgow: Fontana, 1974), pp. 177–78.
[17] Ibid., p. 197.

their position and constitutes a very serious trial of their faith. Flew's whole challenge rested on this assumption, but he missed its significance because he begged the question against the theist on that age-old problem. Mitchell expresses his position by yet another parable.

> In time of war in an occupied country, a member of the resistance meets one night a stranger who deeply impresses him. They spend that night together in conversation. The Stranger tells the partisan that he himself is on the side of the resistance—indeed that he is in command of it, and urges the partisan to have faith in him no matter what happens. The partisan is utterly convinced at that meeting of the Stranger's sincerity and constancy and undertakes to trust him.
>
> They never meet in conditions of intimacy again. But sometimes the Stranger is seen helping members of the resistance, and the partisan is grateful and says to his friends, "He is on our side." Sometimes he is seen in the uniform of the police handing over patriots to the occupying power. On these occasions his friends murmur against him: but the partisan still says, "He is on our side." He still believes that, in spite of appearances, the Stranger did not deceive him. Sometimes he asks the Stranger for help and receives it. He is then thankful. Sometimes he asks and does not receive it. Then he says, "The Stranger knows best." Sometimes his friends, in exasperation, say "Well, what would he have to do for you to admit that you were wrong and that he is not on our side?" But the partisan refuses to answer. He will not consent to put the Stranger to the test. And sometimes his friends complain, "Well if that's what you mean by his being on our side, the sooner he goes over to the other side the better."
>
> The partisan of the parable does not allow anything to count decisively against the proposition "The Stranger is on our side." This is because he has committed himself to trust the Stranger. But he of course recognizes that the Stranger's ambiguous behaviour does count against what he believes about him. It is precisely this situation which constitutes the trial of his faith.[18]

Mitchell is surely correct in his strategy. His position does not resort to descriptions of states of affairs which require religious concepts for their identification. Moreover, one can intensify the appeal to the problem of evil by imagining a world which was much more evil than the present one is. Suppose, for example, we inhabited a world where everyone born lived a life of excruciating pain from birth to death. Suppose we all had unbearable pangs of hunger all the time no matter how much or how often we had food. If this would not falsify the claim that the world was created by an all-powerful benevolent God, nothing would. Moreover, pivotal Christian claims associated with the life, death, and resurrection of Jesus Christ are entirely falsifiable in principle, and anyone remotely acquainted with the strain that the rise of historical study has generated in classical Christian thought is aware of this. It is true, of course, that some theologians will attempt to reinterpret their original religious position or that of the classical past in order to avoid the consequences of empirical investigation. Thus Bultmann in modern times has averred that

[18] Basil Mitchell, "Theology and Falsification," in *New Essays in Philosophical Theology,* eds. Antony Flew and Alasdair MacIntyre (London: SCM, 1955), pp. 103–4.

belief in the resurrection has nothing to do with finding the remains of Jesus in Palestine. But that only shows up the ingenuity of a modern theologian; it does not show that religious language is noncognitive. So long as the believer grants that historical findings can falsify some of his or her cherished theological claims, then the positivist challenge has been met entirely satisfactorily. Theologians and believers who reject this idea will answer for themselves. My own view is that religious language is indeed falsifiable and therefore cognitive.

VALUABLE CONSEQUENCES OF POSITIVISM

If I am correct, then the decks have been cleared to begin a lengthy discussion on the status of the central tenets of what we might call traditional Christian theism. We shall explore the classical and contemporary arguments for and against this position. As we proceed to this, we can be grateful to the positivist tradition that it has forced us to come to terms with a critical issue which is presupposed by such arguments. Indeed, our discussion of the positivist challenge makes the examination of arguments for and against religious belief all that more interesting. After all, if religious claims do concern what ultimately is, then it behooves us to examine their truth or falsehood as sensitively as we can.

It remains to note very briefly some other consequences of the positivist critique of religious language. First, it cautions the theologian to be wary of alliances with substantial metaphysical systems. Thus those theologians who baptized idealism in the past or continue to do so in the present may find themselves in considerable intellectual perplexity. Secondly, it invites theologians to be as clear and precise as they can be in the articulation of their position. Without, in any way, inviting the theologian to adopt the errors of the positivist position, it would surely be a great gain in theology were theologians to share the quest of recent philosophy in its search for greater clarity. For this reason alone acquaintance with the issues of philosophy of religion in general and the issue of religious language in particular may be an essential precondition of the renewal of systematic theology. Exposure to positivism and the discussion it provoked is a refining fire through which the theologian and the philosopher should pass. Thirdly, moving beyond positivism involves the reopening of old questions about the meaning of theological predicates and about the concept of God, which are already very much on the agenda. Theologians and philosophers are being invited to explore the foundations of the Western religious traditions and to expound and criticize them with greater precision. Positivism has cleansed the metaphysical stables, but it has by no means demolished them.

Chapter Three
Natural Theology

Once it is established that religious language is to be interpreted as true or false, it is natural to take up the question of its actual truth or falsehood. It is a truism that intelligent people have come down on both sides of this issue. Some believe and some do not. Why do they believe or disbelieve? Here we leave the realm of the agreed and enter a complex world of argument and counterargument. As we move into this arena, it is imperative that we be as clear as possible about what we are asking.

THE FUNDAMENTAL QUESTION

It is important that we avoid coming to closure too abruptly. In the past it has been the common practice to cast the issue simply in terms of proofs or disproofs of the existence of God. We shall, of course, consider alleged proofs and disproofs of religious belief, but it would be rash to assume that the issue of the truth or falsehood of religion can be settled at this level of rationality. In order to avoid such a rash and uncritical assumption, let us construe the problem as broadly as possible by posing it this way. Is it reasonable to believe the central tenets of the Judaic-

Christian tradition in whole or in part? This is the question which shall occupy us for several chapters.

This question is not to be interpreted as a psychological query about the process which brought a person to belief or unbelief. Nor is it a query about how one might actually bring an unbeliever to faith. Rather it is a question about certain propositions. In other words, our attention is focused quite simply on the truth or falsehood of certain propositions. Thus we can see immediately how irrelevant it is to complain, as religious believers and theologians sometimes do, that arguments never really brought anyone to faith. The issue is the truth or falsehood of certain propositions; it concerns the rationality or irrationality of certain beliefs; it is not about someone's ability to bring people to faith or trust in God.

Although our question cannot be reduced to proofs or disproofs of the existence of God, it is useful to begin there. Many religious believers have held that it is indeed possible to prove that God exists. There is a wealth of material in the history of philosophy and theology which bears witness to this. The core arguments deployed within this tradition have become known as natural theology. They are known as this in contrast to revealed theology because they appeal to considerations which are available to all rather than resting on information made available to some through special revelation. The most famous exponent of natural theology was Thomas Aquinas (1225–74). Aquinas laid out five separate ways to prove the existence of God. He based his proofs in turn on the existence of change, causation, contingency, gradation, and directedness, as he found these in nature.[1] The central proofs for the existence of God are generally, however, reduced to three in number. These are known as the ontological, the cosmological, and the teleological arguments for the existence of God.

As we look at these arguments, it is important to realize what exactly a proof of God's existence involves. God here refers to the God of the classical, Judaic-Christian tradition, understood as a transcendent, personal agent, who as creator of all that exists, is omnipotent, omnipresent, omniscient, eternal, and all-loving. Any proof for the existence of God must satisfy at least two conditions. First, the argument proposed must be a valid argument. That is, the conclusion must follow as a matter of logic from the premises on which it is based. Secondly, the argument must rest on true premises. Here we must either appeal to conceptual considerations about the classical idea of God or go beyond logic entirely and appeal to generally accepted matters of fact about the natural world. The classical arguments for the existence of God have gone in both directions. Moreover, they have been stated in varied forms. This can be confusing initially, but it shows indirectly how enduring and popular they have been over time. Even yet they are a matter for both sophisticated and commonplace discussion. Let us now examine them in turn.

---

[1] A detailed discussion can be found in Anthony Kenny, *The Five Ways* (London: Routledge and Kegan Paul, 1969).

THE ONTOLOGICAL ARGUMENT

The ontological argument for the existence of God rests entirely on considerations of logic. Its most celebrated exponent was Anselm, who was Archbishop of Canterbury from 1093 to 1109. In later times the argument was restated by Descartes (1596-1650). In the modern period the argument has been taken up by the contemporary philosopher Alvin Plantinga. The fascination of this proof of God's existence is unending.

No doubt much of that fascination rests on the exquisite simplicity of its central theme. The argument appeals to the concept of God, inviting us to reflect on what it entails. Anselm's exposition of it is a stroke of genius. He expressed his insight in plain language without recourse to any complicated, technical terms. Beginning with the conviction that God is that than which nothing greater can be conceived, he proceeded to argue that such a being must of necessity exist. Anselm puts it like this:

> O Lord, you who give understanding to faith, so far as you know it to be beneficial, give me to understand that you are just as we believe, and that you are what we believe.
>
> We certainly believe that you are something than which nothing greater can be conceived.
>
> But is there any such nature, since "the fool has said in his heart: God is not"?
>
> However, when this very same fool hears what I say, when he hears of "something than which nothing greater can be conceived," he certainly understands what he hears.
>
> What he understands stands in relation to his understanding (*esse in intellectu*), even if he does not understand that it exists. For it is one thing for a thing to stand in relation to our understanding; it is another thing for us to understand that it really exists. For instance, when a painter imagines what he is about to paint, he has it in relation to his understanding. However, he does not yet understand that it exists, because he has not yet made it. After he paints it, then he both has it in relation to his understanding and understands that it exists. Therefore, even the fool is convinced that "something than which nothing greater can be conceived" at least stands in relation to his understanding, because when he hears of it he understands it, and whatever he understands stands in relation to his understanding.
>
> And certainly that than which a greater cannot be conceived cannot stand only in relation to the understanding. For if it stands at least in relation to the understanding, it can be conceived to be also in reality, and this is something greater.
>
> Therefore, if "that than which a greater cannot be conceived" only stood in relation to the understanding, then "that than which a greater cannot be conceived" would be something than which a greater can be conceived. But this is certainly impossible.

Therefore, something than which a greater cannot be conceived undoubtedly both stands in relation to the understanding and exists in reality.[2]

A recent commentator in Anselm has more formally summarized this argument as follows:

> We believe that God is something than which nothing greater can be thought.
> When an unbeliever hears this he understands it, and what he understands exists in his mind.
> But what exists in the mind and in reality too must be greater than what exists in the mind alone.
> So that than which nothing greater can be thought cannot be that which exists only in the mind.
> So that than which nothing greater can be thought must exist in the mind and in reality, too.
> So God must exist in reality.[3]

The essence of the argument is self-explanatory. God must exist because of who he is. Those who do not see this, according to Anselm, have either distorted or ignored the true sense of who God is. If God is to be that than which nothing greater can be conceived, he must actually exist.

Modern versions of the argument from Descartes to the present, although they have their own distinctive ingredients, ultimately rest on the ideas first propounded by Anselm. Descartes, for example, suggested two analogies to help explain the argument.

> Existence can no more be separated from the essence of God than can its having its three angles equal to two right angles be separated from the essence of a rectilinear triangle, or the idea of a mountain from the idea of a valley; and so there is not any less repugnance to our conceiving a God (that is, a Being supremely perfect) to whom existence is lacking (that is to say, to whom a certain perfection is lacking), than to conceive of a mountain which has no valley.[4]

Just as you cannot conceive of a triangle without three angles or a mountain which has no valley, so you cannot conceive of God without existence. In more recent

---

[2] The ontological argument is located in Anselm's *Proslogion.* The translation used here is that of Arthur C. McGill in *The Many-Faced Argument,* eds. John Hick and Arthur C. McGill (London: Macmillan, 1968), pp. 4–6. Copyright © 1964, 1967 by John H. Hick and Arthur C. McGill.

[3] G. R. Evans, *Anselm and Talking about God* (Oxford: Clarendon Press, 1978), p. 44.

[4] *The Philosophical Works of Descartes,* vol. I, trans. Elizabeth S. Haldane and G. R. T. Ross (Cambridge: Cambridge University Press, 1911). This quote can be found in *The Ontological Argument,* ed. Alvin Plantinga (New York: Doubleday, 1965), pp. 31–35.

times, fresh interest has been aroused by Plantinga's attempt to restate the argument in terms developed by modern modal logicians.[5]

What are we to make of the central thread in this argument? Since it was first published it has elicited a solid body of objections. One way to counter the ontological argument is to explore what else one might prove by the same means. Following a hint of Gaunilo, a contemporary of Anselm, one might argue that one could then prove the existence of anything one wished. For example, could one not argue for the existence of an island than which none greater can be conceived?[6] The problem with this objection, however, is that it is very difficult to conceive of such an island. Plantinga has captured this very wittily.

> No matter how great an island is, no matter how many Nubian maidens and dancing girls adorn it, there could always be a greater—one with twice as many for example. The qualities that make for greatness in islands—number of palm trees, amount and quality of coconuts, for example—most of these qualities have no *intrinsic maximum*. That is, there is no degree of productivity or number of palm trees (or of dancing girls) such that it is impossible that an island display more of that quality. So the idea of a greatest possible island is an inconsistent or incoherent idea; it's not possible that there be such a thing.[7]

May there not, however, be other possible objects or agents which do possess qualities of intrinsic maximum? Suppose we think of a perfect hundred dollar bill. In such a case its perfection consists in its ability to purchase one hundred dollars' worth of goods or whatever. Thus if a shopkeeper refused to accept it, one might rightly argue that it was a perfectly good one hundred dollar bill; one could say this even if, in other respects, it was far from perfect, e.g., its color or its texture. It is difficult to see why, by parity of the reason used by Anselm, this perfect bill should not exist. Perhaps more convincing is the case of an unlimited malevolent being. Consider that agent than which no more evil can be conceived. Such an agent, were he to exist in the mind only, would clearly be inferior in malevolence from one which existed also in reality. Indeed the former agent would be a rather tame affair, capable of doing little evil compared to the real one which exists objectively in the world. If these counterexamples succeed, they provide a way of reducing the ontological argument to absurdity. Unfortunately, it is not always easy to see if they do really succeed.

---

[5] Modal logicians are interested in the meaning of such terms as contingency, possibility, and necessity. The discussion is highly technical and for that reason is not pursued here. Plantinga has offered a good account of his version of the argument in *God, Freedom and Evil* (London: George Allen and Unwin, 1975). Be it noted that Plantinga is just one of the modern philosophers interested in restating the ontological argument. Others include Charles Hartshorne and Norman Malcolm.

[6] Gaunilo originally expressed the objection in terms of that island which is greater than all actual islands. See *The Ontological Argument*, ed. Alvin Plantinga, pp. 6–13.

[7] Plantinga, *God, Freedom and Evil*, pp. 90–91.

By far the most famous and critical objection to the argument was developed by Immanuel Kant (1724-1804). Kant's proposal was directed principally at the Cartesian version of the argument. We can usefully approach Kant's central point by reflecting on the following. Suppose I buy the evening newspaper and, hunting around for a car, find this advertisement: "For sale, 1980 Ford Escort, in good running order, existing, good tires, paint work needs attention, body in excellent condition." We instinctively sense that the claim to existence is totally out of place in the list of attributes given to the car. What Kant basically argued was that Anselm failed to notice that existence is not an attribute or a predicate. Existence is not a quality and therefore cannot add to or detract from the perfection of something. Of course the grammar of our language may suggest that it is, but we must be careful not to be misled at this point. When we say that something, say *x,* exists, what we mean is that *x* (however defined) is to be found in the real world. The verb *exists* has the logical function of asserting that a particular description, whatever it may be, is instantiated in the real world.

Kant expressed this argument in the following terms.

> By whatever and by however many predicates we may think a thing—even if we completely determine it—we do not make the least addition to the thing when we further declare that this thing *is.* Otherwise, it would not be exactly the same thing that exists, but something more than we had thought in the concept; and we could not, therefore, say that the exact object of my concept exists. If we think in a thing every feature of reality except one, the missing reality is not added by my saying that this defective thing exists. On the contrary, it exists with the same defect with which I have thought it, since otherwise what exists would be something different from what I thought. When, therefore, I think a being as the supreme reality, without any defect, the question still remains whether it exists or not.[8]

Kant's argument seems to me to be essentially correct. However, it is extremely difficult to prove conclusively that he is correct. As yet we do not have sufficient agreement on the nature of predication to settle the issue once and for all.

A very telling objection has been propounded of late by Richard Swinburne.[9] Swinburne believes that it is relatively easy to show that the ontological argument fails. If the argument succeeds, it entails the view that "God exists" is logically necessary, that is, true by definition. If "God exists" is logically necessary, then any other sentence entailed by "God exists" must also be logically necessary. Thus the following sentences must be logically necessary: "It is not the case that the only persons are embodied persons"; "It is not the case that no one knows everything about the past." Equally if these statements are logically necessary, their negations must be incoherent. But the negations of these sentences are entirely coherent, hence "God exists" is not logically necessary. To put the point even more sharply, it

[8]Plantinga, ed., *The Ontological Argument,* p. 62.
[9]Richard Swinburne, *The Coherence of Theism* (Oxford: Clarendon Press, 1977), p. 265.

is surely false to say that the sentence "God does not exist" is a self-contradiction on a par with "Bachelor Jones is a married man" or "that square is round." However, if the ontological argument is valid, "God does not exist" is necessarily false. As that is obviously not the case, we should reject the ontological argument.

This does not mean that examination of the ontological argument is a waste of time even within religion. On the contrary, the argument can inspire the believer to explore more fully and self-critically what he or she believes about God. In doing so, one returns to the original spiritual and devotional context where Anselm first placed the argument. This is no bad thing, for the technical and abstract discussions about predication which presently dominate the discussion can easily erode the original insight which Anselm sought to conceptualize. To be sure, the technical issues must be pursued without apology, but technical issues are only a small part of philosophy of religion, and it is disastrous for the discipline as a whole when they become dominant.

THE COSMOLOGICAL ARGUMENT

The cosmological argument for the existence of God, like the ontological argument, can be expressed in various forms. Unlike the ontological argument, it appeals to facts about the world rather than to purely conceptual considerations. Sometimes it is known as the first-cause argument, sometimes as the argument from contingency. Its source can be located in the common experience of wonder at the existence of the world. Thus at various moments we are struck by the sheer existence of the universe. It puzzles us profoundly why there should be a world at all; why there should be something rather than nothing. In its essence, the cosmological argument seeks to relieve our intellectual perplexity by explaining the existence of the cosmos as a product of the activity of God. For many theists this is still a foundational consideration in their commitment.

One philosopher who considers the cosmological argument to be the fundamental metaphysical argument for God's existence is F. C. Copleston, a leading historian of philosophy. He sets out the argument in terms of contingency, dividing it into a series of distinct steps.

> First of all, I should say, we know that there are at least some beings in the world which do not contain in themselves the reason for their existence. For example, I depend on my parents, and now on the air, and on food, and so on. Now, secondly, the world is simply the real or imagined totality or aggregate of individual objects, none of which contain in themselves alone the reason for their existence. There isn't any world distinct from the objects which form it, any more than the human race is something apart from the members. Therefore, I should say, since objects or events exist, and since no object of experience contains within itself the reason of its existence, this reason, the totality of objects, must have a reason external to itself. That reason must be an existent being. Well, this being is either itself the reason for its own existence, or it is not. If it is, well and good. If it is not, then we must proceed

farther. But if we proceed to infinity in that sense, then there's no explanation of existence at all. So, I should say, in order to explain existence, we must come to a being which contains within itself the reason for its own existence, that is to say, which cannot not-exist.[10]

Religious believers often find it confusing and disappointing that what began as an experience of wonder should turn out to be so complex. Not surprisingly, therefore, ordinary people tend to favor that form of the cosmological argument which is expressed in terms of a first cause. What strikes most people as somehow obvious is that there must be something that started the cosmos going. The heart of the argument, as Brian Davies points out, is that there is a cause of the existence of things and this cause does not itself require a cause of its existence outside itself.[11] However, we recall that if we are to speak of any argument as a proof for God's existence, then we must pay the price for a proof by specifying quite clearly what the premises are, by showing the premises to be true, and by establishing that the conclusion sought really follows from the premises as a matter of logic. Hence sooner or later the believer has to deliver the goods in the manner displayed by Copleston. What are we to make of his argument?

The problems in any formal version of the argument are numerous. First, the argument assumes that there must be a reason for everything that exists. How do we know that is so? Perhaps some things exist as a brute fact for which no further reason can be given. Perhaps that is true of the cosmos. It just happens to exist, we know not why, and that is all there is to be said. There is no reason why it exists. Secondly, the argument assumes that it makes sense to ask for a cause for the cosmos. But perhaps the language of causality applies only to entities within the cosmos as a whole. Maybe we are stretching the language of causes beyond its proper context. Bertrand Russell (1872-1970) believed that such stretching was taking place and expressed it in this fashion in his response to Copleston.

Every man who exists has a mother, and it seems to me your argument is that therefore the human race must have a mother, but obviously the human race hasn't a mother—that's a different logical sphere.[12]

Thirdly, the cosmological argument seems to depend in a covert way on the validity of the ontological argument. This fact emerges when one unpacks what is meant by a necessary being. We defined that as a being which contains within itself the reason for its existence. Copleston, however, takes this to involve a being the essence of which is to exist. Such a being must exist and cannot not-exist.[13] It is true that, being what we are, we do not have a clear intuition of God's essence;

[10] John Hick, ed., *The Existence of God* (New York: Macmillan, 1964), p. 168.

[11] Brian Davies, *An Introduction to the Philosophy of Religion* (Oxford: Oxford University Press, 1982), p. 43.

[12] Hick, *Existence of God*, p. 175.

[13] Ibid., p. 172.

therefore we cannot rely on the ontological argument. However, if we really saw who God is, we would necessarily see that God must exist. That is what is at stake when we speak of necessary existence. Therefore the cosmological argument does appeal in the end to a conception of being, which leads by degrees back into the essential ingredients of the ontological argument with all its attendant problems.

One might avoid this problem by abandoning all talk of a necessary being and simply speak of a first cause, which brought everything into existence. To take this route is to leave the frying pan for the fire. How do we know there is just one first cause? Maybe polytheism is true and there are several gods. How we do know that there is not an infinite series of causes going on back for ever and ever? Maybe there is an infinite series of causes and that is the way things ultimately are. Moreover, do we know that the first cause is God? Maybe the first cause is an idiot god or a weak god who is doing the best he can in creating the cosmos. It is only too clear that the cosmological argument fails to prove the existence of God.

THE TELEOLOGICAL ARGUMENT

Does the teleological argument fare any better? Like the cosmological argument, the teleological argument appeals to certain facts about the world rather than to considerations about the concept of God. It appeals to certain operations and features of the world which suggest that there must be a creative intelligence behind them. From time immemorial people have found that the world exhibits an order and design which, they feel, necessarily points to the existence of some intelligent divinity who has brought it into existence. Clearly the argument is very akin in substance to the cosmological argument; both arise out of extreme wonder and bafflement at the existence of things as they are.

One of the most celebrated exponents of the teleological argument was William Paley (1743-1805). He developed his central point by means of a common analogy.

> In crossing a heath, suppose I pitched my foot against a *stone,* and were asked how the stone came to be there, I might possibly answer, that, for anything I knew to the contrary, it had lain there for ever; nor would it, perhaps, be very easy to show the absurdity of this answer. But suppose I found a *watch* upon the ground, and it should be inquired how the watch happened to be in that place, I should hardly think of the answer which I had before given—that, for anything I knew, the watch might have always been there. Yet why should not this answer serve for the watch as well as for the stone? Why is it not as admissible in the second case as in the first? For this reason, and for no other, viz., that, when we come to inspect the watch, we perceive (what we could not discover in the stone) that its several parts are framed and put together for a purpose. . . .

Paley then describes in detail the mechanism of a watch and concludes:

This mechanism being observed, (it requires indeed an examination of the instrument, and perhaps some previous knowledge of the subject, to perceive and understand it; but being once, as we have said, observed and understood) the inference, we think, is inevitable, that the watch must have had a maker; that there must have existed, at some time, and at some place or other, an artificer or artificers who formed it for the purpose which we find it actually to answer; who comprehended its construction, and designed its use.[14]

The application of this to an argument for God is obvious. The indications of contrivance in the watch are matched countless times by the indications of contrivance in nature. Therefore, just as the watch must have a maker, so must the world have a designer and creator. One cannot admit the former without granting the latter on pain of inconsistency.

In recent times proponents of the teleological argument have departed from the emphasis of Paley when he focused on the specific complexity and efficiency, say, of the human eye. Writers like F. R. Tennant (1865-1957)[15] and Richard Swinburne[16] have focused on the orderliness of nature as a whole. They very rightly recognize that particular indications of contrivance can be very adequately explained on evolutionary principles. Evolution itself, however, is a specific example of the general regularity of nature, and it is that which constitutes the basic data for the argument. Does the existence of order in the universe establish the existence of God? The general consensus is that it does not.

The more common grounds for this conclusion were long ago laid out by David Hume (1711-76).[17] Not all of Hume's arguments will hold, but his central objections are very interesting. We can state them this way. First, in cases where we infer a designer for such artifacts as watches, we do so on the basis of experience. It is experience which has taught us that watches are produced by watchmakers. If in doubt, we can go and look at them being made. We have no such experience for the existence of orderliness in the world as a whole. There is no way of checking that our world and its order was made by a designer or creator. Secondly, even if we grant that we can argue from the regularity in the universe, there is no guarantee that its designer is God. Perhaps the universe was designed by a committee of gods; or perhaps it was made by a god who is less than almighty, eternal, omniscient, and so on. Thirdly, even if we establish that there is a single designer behind the universe, we can still legitimately ask if there lies another designer behind that designer, and so on or ad infinitum. It may seem a little odd to believe in a designer behind the designer, but unless such a possibility is ruled out conclusively, the argument from design remains unsuccessful as a proof for God. Alternately, one might simply argue

---

[14] Ibid., p. 99.

[15] F. R. Tennant, *Philosophical Theology*, vol. II (Cambridge: Cambridge University Press, 1930).

[16] Richard Swinburne, *The Existence of God* (Oxford: Clarendon Press, 1979).

[17] David Hume, *Dialogues Concerning Natural Religion* (New York: Hefner, 1948).

that the existence of designlike entities and processes is a simple brute fact. They might have been made by God; but then again, they might not have been made by God. So long as the latter is a possible option, then they do not prove the existence of God. For such reasons as these, I do not find the teleological argument valid.

ANCILLARY ARGUMENTS

This is an important conclusion, for it has relevance to that whole range of ancillary arguments in natural theology which appeal to events, processes, or experiences in life generally. Religious believers have appealed from time to time to various considerations which are not normally included in the data of the cosmological or teleological arguments. They have appealed to extraordinary events like surprising healings subsequent to prayer, to visions of one kind or another, to their sense of obligation and conscience, to the general intelligibility of the universe, to the existence of beauty in nature and art, to their ability to appreciate the complexity and glory of the world, and so on. These arguments are almost without exception variants of the argument from design. They point to events and experiences which seem to require an intelligent source for their existence. Moreover, their general form takes the following pattern of reasoning.

> If God did not exist, phenomena a, b, c . . . n would not exist.
> The phenomena a, b, c . . . n exist.
> Therefore God exists.

This argument is formally valid. The problem lies in the fact that we do not know and cannot prove that its first premise is true. Sceptics can always make one of two moves to avoid the conclusion. They can attempt to show that the phenomena in question can be accounted for in purely natural terms, thus making appeal to God unnecessary; or they can accept the phenomena as brute facts of life for which no explanation is available or necessary. Therefore these arguments fail conspicuously to prove the existence of God.

This is an important conclusion to have reached. It shows how misguided our initial instincts and intuitions may be, for classical natural theology rests on experiences and feelings which are widespread in religious communities. The move from data and experience to their implications is more complex and ultimately more precarious than we might at first believe. Reflection on classical natural theology forces us to clarify our intuitions and test them self-critically for ourselves. This is a chastening experience but one which is surely well worth the effort, despite the fact that it has left many profoundly unsettled about their religious beliefs. It drove David Hume, for example, out of conventional Calvinistic piety. It even led John Wesley (1703-91) to contemplate suicide. Despite this, we do well to follow Wesley's advice to think the issue through for themselves.

But in a point of so unspeakable importance, do not depend upon the word of another; but retire for awhile from the busy world, and make the experiment yourself. Try whether *your* reason will give you a clear satisfactory evidence of the invisible world. After the prejudices of education are laid aside, produce your strong reasons for the existence of this. Set them all in array; silence all objections; and put all your doubts to flight. Alas! you cannot, with all your understanding. You may repress them for a season. But how quickly will they rally again, and attack you with redoubled violence! And what can poor reason do for your deliverance? The more vehemently you struggle, the more deeply you are entangled in the toils; and you find no way to escape.[18]

Wesley stands among those who find classical natural theology religiously unsatisfactory. Even had the arguments for God's existence succeeded, they did not produce the kind of personal assurance he felt was central to the Christian faith. Wesley found such assurance in intimate, personal experience of God. Much modern theology has turned from natural theology to religious experience in the hope of relieving the perplexity caused by the collapse of the classical proofs for the existence of God. Let us now explore this in some detail and determine to what degree religious experience can serve as the foundation for religious belief and assurance.

[18] John Wesley, *The Works of John Wesley*, vol. VI (London: John Mason, 1829), p. 356. The emphasis as in the original.

Chapter Four
Religious Experience

The collapse of natural theology has left a vacuum which self-critical religious believers have not hesitated to fill in modern times. Of the various options open, one of the most important has been the appeal to religious experience. Simple believers and sophisticated theologians have both looked to this as a means of relieving their own doubts and of answering sceptics who wished to know why they continued to believe in God when much traditional thinking had collapsed. We shall examine the appeal to religious experience in some detail in this chapter.

QUESTIONS RAISED BY RELIGIOUS EXPERIENCE

In doing so we shall need to explore several factors. We want to know, for example, what we mean when we speak of religious experience. What is a religious experience? How does it differ from other experiences? Can we identify a common core in all religious experience? We also want to know how religious experience serves to justify religious belief. What kind of argument is being tendered when someone appeals to religious experience? Is there, in fact, an argument at all to offer? If not, how can religious experience be said to justify religious belief? Moreover, we want to know what kind of religious belief religious experience can actually justify. Does it justify belief in a personal god? Does it point to something transcendent and then leave one to describe this reality in detail but on other grounds? These are the principle issues which shall detain us. We begin with the nature of religious experience.

It is far from easy to identify and describe religious experience. Two routes have been taken to reduce the difficulty. One way is to focus on examples of mystical experience. Excellent summaries of these are available.[1] The general approach is to describe the basic character of mystical experience and then explore how far such experience constitutes a warrant for religious belief. It is assumed in this case that any appeal to religious experience outside of mysticism will not be different in logic from that offered in the case of mysticism. A second way to reduce perplexity is to isolate a common core in all religious experience, clarify it as carefully as possible, and then explore its rational implications for religious belief. In a classic study the German theologian Rudolf Otto (1869-1937) took this approach. In *The Idea of the Holy*[2] he argued that religious experience was a unique experience involving an awareness of the numinous reality of God, evoking at one and the same time wonder, ecstasy, and fear.[3] Through such experience we become aware of God. Such awareness constitutes the fundamental basis for religious belief.

Both approaches have their advantages and disadvantages. The former helps the critical question to be raised very sharply, but it tends to make religious experience rather remote and esoteric. The latter keeps religious experience more intelligible and accessible, but it tends to be rather obscure about the role of religious experience as a foundation for religious belief.[4] Let us attempt, therefore, to do justice to both the diversity of religious experience and its critical role in religious belief as we explore what it is.

Suppose someone were to say that he or she had had a religious experience. What might be meant by such a claim? Some have suggested that it could mean anything from laughing at jokes to an experience of the internal witness of the Holy Spirit.[5] This is a strange position to adopt, not least because it fails to distinguish between believing that the divine is present and sensing the presence of the divine. A religious believer might hold, for example, that God was present in the eucharist but have no sense of God's presence when he participated on a particular occasion.

---

[1] See, for example, William James, *The Varieties of Religious Experience* (London: Longmans, Green, 1928), chaps. 16 and 17; Evelyn Underhill, *Mystics of the Church* (Cambridge: James Clarke, 1925); R. C. Zaehner, *Mysticism Sacred and Profane* (Oxford: Oxford University Press, 1956); Geoffrey Parrinder, *Mysticism in the World's Religions* (New York: Oxford University Press, 1976).

[2] Trans. John W. Harvey (London: Penguin, 1959).

[3] Otto used the Latin terms *mysterium, fascinans,* and *tremendum* to describe religious experience. Various English terms can be used to capture what he meant (e.g., mystery, fascination, dread) but it is not at all easy to do justice to their native complexity.

[4] An excellent attempt to clarify Otto's position on this is given by Malcolm Diamond in *Contemporary Philosophy and Religious Thought* (New York: McGraw-Hill, 1974), chap. 5.

[5] See John Stacey, *Groundwork of Theology* (London: Epworth Press, 1977), pp. 67–69. I shall explain shortly what is meant by the internal witness of the Holy Spirit.

Or, to take a more general case, a religious believer would hold that God was present in her room while she slept, but sleeping would not constitute a religious experience. One could multiply such examples very easily. Moreover, in an attempt to make religion seem relevant by insisting that religion and life are one, this approach trivializes religious experience. When one speaks of having a religious experience one speaks of something significant and important. To make every experience a religious experience flies in the face of this fact and encourages loose thinking about its significance. It is more helpful to work with reasonably clear-cut examples rather than to try to make every experience a religious experience. How far such examples can be divided into classes for convenience need not worry us unduly, although classification obviously increases clarity. What matters most is to capture those cases which are manifestly relevant to the justification of religious belief. We can think of several of these.

PARADIGM CASES OF RELIGIOUS EXPERIENCE

A clear example of religious experience is the case of conversion. One of the most famous is that of Augustine (354–430). After years of searching and struggle he at last found peace. He describes his conversion as follows:

> I probed the hidden depths of my soul and wrung its pitiful secrets from it, and when I mustered them all before the eyes of my heart, a great storm broke within me, bringing with it a great deluge of tears. I stood up and left Alypius so that I might weep and cry to my heart's content, for it occurred to me that tears were best shed in solitude. I moved away far enough to avoid being embarrassed even by his presence. He must have realized what my feelings were, for I suppose I had said something and he had known from the sound of my voice that I was ready to burst into tears. So I stood up and left him where he had been sitting, utterly bewildered. Somehow I flung myself down beneath a fig tree and gave way to the tears which now streamed from my eyes, the sacrifice that is acceptable to you. I had much to say to you, my God, not in these very words but in this strain: Lord, will you never be content? Must we always taste your vengeance? Forget the long record of our sins. For I felt that I was still the captive of my sins, and in my misery I kept crying, "How long shall I go on saying 'tomorrow, tomorrow'? Why not now? Why not make an end of my ugly sins at this moment?"
>
> I was asking myself these questions, weeping all the while with the most bitter sorrow in my heart, when all at once I heard the sing-song voice of a child in a nearby house. Whether it was the voice of a boy or a girl I cannot say, but again and again it repeated the refrain "Take it and read, take it and read." At this I looked up, thinking hard whether there was any kind of game in which children used to chant words like these, but I could not remember ever hearing them before. I stemmed my flood of tears and stood up, telling myself that this could only be a divine command to open my book of Scripture and read the first passage on which my eyes should fall. For I had heard the story of Antony, and I remembered how he had happened to go into a church while the Gospel was being read and had taken it as a counsel addressed to himself when he heard the words *Go home and sell all that belongs*

*to you. Give it to the poor, and so the treasure you have shall be in heaven;
then come back and follow me.* By this divine pronouncement he had at once
been converted to you.

So I hurried back to the place where Alypius was sitting, for when I stood
up to move away I had put down the book containing Paul's Epistles. I seized
it and opened it, and in silence I read the first passage on which my eyes fell:
*Not in revelling and drunkenness, not in lust and wantonness, not in quarrels
and rivalries. Rather, arm yourselves with the Lord Jesus Christ; spend no
more thought on nature and nature's appetites.* I had no wish to read more
and no need to do so. For in an instant, as I came to the end of the sentence,
it was as though the light of confidence flooded into my heart and all the
darkness of doubt was dispelled.[6]

A second example of religious experience is represented by cases of visions,
auditions or dreams. Consider the following instance.

Peter went up on the housetop to pray, about the sixth hour. And he became
hungry and desired something to eat; but while they were preparing it, he fell
into a trance and saw the heaven opened, and something descending, like a
great sheet, let down by four corners upon the earth. In it were all kinds of
animals and reptiles and birds of the air. And there came a voice to him,
"Rise, Peter, kill and eat." But Peter said, "No, Lord, for I have never eaten
anything that is common or unclean." And the voice came to him a second
time, "What God has cleansed, you must not call common." This happened
three times, and the thing was taken up at once to heaven.[7]

A third example is that which is technically described as the *testimonium
Spiritus Sancti internum,* the inner testimony of the Holy Spirit. This refers to that
inner assurance of pardon and acceptance which has been central to the evangelical
account of the Christian faith. It is perfectly illustrated by John Wesley's report of
his conversion in 1738.

In the evening I went very unwillingly to a society in Aldersgate Street, where
one was reading Luther's preface to the Epistle to the Romans. About a quar-
ter before nine, while he was describing the change which God works in the
heart through faith in Christ, I felt my heart strangely warmed. I felt I did
trust in Christ, Christ alone for salvation; and an assurance was given me that
He had taken away my sins, even mine, and saved me from the law of sin and
death.[8]

A fourth example is that of a vivid awareness of God in nature or in some
other event such as listening to a sermon, singing hymns, participating in a sacra-
ment, or joining with others in prayer. Jonathan Edwards (1703–58) bears witness
to the first of these in this way:

[6] Saint Augustine, *Confessions,* trans. R. S. Pine-Coffin, (New York: Penguin Classics,
1961), pp. 177–78. Copyright © R. S. Pine-Coffin, 1961.

[7] Acts 10:9–16.

[8] John Wesley, *The Journal of John Wesley* (London: Wesleyan Conference Office,
1875), vol. I, p. 97.

After this my sense of divine things gradually increased, and became more and more lively, and had more of that inward sweetness. The appearance of everything was altered; there seemed to be, as it were, a calm, sweet cast, or appearance of divine glory, in almost everything. God's excellency, his wisdom, his purity and love, seemed to appear in everything; in the sun, moon, and stars; in the clouds and blue sky; in the grass, flowers, and trees; in the water and all nature; which used greatly to fix my mind. And scarce anything, among all the works of nature, was so sweet to me as thunder and lightning; formerly nothing had been so terrible to me. Before, I used to be uncommonly terrified with thunder, and to be struck with terror when I saw a thunderstorm rising; but now, on the contrary, it rejoices me.[9]

The most widely discussed example of religious experience is undoubtedly that of mysticism. Some mystical experiences come very close in description to the one just given by Edwards. In such cases the mystic looks outward through the senses to the natural world. In other cases the mystic looks deep within. It is common, therefore, to find students of mysticism distinguishing between extrovertive and introvertive types of mystical experience. The former see the world of the senses transformed; the latter find the divine within themselves after profound experience of darkness and nothingness. For an example of the former we can turn to Malwida von Meysenbug, a German Idealist, writing in 1900.

I was alone upon the seashore as all these thoughts flowed over me, liberating and reconciling; and now again, as once before in distant days in the Alps of Dauphine, I was impelled to kneel down, this time before the illimitable ocean, symbol of the Infinite. I felt that I prayed as I had never prayed before, and knew now what prayer really is; to return from the solitude of individuation into the consciousness of unity with all that is, to kneel down as one that passes away, and to rise up as one imperishable. Earth, heaven, and sea resounded as in one vast world-encircling harmony. It was as if the chorus of all the great who had ever lived were about me. I felt myself one with them, and it appeared as if I heard their greeting: "Thou too belongest to the company of those who overcome."[10]

The introvertive type is well represented in a passage of Gregory of Nyssa (335-95).

For leaving behind everything that is observed, not only what sense comprehends but also what the intelligence thinks it sees, it keeps on penetrating deeper until by the intelligence's yearning for understanding it gains access to the invisible and the incomprehensible, and there it sees God. This is the true knowledge of what is sought; this is the seeing that consists in not seeing, because that which is sought transcends all knowledge, being separated on all sides by incomprehensibility as by a kind of darkness. Wherefore John the sublime, who penetrated into the luminous darkness says, No one has ever seen God, thus asserting that knowledge of the divine essence is unattainable not only by men but also by every intelligent creature.[11]

[9] Quoted in James, *Varieties of Religious Experience*, pp. 248-9.
[10] Ibid., p. 395.
[11] Gregory of Nyssa, *The Life of Moses*, trans. Abraham Malherbe and Everett Ferguson (New York: Paulist Press, 1978), p. 95.

Reflecting on examples of extrovertive and introvertive mysticism, William L. Rowe suggests that each type of experience has the following list of characteristic features.

THE EXTROVERTIVE TYPE:

1. Looks outwards through the senses
2. Sees the inner essence of things, an essence which appears to be alive, beautiful, and the same in all things
3. Sense of union of one's deeper self with this inner essence
4. Feeling that what is experienced is divine
5. Sense of reality, that one sees things as they really are
6. Sense of peace and bliss
7. Timelessness, no awareness of the passage of time during the experience

THE INTROVERTIVE TYPE:

1. A state of consciousness devoid of its ordinary contents: sensations, images, thoughts, desires, and so forth
2. An experience of absolute oneness, with no distinction or divisions
3. Sense of reality, that one is experiencing what is ultimately real
4. Feeling that what is experienced is divine
5. Sense of complete peace and bliss
6. Timelessness, no awareness of the passage of time during the experience [12]

Such reflection leads Rowe, along with many others, to argue that there is considerable agreement among mystics about their experience. William James's statement of this is especially memorable.

> This overcoming of all the usual barriers between the individual and the Absolute is the great mystic achievement. In mystic states we both become one with the Absolute, and we become aware of our oneness. This is the everlasting and triumphant mystical tradition, hardly altered by differences of clime or creed. In Hinduism, in Neoplatonism, in Sufism, in Christian mysticism, in Whitmanism, we find the same recurring note, so that there is about mystical utterances an eternal unanimity which ought to make a critic stop and think, and which brings it about that the mystical classics have, as has been said, neither birthday nor native land. Perpetually telling us the unity of man with God, their speech antedates languages, and they do not grow old. [13]

What unites these examples is that they all involve a claim to be aware of the divine. They isolate particular experiences where the individual senses the presence of God. Indeed, the language of the senses is the natural language believers will use to report their experience: they see, hear, or feel God present. Experiences of this

[12] William L. Rowe, *Philosophy of Religion* (Belmont, Calif.: Wadsworth, 1978), pp. 66–68.

[13] James, *Varieties of Religious Experience,* p. 419.

sort are widespread in space and time and appear among peoples of varying races, religions, and social conditions.

Because these experiences all constitute examples of claims to be directly aware of God, it is natural to distinguish them from other cases of religious experience. Indeed it is not easy to agree on what other experiences would constitute a religious experience. Perhaps we might include experience of an alleged miracle, e.g., an experience where one observes a miracle in one's own body or is present at a miracle, such as would be the case of the disciples at the resurrection of Jesus. We might also include a conviction of divine providence at work in one's life over the years, or dramatic answers to prayer, or the pull of divine grace drawing one to live a more holy life. The latter is captured very aptly by the early Quaker, Robert Barclay (1648–90).

> For not a few have come to be convinced of the Truth, after this manner, of which I myself in a part am a true witness, who not by strength of arguments, or by a particular disquisition of each doctrine, and convincement of my understanding thereby, came to receive and bear witness of the Truth, but by being secretly reached by this Life; for, when I came into the silent assemblies of God's people, I felt a secret power among them, which touched my heart, and, as I gave way unto it, I found the evil weakening in me and the good raised up.[14]

In such cases as these we cannot rule out the possibility of a claim to be aware of God. However, they can in some instances be construed as religious experiences where there may be no direct sense of the presence of God. At the very least the intensity of the awareness of God tends to be less marked than in the earlier cases cited.

THE ARGUMENT FROM RELIGIOUS EXPERIENCE

This is important because it has a bearing on the logic of the argument from religious experience. In the latter set of examples the argument more readily takes the form of offering an explanatory hypothesis for certain experiences. That is to say, the believer is arriving at the existence of God by way of an inference from experience. If this is the case, we simply have another piece of classical natural theology whose logic is that of the argument from design. As we have already discussed this in the previous chapter, it shall not detain us here.

The argument from the earlier set of examples, however, does not conform to this pattern at all. On the contrary, its value is often claimed to be its explicit rejection of such an argument. Rather than construed as an inference, the existence of God is taken to be *directly* known. The experience is said to be self-authenticating. It is this that accounts for the peculiar attraction of the appeal to religious experi-

[14] Quoted in Elton Trueblood, *Philosophy of Religion* (New York: Harper and Row, 1957), p. 154.

ence. In a sense it is not really an argument at all; rather it is an appeal to first-hand experience. As such it produces a measure of certainty which is especially intense, making the classical arguments of natural theology look rickety by comparison. No less a figure than Aquinas, one of the great architects of natural theology, seems to have taken this position. Prior to his death, he had a mysterious experience after which he refused to continue his discursive, theological writings, insisting that he could not do so because all that he had written seemed like so much straw compared to what he had seen.[15] In modern times this point has been well made by John Hick. After noting that the biblical writers often were vividly conscious of being in God's presence, he continues:

> This experiencing of life as a "dialogue with God" is the believer's primary reason for being sure that God is real. In testing such a reason we must be careful to ask the right question. This is not: do someone's accounts of his experience of the divine presence and activity provide an adequate reason for someone else, who has had no such experience, to be sure that God is real? Or, can one validly infer the existence of God from the reports of religious experiences? The answer in each case is no. But the proper question is whether the religious man's awareness of being in the unseen presence of God constitutes a sufficient reason for the religious man himself to be sure of the reality of God. He does not profess to infer God as the cause of his distinctively religious experience. He professes to be conscious of living in the presence of God; and this consciousness is (in the classic cases) as compelling as is his consciousness of the natural world.[16]

Hick makes clear what is at stake in the modern appeal to religious experience. The claim is fundamentally a perceptual claim. Just as we normally take our perception of the natural world to be veridical rather than illusory, so we should also take our awareness of the spiritual world to be veridical rather than illusory. To be sure not all lay claim to be aware of the divine, but for those who have had religious experience, that experience should normally be considered veridical. At this point the onus of argument lies with the unbeliever. The sceptic must provide good reasons for not taking the perceptual claim as it stands. Meanwhile, the believer has every right to his or her certainty.

This position has been articulated and defended recently by Richard Swinburne.[17] Swinburne agrees that religious experience should be seen as similar to our experience of natural objects. In both cases we operate on the principle of initial credulity, that is, what one seems to perceive is probably so. In other words, how things seem to be is good grounds for how things are. This principle applies quite generally both to our ordinary perceptual awareness and to our awareness of the divine. As Swinburne sees it, attempts to challenge this principle on general grounds

---

[15] This is briefly discussed in Anthony Kenny, *Aquinas* (Oxford: Oxford University Press, 1980), p. 26.

[16] John Hick, *Faith and Knowledge* (Glasgow: Fontana, 1974), pp. 209–10. Emphasis as in original.

[17] Richard Swinburne, *The Existence of God* (Oxford: Clarendon Press, 1979), chap. 13.

or attempts to rule out its application to religious experience are either unjustified or unsuccessful. As we briefly pursue such attempts, we shall review some of the central arguments against the appeal to religious experience. Most of the opponents of the argument from religious experience concentrate on the inapplicability of the principle to claims to be aware of the divine.

INITIAL OBJECTIONS REBUTTED

Some initially feel that the very phrasing of the appeal begs the question in advance. In order to identify religious experience, the believer has to make use of the very language which is in dispute. Thus the first-hand reports we cited earlier involve the use of descriptions which assume the existence of the divine. They involve reports to have been aware of God or his activity. This is precisely what is at issue, however, hence the appeal to religious experience has begged the question at the outset. Alternatively, one might say that the appeal to religious experience cannot get off the ground, for in order to report it, one will need to refer to the very object whose existence is to be established.

This argument fails, however, for at least two reasons. First, the same applies to our experience of ordinary objects. We speak of seeing a chair, hearing the noise of the car outside my window, and so forth, without accepting that this begs the question in advance against an appeal to experience when challenged to justify our beliefs about the chair or the noise of the car outside my window. Secondly, there is a simple way of rephrasing the descriptions to avoid any *petitio principii.* As Swinburne points out, we can move from external to internal descriptions.[18] Rather than say, "I was aware of the divine," we can say, "It seems to me that I was aware of the divine." That way the principle of initial credulity can still be applied without any difficulty.

A second way to challenge the appeal to religious experience is to draw a distinction between experience and the interpretation of experience. In this case the sceptic accepts that reports of religious experience show that something very important has happened to those who give them but insists that what has actually happened may well be entirely subjective. The report really describes internal mental states rather than any external, objective reality. Thus the claim to be aware of the divine is erroneous. Such a claim is an interpretation of experience; it is really an inference from experience to God; it is an attempt to explain causally the origin of one's religious experience. If one is to accept the religious interpretation, there must be independent reasons outside the experience itself for doing so.

It is not easy to know exactly how to evaluate this objection. We certainly do often accept that we need to distinguish between our experiences and the interpretation of our experiences. Thus when out for a walk, I may see a light in the distance. I may construe this light as a lighthouse or a stationary car or a lamppost.

---

[18] Ibid., p. 245.

Here one can certainly speak of an experience and its interpretation. However, the objection suggests that we can distinguish between experience and interpretation in all cases, including that of religious experience. That is highly questionable. It is very difficult to conceive of our experiences as not involving some level of interpretation. After all, some set of concepts will have to be used once we report our experience, and once we speak of concepts, we are involved in interpretation. Also, we need to remember that the whole thrust of reports of religious experience is that they do not involve an inference. They embody direct awareness of the subject described. To construe religious experience as a case of inference on purely a priori grounds ignores this fact and therefore fails to reckon with the full force of the claim.

Equally unsatisfactory is any general argument from illusion, hallucination, and the use of drugs as the true explanation for reports of religious experience. We do not generally believe that because some reports of ordinary natural objects sometimes involve illusion, hallucination, and the like, then all reports do so. If we insist that they apply only to religious experience, then we face the embarrassing fact that we apply standards in the religious sphere which we do not apply elsewhere. Such a move would seem to exhibit irrational prejudice rather than good critical judgment. It looks as if we are insisting that religious experience must always be seen as guilty until proven innocent. Generally, as the principle of initial credulity suggests, we operate quite differently.

Perhaps there are good reasons, however, for construing religious experience as ultimately illusory. Prima facie it should be taken seriously as evidence for the divine, but when we examine it in detail there are good reasons for either rejecting it or becoming agnostic. Note, however, that it is far from easy to turn this logical possibility into actuality. It is not enough to point out what might be the case about religious experience. The experience itself outweighs such abstract possibilities, for it provides evidence in its own right for the existence of the divine. Moreover, there are independent considerations which quite naturally provide reasons for taking religious experience as reported.

Elton Trueblood draws attention to such considerations when he isolates four separate elements involved.[19] First, there is the number of people involved. Many people across space and time claim to be aware of God; it is not just an isolated few. Secondly, there is the character of those who report that they have been aware of God. They fall into a host of psychological groups and include a large number who cannot be discounted on the grounds of insanity, inability to weigh evidence, or gullibility. A third factor is the remarkable change in life-style which generally accompanies religious experience. If it seems to you that a particular object exists, then, as Swinburne points out, you will believe that that particular object exists.[20] In turn, if you believe that that particular object exists, that will make a difference

---

[19] Trueblood, *Philosophy of Religion*, pp. 156–58.
[20] Swinburne, *Existence of God*, p. 273.

to your behavior in appropriate circumstances. This general pattern is well exemplified in the case of religious experience. Those who claim to be aware of God have found it more natural to act accordingly. Self-sacrifice, worship, and prayer, for example, become a central part of their lives. A final reason for taking religious experience at its face value is the degree of unanimity in reports of religious experience. At a minimum, religious experience speaks of some kind of mysterious order of immense significance and majesty, which should not be confused with the natural world. For these reasons, Trueblood believes that the testimony of religious experience is the strongest and most direct of all evidence for the existence of God.

Does it constitute evidence for someone who has had no awareness of God? Hick, we recall, argued that it only provided evidence for the recipient of religious experience. It gave the religious person the right to be sure of God but not the person who did not have any religious experience. This is a strange position to adopt. To be sure, religious experience would not in the latter case be first-hand evidence for the existence of God, but not all evidence need be of this nature. Clearly we often believe that certain things exist not because we have experienced them ourselves but because others report to us that they have experienced them. As Swinburne points out, we generally operate at this level on the principle of testimony, that is, in the absence of special considerations, the experiences of others are probably as they report them.[21] In other words, unless we have reason to believe otherwise, we have good grounds to believe what others tell us about their experiences. Religious experience, therefore, constitutes evidence for all to believe in the existence of God and not just for the few who actually report a religious experience.

Critics of religious experience have not generally worried about how far religious experience can be relied on by those who make no claim to be aware of God themselves. That is understandable, for those who have deployed the argument have not made much of it. Critics have focused, on the whole, on the value of religious experience for the religious believer who has had some kind of awareness of God. It is strategically important that critics do that, for religious experience is the foundation for any version of the argument relevant to those who report no awareness of God.

FURTHER OBJECTIONS CONSIDERED

Many theists have themselves objected to the appeal to religious experience. Among those who have done so recently is Brian Davies. Davies focuses on the unique nature of what is supposed to be known in religious experience.

> Experience of dogs and cats and people is one thing; but experience of what God is supposed to be seems quite different. It is far from clear that its nature can even be elucidated, let alone judged as something to which one could appeal as providing a reasonable ground for belief in God.[22]

[21] Ibid., p. 271.

[22] Brian Davies, *An Introduction to the Philosophy of Religion* (Oxford: Oxford University Press, 1982), p. 76.

This is a puzzling objection. To be sure, the object of religious experience is a mysterious object, and religious people readily admit that it is often extremely difficult to describe the content of their experience. They are not, however, entirely at a loss, as the examples given earlier make clear. Perhaps those who lay claim not to have had any religious experience may have to draw on their imagination to grasp what is at issue, but this says nothing against the possibility of elucidating the object of religious experience. Reasonably clear accounts of what is experienced are readily available. Besides, religious believers can suggest how best one might become aware of the divine so that the exercise of understanding need not be an entirely cerebral affair.

Antony Flew is a more hostile critic of religious experience. He writes as follows:

> There is no need in general to dispute the claims to have enjoyed vivid experiences, experiences which make it hard for the subject to doubt that he has been in contact with some corresponding object. The vital issue is whether any such private experiences can be furnished with adequate credentials; and this is a question which should be asked as urgently by those who have as by those who have not enjoyed such experiences. Its importance is underlined by two facts which should be familiar but are often ignored: first that religious experiences are enormously varied, ostensibly authenticating innumerable beliefs, many of which are in contradiction with one another or even themselves; and, second, that their character seems to depend on the interests, background and expectations of those who have them rather than upon anything separate and autonomous. First, the varieties of religious experience include, not only those which their subjects are inclined to interpret as visions of the Blessed Virgin or senses of the guiding presence of Jesus Christ, but also others more outlandish presenting themselves as manifestations of Quetzalcoatl or Osiris, of Dionysius or Shiva. Second, the expert natural historian of religious experience would be altogether astounded to hear of the vision of Bernadette Soubirois occurring not to a Roman Catholic at Lourdes but to a Hindu in Benares, or of Apollo manifest not in classical Delphi but in Kyoto under the Shoguns.[23]

It should be noted that Flew, by insisting on credentials, is making demands which are by no means agreed to be essential. Indeed, if our earlier argument is correct, Flew is making demands in the case of religious experience which we do not usually make for other experience. His argument, therefore, does not constitute a wholesale attack on the appeal to religious experience. At best, it discredits the last of the four independent reasons for treating religious experience as veridical, which were mentioned earlier. As such, it is not conclusive.

The key issue is the internal conflict within reports of religious experience. How can a reasonable person treat them all as veridical? Does the argument from religious experience not ultimately commit one to believe in the whole pantheon of comparative religion? Flew is correct to press this point. Reports of religious experience are diverse. Accounts of mystical experience illustrate this. Despite the fact that we can discern patterns of resemblance between different kinds of mystical

---

[23] Antony Flew, *God and Philosophy* (London: Hutchinson, 1966), pp. 126–27.

experience, these patterns are not always compatible. Thus some are couched in monistic terms and some in theistic terms.[24] If we apply the principle of initial credulity to such claims, then Flew's fears will be realized. When we extend the principle of credulity to other cases, the situation seems to be worse, for we will indeed be committed to a whole pantheon of divine agents.

It is not, however, beyond repair. If a religious tradition involves human reflection, it is entirely natural that different concepts may be used to describe one's experience of the divine. This would partially account for the diversity. Moreover, diversity itself need not entail incompatibility. The divine may be known under different names in different cultures. Even where there is incompatibility, the theist need not abandon the appeal to religious experience. If one has good reason, one may reject the conflicting account of religious experience as false, or one may invite its recipient to redescribe it in terms compatible with theism. Obviously this adjustment makes the appeal to religious experience more complex but it by no means discredits it. As Swinburne correctly points out:

> The fact that sometimes descriptions of the object of a religious experience are in conflict with descriptions of the object of another religious experience, only means that we have a source of challenge to a particular detailed claim, not a source of scepticism about all the claims of religious experience.[25]

When those claims are examined with care, taking into account the hard cases, there is still a large range of testimony which remains impressive.

The argument from religious experience can then be rescued from Flew's criticisms but only at the expense of weakening the principle of credulity. The conflict within reports of religious experience is too great for all of them to stand as veridical. The reports are theory laden to a highly significant degree so that experience alone cannot establish that they are correct. Other considerations will have to be presented if the descriptions commonly found in accounts of religious experience are to be accepted as true. So initially there is good reason to take religious experience very seriously, but in the last analysis the whole tradition in which it is embedded will have to be carefully examined to see how far it can be supported by independent considerations. The positive assessment of religious experience can be expressed then in one of two ways. We can say that it is too dogmatic to claim that religious experience is totally reliable or totally unreliable; the truth lies somewhere in between these two poles. Equally we might say that religious experience points to the existence of some kind of religious object but cannot in itself provide a detailed description of that object.[26]

---

[24] This is very clearly presented by Zaehner in *Mysticism Sacred and Profane*.

[25] Swinburne, *Existence of God*, p. 266.

[26] Gary Gutting has presented the argument from religious experience in such terms in *Religious Belief and Religious Skepticism* (Notre Dame: University of Notre Dame Press, 1982).

THE NEED FOR CAUTION

So there are grounds for caution in the appeal to religious experience. First, the appeal cannot be decisive in any simplistic sense. As we have seen, the appeal rests on principles which have to be carefully laid out and defended. For this reason it is confusing and exaggerated to argue that religious experience is self-authenticating. Secondly, throughout our discussion we have kept the conclusion as minimal. Religious experience gives reason to believe in the existence of the divine, but how the divine is to be further described cannot be decided by religious experience alone. This has far-reaching theological consequences for it casts suspicion on all those theologies which make religious experience the exclusive warrant for religious belief. Even those who appeal to it in a nonexclusive fashion need to be much clearer on how it operates than is currently fashionable.

One last point needs to be made. It is very obvious that in the appeal to religious experience we have made use of criteria of rationality which are radically different from those presupposed in the classical proofs for the existence of God. Aside from appealing to direct experience, we have spoken of confirming our experience by other considerations or reasons. This surely demands further critical analysis. We shall return to this point in due course but not before we have looked at a fascinating tradition in modern philosophy and theology which would reject the attempt to offer reasons for religious belief. Before that we must examine those arguments which embody positive objections to religious belief.

Chapter Five
Natural Atheology

Arguments against the existence of God have not been nearly so well organized as those for the existence of God. In the latter case we have a body of material which is sufficiently well known to merit its own label and place in both theology and philosophy of religion. Most educated people have at some time or other come across the classical arguments for the existence of God, and they have probably heard of natural theology. In the former case the situation is more complex. There does not exist an agreed body of arguments against the existence of God. Even the most widely discussed argument in this field, namely, the problem of evil, tends to be seen as a problem for the theist rather than a full-blooded disproof of theism. Moreover, some of the arguments against the existence of God can crop up in places where the primary context of the discussion is not necessarily the rationality of religious belief. For example, one of the more common arguments against theism in recent times has been the claim that religious language is meaningless; yet we have examined this question already.[1]

Arguments against the existence of God may not be well organized but they are well presented and carefully developed nonetheless. Certainly they deserve as much attention as those for the existence of God. Following Alvin Plantinga, we shall call such arguments natural atheology.[2] We might define natural atheology

[1] See chap. 2. Other objections to religious belief will crop up in various chapters to follow.

[2] Alvin Plantinga, *God, Freedom and Evil* (London: George Allen and Unwin, 1975), p. 3.

very broadly as those arguments which seek to show that belief in God is demonstrably irrational or unreasonable. In this chapter we shall look at a representative sample of antitheistic arguments. In the next we shall focus more specifically on the problem of evil.

FORMS OF NATURAL ATHEOLOGY

Arguments against theism take many forms. Some have felt it sufficient simply to undermine all arguments for theism. Thus opponents of theism have been quick to show up the inadequacy of natural theology. Bertrand Russell took this line in a famous lecture in 1927.[3] The logic behind this move is obvious. If there are no good reasons to believe in God, then belief in God must be deemed irrational. The implied assumption behind this argument is that any belief is irrational if no good reason can be presented for it. As theism has insufficient evidence in its favor, it is not worthy of rational commitment. Antony Flew has summed this up very succinctly.

> If it is to be established that there is a God, then we have to have good grounds for believing that this is indeed so. Until or unless some such grounds are produced we have literally no reason at all for believing; and in that situation the only reasonable posture must be that of either the negative atheist or the agnostic.[4]

This move is far from being satisfactory. First, any claim that rationality necessarily demands the giving of reasons is itself irrational. We have many beliefs, ordinarily deemed rational, which are not supported by reasons. For example, I believe correctly that I can now see with my eyes, that $2 + 2 = 4$, that pointless punishment of innocent children is wicked, that there has been a past, and so on, and yet I can give no reasons for such beliefs. Perhaps belief in God falls into this class of beliefs. Until it has been clearly established that it does not, then belief in God may be entirely rational.[5] Secondly, this proposal does not touch those who hold that religious belief is a matter of faith rather than reason. Such thinkers welcome the collapse of natural theology and may well assist in its demolition. But they would argue that this is a good thing, for it exhibits the true nature of religious belief rather than establishing its falsehood. Equally this position does not rule out the possibility that religious belief rests not on argument but on direct awareness of God in religious experience. For these reasons it is clear that any natural atheology which simply seeks to discredit the classical arguments for the existence of God is not very successful.

[3] Bertrand Russell, "Why I am not a Christian," in *Why I am not a Christian* (London: George Allen and Unwin, 1967), pp. 13–27.

[4] Antony Flew, *The Presumption of Atheism* (London: Pemberton, 1976), p. 22.

[5] We shall examine this in greater detail when we look at the recent work of Alvin Plantinga in chap. 8.

Writers like Russell and Flew implicitly agree with this when they deploy further arguments which set out the positive evidence against theism. These arguments fall into two broad categories. There are those arguments which seek to show that belief in God is incoherent. These constitute a very definite attempt to disprove the existence of God a priori. Generally they seek to show that language about God is self-contradictory. In addition, there are those arguments which are a posteriori in character, for they draw on evidence about the world in order to show that belief in God is unreasonable or illusory. The views of Sigmund Freud are a well-known example of the latter. We shall expound and examine some of these arguments shortly.

GENERAL SCEPTICISM

Before we do so we need to pause and note that there have been philosophers who have argued against theism on the grounds that no knowledge of any kind is possible. In this instance we are confronted with a very general sceptical tradition rather than the more limited scepticism directed at religious belief. Any adequate treatment of this general sceptical tradition demands much more attention and space than we can give it here, but it is surely salutary to mention some of the more obvious problems inherent in it.[6]

If we take scepticism to be the view that no knowledge is possible, it is open to the following objections.[7] To begin, such a claim is self-contradictory. The sceptic says that no knowledge is possible; but this itself constitutes a claim to knowledge; hence such scepticism is self-refuting. Indeed, even to state his or her case the sceptic has to make an implicit claim to knowledge for one cannot state any sceptical thesis without knowing the rules governing the concepts used to express that thesis. Moreover, if I am to attend to what the sceptic says, then I must be able to trust some of my senses, for without reliable information from my senses I could never hear or see what the sceptic believes. Here again, the sceptic has to assume what is said to be unknowable.

In addition, the sceptic faces the following dilemma. If I am to accept scepticism as true, I can do so only if the sceptic can present some kind of argument for it. The reason is that general scepticism is so counterintuitive that it would be irrational to accept it without good evidence. Certainly, scepticism is not a self-evident truth. But once the sceptic presents some sort of evidence, then he or she is implicitly saying that some propositions can be known as true or rationally acceptable. Alternatively, it looks as if we simply have to take the sceptic's word for scepticism; that, surely, is a piece of dogmatism which need not detain us.

---

[6] Helpful discussions of scepticism can be found in Richard H. Popkin, *The History of Scepticism from Erasmus to Spinoza* (Berkeley: University of California Press, 1979); and Franklin L. Baumer, *Religion and the Rise of Scepticism* (New York: Harcourt, Brace and World, 1960).

[7] I do not address directly here that form of scepticism which claims that we cannot even know that knowledge is impossible. However, some of the arguments presented here can be applied to it without too much difficulty.

In the past sceptics have presented arguments in their favor. They have constantly drawn attention to the lack of agreement there has been on various issues, and they have pointed out that we have all made mistakes because of faulty reasoning, illusion, madness, dreams, illness, and so on. By such means they have sought to show that every fundamental belief has been contested by somebody somewhere. Again, sceptics are hoist with their own petard. Such arguments rest on historical claims which sceptics must claim to know; these historical claims in turn rest on claims to knowledge mediated through the senses. For such reasons as these any absolute sceptical position has only bleak prospects of success. Hence it does little to enhance the case for atheism. How does the more limited scepticism which restricts itself to religious belief fare? Let us pursue this question by looking at some of the main arguments against the existence of God. We shall look at three in all.

THE ONTOLOGICAL DISPROOF

Recently J. N. Findlay attempted to disprove the existence of God in an argument which has obvious affinity with the ontological proof for the existence of God. Findlay presents his position as one who is genuinely sympathetic to religion. He is not at all keen to shake faith or overturn altars. He expresses this as follows.

> I am by temperament a Protestant, and I tend towards atheism as the purest form of Protestantism. By Protestantism I mean the conviction—resting, as it seems to me, on elementary truisims—that it isn't *essential* in order to be a sound or "saved" person, that one should pay deference to institutions, persons, books, ceremonies and so forth, or do anything more than develop those qualities in which being a sound or "saved" person consists.[8]

This may seem to many to be a bizarre if understandable account of Protestantism; fortunately, it is not relevant to our interests here, and it does not at all affect Findlay's central argument.

Findlay begins by exploring what it is to worship. True worship is characterized by certain attitudes and convictions. In worship, for example, we bend and bow the knee, we wholly defer to the object of worship, we give total allegiance. Such attitudes assume certain characteristics in the object worshipped if they are to be appropriate rather than misplaced. Thus they presume that God is of surpassing greatness, that there is none other beside him in all creation. They presume that he towers infinitely over all objects; somehow God must be all-comprehensive as a source of all existence and virtue. Indeed, true worship implies that God does not merely happen to exist.

> The true object of religious reverence must not be one, merely, to which no *actual* independent realities stand opposed: it must be one to which such

[8] J. N. Findlay, "Can God's Existence be Disproved?" in *New Essays in Philosophical Theology,* eds. Antony Flew and Alasdair MacIntyre (New York: Macmillan, 1955), pp. 74–75. Reprinted with permission of Macmillan Publishing Company.

opposition is totally *inconceivable*. God mustn't merely cover the territory of the actual, but also, with equal comprehensiveness, the territory of the possible. And not only must the existence of *other* things be unthinkable without him, but his own non-existence must be wholly unthinkable in any circumstances. There must, in short, be no conceivable alternative to an existence properly termed "divine": God must be wholly inescapable, as we remarked previously, whether for thought or reality. And so we are led on insensibly to the barely intelligible notion of a Being in whom Essence and Existence lose their separateness. And all that the great medieval thinkers really did was to carry such a development to its logical limit.[9]

Equally not only must God exist necessarily, any characteristics God possesses cannot be possessed accidently. Rather he must be wise, good, powerful in some necessary manner. To worship an object which has less than this would be idolatry. Thus, argues Findlay, we are led on ineluctably to the view that God is not merely good but somehow indistinguishable from his own and anyone else's goodness.

These consequences of worship are fatal for the rationality of belief in God. Certain modern philosophical views make it absurd to speak of such a being. Findlay sums up his position this way:

We may accordingly deny that modern approaches allow us to remain agnostically poised in regard to God: they force us to come down on the atheistic side. For if God is to satisfy religious claims and needs, he must be a being in every way inescapable, One whose existence and whose possession of certain excellences we cannot possibly conceive away. And modern views make it self-evidently absurd (if they don't make it ungrammatical) to speak of such a Being and attribute existence to him. It was indeed an ill day for Anselm when he hit upon his famous proof. For on that day he not only laid bare something that is of the essence of an adequate religious object, but also something that entails its necessary non-existence.[10]

What Findlay is arguing here is that the religious believer, as a worshipper, must assume that it is logically impossible for God not to exist. However, this idea of a being whose existence is logically necessary is itself plain nonsense. It is ruled out by the principle that all statements about particular objects existing are always contingent; they are never true as a matter of logic. Consequently, the God required by proper worship cannot exist. The very idea of such a God is incoherent or self-contradictory.

Findlay's argument is now generally known as the ontological disproof of the existence of God. Is it successful? Very few have been convinced that it is. The following comments will show why. A very obvious objection to it is that it is not at all clear that worship of God has the consequences that Findlay thinks it has. Findlay insists that worship of any object other than God as he defines him would not be worship but veneration or idolatry. This he argues as a matter of logic rather than, say, of revelation. His argument is simply unconvincing. The Israelites, for ex-

[9] Ibid., p. 52. Emphasis as in original.
[10] Ibid., p. 55.

ample, were told not to worship anyone other than the God who brought them out of Egypt (Exod. 34:14). This command would make no sense whatsoever if the God of Israel could alone as a matter of logic be worshipped. On the contrary, religious believers have accepted that genuine worship can be directed at objects other than the true God. Idolators have not made a mistake in logic but a mistake in fact, giving their allegiance to the wrong source.

A second, and even more important, objection to Findlay's position is that it rests on a confusion about the meaning of necessary existence. Findlay has overlooked the fact that *necessary* does not have the same meaning when applied to God as it does when it is applied to propositions. Philosophers have long debated what is meant by *necessary* when used of propositions. It is generally agreed that a necessary proposition is one which is known to be true by virtue of the meaning of the concepts involved. Contingent propositions, on the other hand, lack this kind of necessity.[11] When applied to God, the term *necessary* has an entirely different meaning. It does not mean that the proposition "God exists" is necessary; it means that God is not dependent on anything or anyone for his existence. On the contrary, all else is contingent upon God and his power. Insofar then as theists speak of God's existence being necessary, they are not open to the charge of logical absurdity posited by Findlay.

Equally theists do not need to insist that "God is good" and "God is love" are necessary truths. Such claims may rest not on pure logic but upon God's revelation of himself in history and upon the believer's experience of divine grace. To argue that these claims rely on pure reason is false. Worship of the divine does, of course, depend on the truth of such claims in the sense that they provide the reasons for the network of activities and attitudes inherent in worship, but it does not depend on some precise theory about their logic or foundation.

THE SOMATOLOGICAL DISPROOF

Let us now turn to a second attempt to disprove the existence of God. This attempt assumes that in thinking and speaking of God, we conceive of him fundamentally and essentially as an agent, i.e., as one who performs certain acts intentionally. Equally we think of God as invisible and incorporeal, i.e., he does not have a body. The objection to theism we now want to examine argues that these two commitments are logically incompatible. In other words, the idea of a disembodied agent is incoherent. Let us call this argument the somatological disproof of the existence of God.[12]

Paul Edwards develops this argument in this manner:

> I have no doubt that when most people think about God and his alleged activities, here or in the hereafter, they vaguely think of him as possessing some

---

[11] Terence Penelhum makes this point very clearly in "Divine Necessity," in *Philosophy of Religion,* ed. Basil Mitchell (Oxford: Oxford University Press, 1971), p. 189.

[12] This is a neologism drawing on the Greek word for body.

kind of rather large body. Now, if we are told that there is a God who is, say, just and good and kind and loving and powerful and wise and if, (a) it is made clear that these words are used in one of their ordinary senses and (b) God is not asserted to be a disembodied mind, then it seems plain to me that *to that extent* a series of meaningful assertions has been made. And this is so whether we are told that God's justice, mercy, etc. are "limitless" or merely that God is superior to all human beings in these respects. However, it seems to me that all these words lose their meaning if we are told that God does not possess a body. Anyone who thinks otherwise without realizing this, I think, is supplying a body in the background of his images. For what would it be like to say, just, without a body? To be just, a person has to *act* justly—he has to behave in certain ways. This is not reductive materialism. It is a simple empirical truth about what we mean by "just." But how is it possible to perform these acts, to behave in the required ways without a body? Similar remarks apply to the other divine attributes.[13]

Edwards's argument runs like this. The attributes commonly applied to God, e.g., loving, just, forgiving, and so on, rest on claims about what God has done. Action, in turn, is only logically possible where the agent has a body. God, however, does not have a body. Therefore it is nonsense to speak of God acting. Hence it is impossible to secure the descriptions normally predicated of God. The God described by these predicates cannot, therefore, exist.

Implicit in the argument, as I have articulated it, is the thesis that one way to secure reference to a disembodied agent is to make use of descriptions which refer uniquely to that agent. Clearly we cannot refer to God by pointing, for God is not a part of the physical universe. We refer to God by speaking of "The Creator of heaven and earth," "The One who raised Jesus Christ from the dead," "He who meets us in religious experience." Thus God is distinguished from other subjects of discourse by means of his unique characteristics, which in turn are related to statements to what he has done. It is precisely these statements that Edwards deems incoherent. Hence, his argument is skillfully directed at the very heart of theism. What are we to make of this challenge?

It is correct to note that this problem cannot be solved by appeal to the Christian doctrine of the incarnation of God in Jesus Christ. To be sure, God is said to have become a human being in Christ and thus to have assumed embodiment in history. But this does not help because to speak of incarnation is to speak of further divine action, and it is all such talk that Edwards argues is unintelligible. Nor will it do to soft-pedal or abandon the claim that God is an agent, for the concept of agency is constitutive of theism. Replacing *agent* by concepts like *Process, The Absolute, Being,* and the like, undermines the personal nature of God as one who creates, forgives, redeems, promises us eternal life, and so forth. Edwards's argument demands a very different response on the part of the theist.

The first problem in Edwards's position is that it is false to say, as he does, that when most people think of God they vaguely think of him as possessing some

---

[13] Paul Edwards, "Some Notes on Anthropormorphic Theology," in *Religious Experience and Truth,* ed. Sidney Hook (New York: New York University Press, 1974), pp. 242–43. Emphasis as in original.

kind of large body. Edwards simply gives this as his opinion about the psychology of religious believers, and he produces no evidence for his claim. Even were he to produce evidence, it would be irrelevant; what it would reveal is the immaturity of the believers he has studied. The mature theist does not try to imagine God in the same way he might try to imagine an absent friend or a childhood home. Those who do so have not grasped who God is. There is nothing peculiar about this. After all, we do not try to imagine physically such things as numbers, the unconscious, time, or justice. It looks as if Edwards is supplying the theist's imagination with a body because that is how he imagines the theist must think, given his philosophical conviction about the meaning of agency. How secure is this conviction?

Edwards tells us that he cannot conceive of action without a body. Indeed, he asserts, a body is part of the very concept of agency or action. But how does Edwards know this? Theists are perfectly within their rights to reject this as a piece of linguistic dogmatism. Certainly ordinary language allows one to speak of agents who do not have bodies, God being the prime example of the very point at issue. Moreover, stout atheists like Bertrand Russell have no difficulties speaking of the devil.[14] This being so, the task of the philosopher is not to lay down the law about what is essential to the concept of agency in advance but to articulate fully and carefully an account which does justice to the way the concept is actually used. Thus theism is not at all shown to be incoherent by the argument deployed by Edwards.

It should also be remembered that it is possible to think of actions which do not involve any bodily movements, e.g., concentrating, deciding, or even telekinesis. Indeed, the concept of agency cannot logically be identified simply with that of bodily movement. W. D. Hudson has drawn attention to this point recently.

> There is always a logical gap between an agent as such and what may be called his situation. Suppose Smith's situation is that he is bankrupt. It makes sense to ask Smith, "What are you going to do about your bankruptcy?" The idea of Smith, the agent, "stepping back" so to speak from his situation and forming some intention as to how he will deal with it makes perfectly good sense. Now, the point to take is that exactly the same will be true if Smith's situation is that he has a broken leg or is suffering from kleptomania, for example. That is to say, Smith's body and indeed Smith's psyche can be conceived as part of Smith's situation from which as agent he is logically distinct. He, as agent, is not to be identified with his broken leg or his compulsive psychological mechanism any more than with his bankruptcy. There is, that is to say, some kind of Cartesian parallelism in the last analysis between mind and body even in the case of human agents. Mind and body cannot (logically) be reduced either to other or both to some unifying concept. If an agent is logically distinct from his body and if the latter can be regarded as part of his situation, then why not a like parallelism between certain intentional acts of God and certain spatio-temporal events in the world?[15]

[14] Russell, *Why I am not a Christian*, p. 19.

[15] W. D. Hudson, *A Philosophical Approach to Religion* (London: Macmillan, 1974), p. 174.

THE PSYCHOLOGICAL ARGUMENT

If Edwards's attempted disproof fails, are there any a posteriori arguments against the existence of God which would be decisive in the debate between theists and athesists? Can a candidate for this position be found in the views of Sigmund Freud (1856-1939)? Let us see if it can.

Freud's account and assessment of religion is complex. Freud was, for example, interested at least theoretically in the origins of religion in antiquity. As his views on this subject have not won much support, they shall not detain us here. Of greater interest is his account of why religion arises and is sustained over time. He fundamentally offered a psychological explanation of the origin of religious belief.

According to Freud, religious belief is an attempt to cope with the harsh realities of life. For example, it is obvious that we live in a world where we face considerable threat from the forces of nature. There are diseases, natural disasters, and ultimately death. These clearly threaten our well-being and even our existence. Fear of such harsh realities drives us to personify the hostile forces of nature. By treating them as personal agents, i.e., as gods, demons, angels, and so on, we can try to adjure them, appease them, or bribe them.

Not only do we face hostile natural forces, we also face demanding human agents and institutions in society at large. We live in a web of rules and authorities, which calls for great sacrifice and privation if the common life we inhabit is to endure. Religious belief, says Freud, arises in order to give sanction to the common rules of society and to help people cope with the demands laid upon them. Thus religion promises life in a world to come as a compensation for the sacrifices we must endure here and now.

How does it happen then, that religion involves belief in a supreme reality which is omnipotent, benevolent, omniscient? According to Freud, this belief arises because of people's longing for a father figure. Just as children turn to their earthly father for protection, so when they become adults they require a heavenly father to protect them from the sufferings imposed by nature and society. Freud explains this as follows:

> When the growing individual finds that he is destined to remain a child for ever, that he can never do without protection against strange superior powers, he lends those powers the features belonging to the figure of his father, he creates for himself the gods whom he dreads, whom he seeks to propitiate, and whom he nevertheless entrusts with his own protection. Thus his longing for a father is a motive identical with his need for protection against the consequences of his human weakness. The defence against childish helplessness is what lends its characteristic features to the adult's reaction to the helplessness which *he* has to acknowledge—a reaction which is precisely the formation of religion.[16]

---

[16] Sigmund Freud, *The Future of an Illusion*, trans. W. D. Robson-Scott, rev. ed., James Strachey (London: Hogarth Press and Institute of Psycho-Analysis, 1978), p. 20.

What all this means is that religious belief is an illusion. Normally we take an illusion to be a deceptive appearance or a false perception. Freud does not mean quite that. Illusions are not necessarily errors or delusions where what is believed is false. An illusion is a belief which has wish fulfilment as a prominent factor in its motivation and which is held in the absence of good reasons in its favor. Religious belief is an illusion in this sense. It arises out of the desire for protection, and it is held without adequate rational support. We know the latter to be true because, when the issue of evidence is broached, religious believers either reject any interest in evidence as sinful or appeal to the authority of either their ancestors or some ancient book.

Does this show that religious belief is irrational? Certainly it does not *prove* that religious belief is false. Freud himself saw this, and as we have seen, he describes religious belief as an illusion rather than an error or a delusion. However, it does seem that Freud very definitely believed that religious belief was irrational in the sense that it was unworthy of rational commitment. Thus Freud not only advocated that civilization should abandon religion, he predicted that one day it would. Mature human beings would not need religion as a kind of psychological crutch to lean on. He expected the truth about the origin of religion to have an impact on our attitude towards it. Certainly he thinks it will be harder for those in the know to believe.

> We know approximately at what periods and by what kind of men religious doctrines were created. If in addition we discover the motives which led to this, our attitude to the problem of religion will undergo a marked displacement. We shall tell ourselves that it would be very nice if there were a God who created the world and was a benevolent Providence, and if there were a moral order in the universe and an after-life; but it is a very striking fact that all this is exactly as we are bound to wish it to be. And it would be more remarkable still if our wretched, ignorant and downtrodden ancestors had succeeded in solving all these difficult riddles of the universe.[17]

It is difficult to avoid the conclusion, therefore, that Freud intended to offer an argument against the rationality of religious belief. Let us call that argument the psychological argument against the existence of God. Its essence is that this belief arises out of wish fulfilment and is held without rational support.

How strong is this argument? Some have suggested that we can accept all that Freud says and keep our theistic beliefs undisturbed. John Hick even suggests that Freud's analysis would illuminate rather than disprove belief in God.

> Perhaps the most interesting theological comment to be made upon Freud's theory is that in his work on the father-image he may have uncovered the mechanism by which God creates an idea of himself in the human mind. For if the relation of a human father to his children is, as the Judaic-Christian

---

[17] Ibid., p. 29.

tradition teaches, analogous to God's relationship to man, it is not surprising that human beings should think of God as their heavenly Father and should come to know him through the infant's experience of utter dependence and the growing child's experiences of being loved, cared for, and disciplined within a family. Clearly, to the mind which is not committed in advance to a naturalistic explanation there may be a religious as well as a naturalistic interpretation of the psychological facts.[18]

This is an interesting suggestion. Unfortunately, as it stands it is speculative. Hick has not shown that we come to know God as a father in the way suggested; hence this does not alleviate the doubts raised by Freud.

Nor does it help to argue that Freud has fallen prey to the genetic fallacy, i.e., that he has argued religious belief is false because of its causal origins in wish fulfilment. As we have seen, Freud's argument is more subtle, for he insists that religious belief not only arises from desire but continues to be held in the absence of good evidence. It is both of these taken together which seems to bother Freud in his assessment of the truth of religion. Without disproving religious belief, they seem to render it less than rationally acceptable.

Freud is surely correct in the formal structure of his argument. Normally we are suspicious of those beliefs which are generated by our wishes and especially so in those cases where the believer either offers irrelevant evidence or expresses disinterest in examining the truth or rationality of his position. The problem with Freud's position is that he has not shown that this is always the case with religious belief. If anything, the evidence counts seriously against him. Thus it is difficult to show that belief in original sin is a product of wish fulfilment; likewise with belief in the Trinity, the deity of Christ, divine punishment, and so on. One can, of course, always try to invent a wish as the father of these beliefs, but without good evidence such invention is a matter of speculation.

Equally Freud has not shown that religious belief is held in the absence of adequate evidence. Freud's account of the grounds which religious believers have offered for their position, although not entirely inaccurate, does not get at the heart of the issue. Freud simply ignores the possible reasons that mature religious believers might offer. At this point he betrays an ignorance of the history of religious thought, which is astonishing for someone possessing his genius. To make out his case, Freud would have to show that all attempts to defend the rationality of religious belief have failed and must fail. In this he is unsuccessful.

This is an important consideration, for it touches not just Freud's psychological argument against religious belief but others of a similar nature. Normally we only look for the causal origins of a belief when we are relatively certain that there are no good reasons for that belief. To take an example: I look for a cause of Jones's belief that his friends are out to kill him only when I know that his belief is false and that Jones cannot produce any good evidence for his claim but utterly refuses to attend to the clear evidence against it. At the very least, it is only in such circum-

[18] John Hick, *Philosophy of Religion* (Englewood Cliffs, N.J.: Prentice-Hall, 1973), p. 36.

stances that a causal explanation of Jones's belief, say, in terms of some mental illness or whatever, discredits it. This case is relevant to Freud's argument, for, contrary to what we normally do, he has assumed religious belief to be false at the outset. It also applies to other arguments in modern atheology which incorporate the same fundamental structure of Freud's position. I have in mind here especially those who have appealed to sociological factors to explain away religious belief.[19]

Our conclusion in this chapter is that some standard arguments against the existence of God do not succeed. Neither the ontological disproof, nor the somato-logical disproof, nor the psychological argument of Freud show religious belief to be irrational or incredible. All these arguments are highly sophisticated and some-what remote from the ordinary person in the street. In this respect they resemble the classical arguments of natural theology. We turn now to an issue which, although equally complex, rests on experiences all human beings encounter. We look, that is, at the problem of evil.

[19] Feuerbach, Marx, and Durkheim are relevant examples. Marx's critique of religion is examined below, chap. 19. This objection would also apply to composite theories which bring together elements from various psychological and sociological theories. J. L. Mackie takes this approach in *The Miracle of Theism* (Oxford: Clarendon Press, 1982), pp. 187–98.

Chapter Six
The Problem Of Evil

The oldest and most formidable weapon in natural atheology is the existence of evil. Most religious believers themselves have felt the force of this issue in their own minds. If they have not, then the story of the agony of Job serves as a sharp reminder that they cannot set it aside lightly. For Job the issue is in part existential and intimate, for Job has to wrestle personally with the ravages of pain and misery. This aspect is one dimension of evil which religious believers, like all human beings, have to face. Clearly evil poses a problem of pastoral care, and within religious communities much energy is devoted to this matter.

THE NATURE OF THE PROBLEM

That is not, however, what concerns us here. We are not proposing, that is, to offer advice on how to cope with evil. Nor are we interested in many of the other questions evil provokes, e.g., Will there always be evil? Is my sickness due to my sin? Does God heal everybody who has faith? Is demon possession another name for psychiatric disorder? These are entirely legitimate and important matters, but they are not what is at stake here. The issue here is evil as an argument in natural atheology. We wish to know whether the existence of evil disproves the existence of God or whether the existence of evil makes it unreasonable or implausible to disbelieve in God.

It needs to be emphasized that evil poses a serious problem to theists only because they are committed to the view that God is both omnipotent and all-good. Clearly if God is omnipotent he should be able to eliminate evil from the world. Equally if God is all-good it would seem that he would want to eliminate evil from the world. How then is there any evil at all in the universe? J. L. Mackie states the problem this way:

> In its simplest form the problem is this: God is omnipotent; God is wholly good, yet evil exists. There seems to be some contradiction between these three propositions, so that if any two of them were true the third would be false. But at the same time all three are essential parts of most theological positions; the theologian, it seems, at once *must* adhere and *cannot consistly* adhere to all three.[1]

If Mackie is correct, theism is in serious intellectual trouble. Not surprisingly Mackie and many others have argued that theism is so inconsistent that it was best from a rational point of view to reject it entirely. We could, of course, avoid this conclusion by exercising our logical rights to abandon or modify any of the three propositions which seem to be in conflict, or all of them. But none of these options are particularly attractive.

INADEQUATE SOLUTIONS

We could, for example, try to argue that evil does not exist. It only appears, that is, to exist. This is manifestly false, for evil does exist, and most religions put a strong emphasis on its reality and power. In any case, the widespread illusion about evil demanded by this solution would itself be a gross evil, so the basic premise of the atheist's argument remains secure. Equally we could abandon either the omnipotence or goodness of God to resolve our dilemma.

Of these options, it is much more common to abandon the omnipotence of God. Rabbi Harold S. Kushner, whose son, Aaron, died of rapid aging, has recently suggested such a solution. He writes:

> I believe in God. But I do not believe the same things about Him that I did years ago, when I was growing up or when I was a theological student. I recognize His limitations. He is limited in what He can do by laws of nature and by the evolution of human nature and human moral freedom. I no longer hold God responsible for illnesses, accidents, and natural disasters, because I realize that I gain little and I lose so much when I blame God for those things. I can worship a God who hates suffering but cannot eliminate it, more easily than I can worship a God who chooses to make children suffer and die, for whatever exalted reason. Some years ago, when the "death of God" theology was a fad, I remember seeing a bumper sticker that read "My God is

---

[1] J. L. Mackie, "Evil and Omnipotence," in *The Philosophy of Religion,* ed. Basil Mitchell (Oxford: Oxford University Press, 1971), p. 92. Emphasis as in original.

not dead; sorry about yours." I guess my bumper sticker reads "My God is not cruel; sorry about yours."[2]

The problems in this solution are all too obvious. First, it involves abandoning a central tenet of the Judaic-Christian conception of God which seems to be well grounded in the biblical tradition. Secondly, although initially it seems quite an attractive position, for it construes God in more sympathetic terms, it offers no markedly better conception of God in the end. Kushner, in fact, even suggests that we may need to forgive God for not making a better world. He asks very pointedly at the close of his sensitive discussion:

> Are you capable of forgiving and loving God even when you have found out that He is not perfect, even when He has let you down and disappointed you by permitting bad luck and sickness and cruelty in His world, and permitting some of these things to happen to you?[3]

Thirdly, this solution becomes less inviting when one asks how God's power is now to be specifically delimited. What in the revised theology can God do and not do? Presumably God cannot rid the world of various diseases like rapid aging. But suppose in twenty years' time some doctor discovers a cure for this disease and cures someone. Then God turns out to be less powerful than human doctors. But why should we limit God's power only in the case of certain diseases? If we revise our conception of God in a finite direction to resolve the evil caused by rapid aging, there seems no good reason not to revise further in the face of all the varied evils we meet. In that case we end up with a thoroughly incompetent deity, who deserves more of our pity than our forgiveness. It is surely not surprising that religious believers have not been very keen to worship such an agent. They have been even less enthusiastic about partially good deities, for similar reasons. In both cases the problem of evil seems to drive one out of the frying pan into the fire.

It is generally agreed that this is also the case where the proposed solution is more complex. Thus positing some kind of eternal, malevolent force over against God as the cause of evil or arguing that the concepts we apply to God are incomprehensible have fallen on hard times of late. Certainly most theists look elsewhere for a solution to the dilemma posed by modern atheologists. As we explore their work, we need to pause and give a brief analysis of the kinds of evil that confront us.

It is usual to distinguish between two broad classes of evil. There are moral evils and natural evils. The former refers to those evil states and processes brought about by the deliberate choice of human agents. Examples of moral evil would be murder, bank robbery, and cruelty to animals. Natural evils are those evils which are not brought about by the deliberate choice of human agents. Examples, in this case,

---

[2] Harold S. Kushner, *When Bad Things Happen to Good People* (New York: Shocken, 1981), p. 134. Reprinted by permission of Shocken Books Inc. Copyright © 1981 by Harold S. Kushner.

[3] Ibid., p. 148.

would be earthquakes, diseases, inflation, and animal pain. One reason for making this distinction is that it allows the protagonists to focus the issue more sharply. In turn the theist can attempt to turn the edge of the atheological argument from evil by showing that each kind of evil is compatible with belief in God.

THE FREE-WILL DEFENSE

How might this be done in the case of moral evil? The standard line of the theist is that such evil results from God's creating human agents who are significantly free. God himself does not cause such evils. The evils are brought about by persons acting contrary to God's will, having chosen to act as they do. God could, of course, have prevented such evils either by restricting human choice or refusing to create human beings at all. But God cannot create genuinely free human beings and then not permit them to bring about moral evils. As the creation of persons with genuine choices is a good thing, then the existence of moral evil is both logically and rationally consistent with belief in God. Alvin Plantinga's summary of this position is impeccable.

> A world containing creatures who are significantly free (and freely perform more good than evil actions) is more valuable, all else being equal, than a world containing no free creatures at all. Now God can create free creatures, but He can't *cause* or *determine* them to do only what is right. For if He does so, then they aren't significantly free after all; they do not do what is right *freely*. To create creatures capable of *moral good,* therefore, He must create creatures capable of moral evil; and He can't give these creatures the freedom to perform evil and at the same time prevent them from doing so. As it turned out, sadly enough, some of the free creatures God created went wrong in the exercise of their freedom; this is the source of moral evil. The fact that free creatures sometimes go wrong, however, counts neither against God's omnipotence nor against His goodness for He could have forestalled the occurrence of moral evil only by removing the possibility of moral good.[4]

Various objections have been made to this argument. One of the most original was developed by J. L. Mackie. Mackie posed the question whether it is not possible for God to make a world in which human beings always freely do what is good. He expresses this as follows:

> If God has made men such that in their free choices they sometimes prefer what is good and sometimes what is evil, why could he not have made men such that they always freely choose the good? If there is no logical impossibility in a man's freely choosing the good on one, or on several occasions, there cannot be a logical impossibility in his freely choosing the good on every occasion. God was not, then, faced with a choice between making innocent

---

[4] Alvin Plantinga, *God, Freedom and Evil* (London: George Allen and Unwin, 1975), p. 30.

automata and making beings who, in acting freely, would sometimes go wrong; there was open to him the obviously better possibility of making beings who would act freely but always go right. Clearly, his failure to avail himself of this possibility is inconsistent with his being both omnipotent and wholly good.[5]

The flaw in this objection is not too difficult to detect. Consider the situation Mackie envisages. We can think of it as the case where Adam, faced with a choice between good and evil, freely chooses what is good. By extension we can think of Adam as always choosing what is good. Here is a case where God creates Adam, and Adam always freely chooses what is good. What Mackie requires, however, is something much stronger. What is needed is the case where God creates Adam and God always *ensures* that Adam will choose what is good. In the latter instance it is very strange to speak of Adam's possessing any freedom whatsoever. If God always ensures that Adam will choose what is good, Adam is not genuinely free. Yet it is this latter possibility which Mackie needs. As it turns out, human beings have not always chosen what is good. But that is their fault; it is not God's responsibility in any direct culpable sense.

Mackie raises a further question about the free-will defense. He asks why it is that God does not leave human beings free when they will rightly but intervene when he sees them beginning to will wrongly.

> If God could do this, but does not, and if he is wholly good, the only explanation could be that even a wrong free act of will is not really evil, that its freedom is a value which outweighs its wrongness, so that there would be a loss of value if God took away the wrongness and the freedom together. But this is utterly opposed to what theists say about sin in other contexts. The present solution of the problem of evil, then, can be maintained only in the form that God has made men so free that he *cannot* control their wills.[6]

The difficulty in this argument is the same as in Mackie's first objection. If God intervenes to prevent human beings from doing anything evil, then they attain only a very limited freedom indeed. To be sure, there would be no evil, but equally the range of choice would be trivial and insignificant. That God allows evil choices does not diminish their evil nature. Rather it is the potential price that has to be paid if freedom is to be substantial and significant.

A very different objection to the free-will defense has been offered of late by Brian Davies. Davies focuses on the fact that a free act is one that by definition cannot be caused by God. In this he is surely correct, for a free act is usually construed as one which is not determined by preceding conditions; rather it is an act performed by an agent for certain intentions or purposes. According to Davies, this account of free action is inconsistent with some other beliefs of the theist.

[5]Mackie, "Evil and Omnipotence," p. 100.
[6]Ibid., p. 101.

The assumption that God does not cause free actions is difficult to reconcile with classical theism. For whatever a free act is (and that is a big philosophical question in its own right), it is necessarily an act of somebody. And the notion of somebody acting without being caused to do so by God is hard to accept if we are thinking in terms of classical theism. This holds that God's creative causality is not something exercised in the past. It thinks of it as something that is operative as long as anything apart from God exists at all. Thus, we hear it said that everything depends on God for its existence, that the sheer fact of there being anything at all is ultimately due to God's activity, that God is the first cause lying behind all the causal processes that are distinct from his own being.[7]

The crux of this argument against the free-will defense, then, is that it is incompatible with the Christian view that God is causally operative in all things, including the activities of human beings. As God is the cause of all human action, that action is no longer free in the sense required. Thus the free-will defense is useless.

In taking this view Davies seems to be fully prepared to accept the interesting corollary that even human sin is in some sense brought about by God. In doing so he is in exceptionally good company, for as he points out, Aquinas shared this conviction.[8] Even so, this consequence of Davies's argument is good reason for calling the argument in question. Surely any view which makes God the author of sin is inconsistent with any account of his goodness. Yet as we have seen, it is only because of his goodness that evil poses a problem for the theist. What has gone wrong with Davies's argument?

The crucial weakness in it is that Davies, along with Aquinas, has equated God's creative activity with God's bringing about or causing human actions. It is true that human beings could not act if God did not create and sustain them. But this in no way entails the view that God somehow performs the acts done by human agents. A father, for example, could sustain his son in business, and yet the son could still act on his own and be accountable for his actions. What God does to sustain human agents will be more complex than such a case, but the logic of the concept when applied to God leaves room for human initiative and action. How far God might influence or inspire human beings without fully causing their actions is a matter which needs to be pursued in its own right and does not materially alter the present issue.[9]

Theists, therefore, are right to argue that the existence of moral evil is compatible with belief in God. The free-will defense is essential to that argument. Without it their case is extensively weakened, for moral evil is a formidable and universal

---

[7] Brian Davies, *An Introduction to the Philosophy of Religion* (Oxford: Oxford University Press, 1982), p. 21.

[8] Ibid.

[9] Its most natural home is the discussion on the relation between grace and freedom. For the latter see chap. 12.

reality. What of natural evil? How can we reconcile it with belief in an omnipotent, all-good God? Many moves have been made to cope with this problem.

It has always been popular to extend the free-will defense to deal with it. For example, thinkers as far apart in time as Augustine and Wesley believed that natural evil was a just punishment for man's fall into sin. Few would deny that there may be some truth in this belief. Human sin does have physical consequences, such as when greed leads people to pollute the environment. However, it is implausible to believe that all natural evil can be construed as punishment for sin. Some natural evil, e.g., animal pain, existed before there were any human beings to punish, and much natural evil seems unrelated to prior human sin. Innocent people suffer, and volcanoes do not only burn up the wicked.

Another way to use the free-will defense to explain natural evil is by appeal to the activity of the devil. Plantinga takes this position in the following passage. Responding to those who argue that physical or natural evil is inconsistent with the existence of God, he writes:

> To make this claim, however, is to overlook an important part of traditional theistic belief; it is part of much traditional belief to attribute a good deal of the evil we find to Satan, or to Satan and his cohorts. Satan, so the traditional doctrine goes, is a mighty non-human spirit, who, along with many other angels, was created long before God created men. Unlike most of his colleagues, Satan rebelled against God and has since been creating whatever havoc he could; the result, of course, is physical evil. But now we see that the moves available to the Free Will Defender in the case of moral evil are equally available to him in the case of physical evil.[10]

Plantinga is well aware that this argument may seem very strange in modern times. It looks like an ad hoc arrangement brought in as a last-ditch effort to save the theist from criticism. Moreover, belief in the devil is not as popular as, say, belief in the theory of relativity. Against the first rejoinder Plantinga would simply reply that belief in the devil has been a part of the Christian tradition for centuries, so it is not something invented at the last minute to rescue the theist from danger. As to the second rejoinder, he points out that the theist does not have to show that belief in the devil is probable or even true. All that needs to be shown is that it is not inconsistent with the proposition that God exists.

In terms of strict logic Plantinga is entirely correct. To save theism from the charge of contradiction, all that the theist has to do is to argue that natural evil is possibly due to the activity of Satan. The problem with this solution, however, is that it is thoroughly implausible to argue that all natural evil is due to the devil. Plantinga is insensitive to this problem and leaves the impression that his primary concern is to save theism fror . inconsistency no matter how strange the consequences. Plantinga may reject this counter-argument on the ground that appeal to plausibility is much too vague and subjective. He may also hold that common scepti-

[10]Alvin Plantinga, "The Free Will Defence," in *The Philosophy of Religion,* ed. Basil Mitchell, p. 119.

cism about the devil is a purely sociological fact unrelated to rational considerations. Whatever the case, he may insist that his opponent must actually show that natural evil is not caused by Satan. That, of course, is a heroic feat to perform, and Plantinga knows that. But this insistence only saves him because he fails to acknowledge that his own positive beliefs about the devil call for justification. It is not enough just to affirm that it is possible Satan exists and that he brings about all natural evil. We want to know if there is any good reason for such beliefs. Hiding behind logical possibilities is an evasion of this issue. Indeed, if the theist is not careful here, he or she may appear to be dishonest or even insincere.

It is not surprising, therefore, that many theists have sought more than a logically possible defense of theism. Rather they have been at pains to provide a theodicy. They have tried, that is, to say why God might have created a world which contains natural evil. This is not to say that the theodicist is claiming to know why God created as he did. Rather he or she is arguing that God may well have had good reason for creating natural evil; its existence does not therefore show theism to be irrational.

THE IRENAEAN THEODICY

By far the most significant move in this regard stems from as far back as Irenaeus (ca. 130–ca. 202). The central point enunciated by Irenaeus and developed by those who take their cue from him is that God makes a world where human agents have an environment which is appropriate for spiritual growth.[11] This world is not a hedonist's paradise, as is often presupposed by atheists who appeal to the existence of natural evil; it is a world which provides a context where there can be genuine moral development; or, to use the classical phrase, this world is a vale of soul making.

The obvious objection to be made against this general argument is that it raises questions about God's omnipotence. Why, it might be asked, could not God achieve the same result, that is, moral and spiritual maturity, without having to create natural evil? If God is omnipotent, then it would seem that he could causally organize affairs to bring that about without having to produce natural evil. Pursuing this issue takes us into the details of the theodicist's case.

That case claims not that natural evil is simply causally necessary for real spiritual development but that it is logically necessary. If there are to be such virtues as courage, patience, sympathy, generosity, loyalty, self-sacrifice, bravery, self-reliance, and cheerfulness, then it is essential that there be an environment which contains natural evil. Equally, natural evil provides numerous temptations to become hard, bitter, depressed, selfish, cowardly, dependent, insensitive, and so on. This being so, human agents are faced with genuine choices about what kind of character they will acquire. Such character as is formed is not forced upon them, and yet

---

[11] The Irenaean tradition is well summarized in John Hick, *Evil and the God of Love* (London: Macmillan, 1968), pp. 207–41.

genuine, unavoidable decisions have to be made. Living in a world where there is natural evil makes possible, therefore, the growth of crucial moral dispositions.

It also enlarges the scope of human freedom and responsibility. Suppose, for example, that God had made a perfectly complete and totally finished universe. In such a case there would be nothing that we could do to improve matters. As it is, we live in an incomplete, half-finished universe where disease, for example, has to be eradicated. In this case we are drawn into the very creative activity of God, becoming cocreators with him rather than spectators on the sidelines.

Moreover, the existence of natural evil furnishes humankind with good reason to find out how nature operates. We are invited to discover for ourselves the secrets of the world, yet without being coerced into doing so, as would be the case were we equipped with an utterly insatiable thirst for knowledge. Greater knowledge in turn means more significant choices. Thus further scientific advance opens up greater opportunities for cooperation and mutual care. Equally it increases the range of our responsibilities. We now live at a time when the option of destroying planet earth is no longer a dream. God allows us therein to make crucial decisions about the very future of the universe. So by making a world where there is natural evil, God has increased our range of choice and the responsibility which goes with it to truly awesome proportions.

In fact, our knowledge of how to bring about evil or prevent it from happening may well depend on the existence of natural evil. Richard Swinburne has argued this point at length of late.[12] He points out that God could give knowledge of the effects of our actions by means of special revelation. However, if that were the case, then any decision on our part to seek out such knowledge would be impossible. Also, it would immediately mean a world with much less temptation, for God's existence would be a common item of knowledge and obedience to him would be overwhelmingly prudent. Similar considerations would apply to the case where such knowledge was intuitive or given with nature. It was better, therefore, that such knowledge be given through experience. By means of induction from past experience we can come to know how to cause evils or prevent them. In this instance natural evil on a relatively large scale is essential. By observing these evils and their impact both on other human beings and on animals we can come to know how to inflict or hinder such occurrences.

Swinburne furnishes an example which helpfully explains this general point.

> We know that rabies causes a terrible death. With this knowledge we have the possibility of preventing such death (e.g., by controlling the entry of pet animals into Britain), or of negligently allowing it to occur or even of deliberately causing it. Only with the knowledge of the effects of rabies are such possibilities ours. But for us to gain knowledge of the effect of rabies it is necessary that others die of rabies (when the rabies was not preventable by

[12] Richard Swinburne, *The Existence of God* (Oxford: Oxford University Press, 1979), pp. 202-14. © Oxford University Press 1979. Reprinted by permission of Oxford University Press.

man), and be seen to have done so. Generally, we can only have the opportunity to prevent disease affecting ourselves or others or to neglect to do so, or the opportunity to spread disease deliberately (e.g., by indulging in biological warfare), if there are naturally occurring diseases. And men can only have the opportunity to prevent incurable diseases or to allow them to occur, if there are naturally occurring incurable diseases.[13]

How are we to assess this attempt to defend theism in the face of natural evil? I am generally in favor of some kind of theodicy. It is surely correct for theists to pursue this line of reasoning and see where it leads. Such reflection shows that natural evil does make possible the development of virtues and dispositions which would otherwise be impossible. It also creates opportunities for a wide range of freedom, choice, and responsibility.

As I have stated it, the proposed defense of theism requires the careful elaboration of a doctrine of creation. Thus it naturally leads into work in systematic theology. Brief though it is, it does not necessarily involve a mistake to which Irenaean theodicies are often prone. I have in mind here especially the argument of some liberal Protestant thinkers that somehow the fall of human beings is inevitable if not a good thing in itself. John Hick expresses it in this manner:

> Man can be truly *for* God only if he is morally independent of Him, and he can be thus independent only by being first *against* Him! And because sin consists in self-centered alienation from God, only God can save us from it, thereby making us free from Himself. Thus man must come to heaven by the path of redemption from sin.[14]

This view surely takes sin too lightly to be acceptable to the Christian theist. Hick realizes the force of the problem, for he does acknowledge the heinous reality of evil.[15] However, it is not clear how he reconciles this with his superficial analysis of human revolt against God, and in the end he has to return to a more realistic account of the exceeding sinfulness of human sin.[16]

It should also be noted that the proposed defense is not undermined by the fact that natural evil often leads to negative reactions. Much has been made of this by D. Z. Phillips.[17] We can agree with Phillips that suffering has made people more selfish, mean, petty, and suspicious. We can even agree that goodness itself can be the occasion for evil. As Phillips points out,

> The depth of a man's love may lead him to kill his wife's lover or to be destroyed when the object of his love is lost to him. A man whose love was mediocre would not have done either of these. Love has as much to do with

---

[13] Ibid., p. 207–8.

[14] Hick, *Evil and the God of Love*, p. 323. Emphasis as in the original. Cf. p. 389.

[15] Ibid., p. 324.

[16] Ibid., p. 396.

[17] D. Z. Phillips, "The Problem of Evil," in *Reason and Religion*, ed. S. C. Brown (Ithaca, N.Y.: Cornell University Press, 1977), pp. 103–21.

the terrible as with the wonderful. The presence of goodness in some may be the cause of hatred in others. Budd's goodness is more than Claggart can bear and it is the very possibility that deep love may be a reality which Iago cannot admit into his dark soul.[18]

All this is true, but what it shows is that natural evil and goodness may lead to further evil. It does not prove that it necessarily has to do so.

REMAINING DIFFICULTIES

There are, however, several difficulties which cannot be so easily answered. Foremost is that this kind of theodicy involves an account of moral judgment which is by no means agreed. It requires a very definite commitment to a utilitarian type of moral theory. Natural evil, on the view proposed, is justified on the grounds that it leads to greater good in the long run. Certainly we do often appeal to consequences to justify our actions, as when a doctor amputates a leg to prevent death. But is this always the case? And can we apply it in the case of all natural evil?

It becomes increasingly more difficult to do so when we seek to come to terms with particular cases of natural evil. What do we say in the case of a child who is born with incurable cancer or with only half a brain? According to Swinburne, such cases must be seen as victims of the system as a whole. Examples like these give people the opportunity to choose whether they shall help the helpless or not. They provide situations where they can be deeply responsible for the innocent and make crucial decisions about the future of certain individuals. However, it can still be asked if the cost to the individuals involved outweighs the long-term potential good made available. One can even understand those who would look upon such utilitarian reasoning as morally corrupt. To have a world where such evil exists is bad enough; to argue that it was put there by God for a purpose might lead one to think of God as unspeakably cruel.

Similar considerations apply to those situations where there seems to be so much natural evil. One can think in terms of the intensity of suffering an individual may have to endure or in terms of the magnitude of natural evil seen in the world as a whole. Plantinga has sought to answer this by requesting that the critic quantify the argument. He invents a measure of evil, known as a turp, and supposing that the amount of evil equals 10 turps, he insists that it is evident that the existence of this amount of evil does not disconfirm theism.[19] The critic is of course in a quandary, for it is virtually impossible to know exactly how much evil would show theism to be unlikely. However, the problem for the critic is that it seems morally insensitive to dismiss the issue beca.se of that impossibility. So long as we keep the issue in terms of abstract, artificial quantities, then we can evade the perplexity which the sheer intensity and quantity of evil normally engenders in us.

[18] Ibid., p. 114.
[19] Plantinga, *God, Freedom and Evil*, p. 63.

The point I am seeking to make here is that I can go a long way down the road proposed by the theodicist, but I cannot go all the way. I can understand why God should permit the moral evil that there is; here the free-will defense is entirely adequate. Moreover, I can understand why God should create a world which has within it natural evil; here a version of the Irenaean theodicy makes much sense. What I cannot fully understand is why there has to be so much natural evil, some of which is utterly useless to the individuals who experience it. In the latter instance there is grave danger that the theodicist, seeking to explain it as part of a wider whole, may become insensitive to the sheer brutality of evil around us. I would prefer that the theist leave such natural evil as a genuine problem or mystery rather than risk embracing a shallow optimism about an ultimate order where everything has its duly allotted purpose.

Natural evil poses, therefore, a serious problem for the theist. There is suffering which even on the most careful human analysis remains haphazard, inexplicable, and cruelly excessive. John Hick agrees and seeks to make a virtue of this.

> The mystery of dysteleological suffering is a real mystery, impenetrable to the rationalizing human mind. It challenges Christian faith with its utterly baffling, alien, destructive meaninglessness. And yet at the same time, detached theological reflection can note that this very irrationality and this lack of ethical meaning contribute to the character of the world as a place in which true human goodness can occur and in which loving sympathy and compassionate self-sacrifice can take place. "Thus, paradoxically," as H. H. Farmer says, "the failure of theism to solve all mysteries becomes part of its case!"[20]

This is surely a spurious virtue. Failure to solve the problem of evil counts against theism, not for it. Theists should own up to the difficulty and live with it.

But can the theist live with the difficult with intellectual integrity? Should the theist not cease to be a theist and become an agnostic or an atheist? To say yes to these questions is to assume that the existence of some natural evil counts decisively against theism. This, however, has by no means been established. To achieve that, the natural atheologian must proceed to do much more than show that there is a difficulty. He must establish that God could have no morally sufficient reason to create the amount of natural evil which exists. I have argued that I have not found any satisfactory account of God's will which displays such morally sufficient reasons, and to that extent the theist has a genuine problem. However, the critic must go further and clearly establish that no such reason exists. Because of the contested character of moral theory and our limited ability to know all that needs to be known about natural evil, I believe it is highly unlikely that this will ever be shown conclusively. The theist, therefore, can accept that there is evidence against his position without thereby conceding that the atheistic or agnostic alternative has been automatically established.

This is especially so if the theist is convinced that there is good evidence

---

[20] Hick, *Evil and the God of Love*, p. 371–72.

gained from elsewhere for his or her beliefs, say, from religious experience, putative revelation, the existence and character of the universe, and so on. In this instance the theist might quite legitimately judge that the case for theism far outweighs the case against it. We shall take up this option later. Before that, we must explore the fideistic approach to the rationality of religious belief. At this juncture, however, we must conclude that the classical arguments of natural atheology are not successful. Theism remains a live option despite the existence of evil.

Chapter Seven
Theological Fideism

Arguments for and against the existence of God are a long-winded and complex affair. Where in the end do they leave us? It is tempting to conclude that they take us nowhere. On the one hand, there is no agreed proof or disproof of the existence of God. Indeed we have argued that the classical proofs and disproofs are unsuccessful. On the other hand, we have seen that both theist and atheist can lay claim to some support for their respective positions. The widespread, intimate awareness of God's presence attested abundantly in varied religious experience must surely lead sensitive and unprejudiced atheists to think twice about their position. Equally the existence of widespread, gratuitous natural evil can torture the faith of most believers when they reflect on it. So we seem left to halt lamely between two opinions.

Formally this is very close to the position of the agnostic, who takes the view that there is no rational way of knowing theism to be true or false. In the absence of good evidence for belief in God, one must suspend belief. Materially the difference between this and outright atheism is very slight. For all practical purposes the agnostic lives as if God does not exist. An agnostic might of course live in the hope that God does exist, but it is rare to find this attitude in real life, a fact reflected in those dictionary definitions which make belief in material phenomena a mark of agnosticism. In other words, agnostics remind one of the saying, "He who is not with me is against me."[1] Suspending belief, therefore, brings one down on the

[1] Luke 11:23.

sceptical side of the religious fence. This is where the route we have taken so far seems to lead. As we have examined the varied arguments, there are no demonstrative proofs either way, and any evidence there is on one side seems canceled out by evidence for the other side.

THE FIDEISTIC ALTERNATIVE

But should we have taken this route in the first place? We have assumed all along that the rationality of religious belief is to be judged by examining arguments for and against it. Religious belief to be rational must pass certain tests. But what if this whole enterprise is misguided? Are religious doctrines a matter of reason at all? What if they do not rest on evidence in the first place? Perhaps they are held as a matter of faith. There is a venerable tradition which has long maintained that this is precisely the case. I shall define this tradition very broadly as fideism. By fideism I mean any view which holds that significant religious beliefs are a matter of faith rather than argument.

It is extremely important to realize that I do not intend this term to be construed as negative or pejorative. I am therefore departing from the common meaning of the word. Van A. Harvey, for example, says that fideism "refers generally to the doctrine that Christian assertions are matters of blind belief and cannot be known or demonstrated to be true."[2] This is too narrow and likely to cast fideism in a bad light at the outset. So I propose that we define a fideist as one who holds that religious belief is not rational in virtue of certain arguments, inference, or evidence; rather religious belief is intrinsically rational and known so as a matter of faith.

We should note several general points before we look at any particular fideistic position. First, fideists rarely if ever claim that reason is useless in any universal sense. Normally fideists will rely on argument and reason in mundane matters and in the average academic discipline like history, physics, and geography. Some fideists have been sceptics about reason's role in such matters, but it is not essential to fideism to take this view. What is crucial to fideism is that it insists that reasoned argument is either useless or only partially essential to the truth of significant religious doctrines. Reason is all right so far as it stays within its limits; it becomes a snare only when it seeks to be positively decisive in the realm of faith.

Secondly, it is clear that there can be weaker or stronger versions of fideism. One can, for example, be a hard or extreme fideist. In such a case one might hold that all religious belief is contrary to what we otherwise think to be true. In this view, where faith and reason clash on matters of religious importance, faith is to be preferred and reason rejected if not denigrated. Here religious belief will be construed as absurd to normal canons of thought. On the other hand, one can be a moderate or soft fideist. In this case one might hold that religious belief can only be fully justified by considerations which are internal to a religious tradition. Here

[2]Van A. Harvey, *A Handbook of Theological Terms* (New York: Macmillan, 1964), p. 99.

reason may not clash with religious belief, but it would be insufficient on its own to show religious belief to be true, and thus it makes sense to speak of some kind of appeal to faith. These are just two possibilities, and they are intended to make clear that fideists come in many colors.

Thirdly, it is important that fideism not be seen as always antithetical to the use of reason in religion. Fideists make use of reason within theology and religion. They argue and discuss as passionately as anyone else. What is at issue is whether the foundations of theology are to be shown to be true by evidence, argument, and the like. This fideists will generally deny. In doing so, however, they do not also deny that these foundational beliefs are true or rational. On the contrary, they confidently hold these beliefs to be most certainly known. What they deny is that these beliefs have to be shown to be true by further evidence outside the beliefs themselves. The beliefs are held to be intrinsically true, not needing any kind of external justification.

THE BARTHIAN VERSION

In this chapter I shall outline and evaluate that version of fideism developed by Karl Barth. After some introductory remarks I shall set out a series of arguments Barth has deployed against any attempt to ground religious belief in anything outside itself. Only then shall I critically examine his doctrines. Throughout it should be borne in mind that this analysis is tentative as an interpretation of Barth's position. Perhaps it might be better described as the outline of a set of fideistic arguments inspired by Barth. I believe that they capture some of Barth's most important ideas on natural theology, but whether they do is not crucial to what follows. My primary concern is to explore the fideistic tradition in some detail; the arguments to come serve that purpose admirably.

Barth is undoubtedly one of the most distinguished representatives of fideism in modern times. He belongs to that illustrious school of thought known as neo-orthodoxy. The title is descriptive of the intention of its adherents: they desire to be orthodox, for they call for a return to the Bible, but they are also contemporary or new, for they want to speak to the world of today and not the world of yesterday. Not all neoorthodox theologians are fideists. Indeed Barth and Brunner had an acrimonious and futile debate about the legitimacy of natural theology. In the main, however, neoorthodoxy is opposed to natural theology as a matter of principle. It is not that theologians like Bultmann, Barth, and Niebuhr examine the classical arguments and, noting that they fail as proofs, conclude that natural theology is not possible. Their thesis is far more radical. They argue that natural theology is religiously unacceptable; natural theology as a matter of principle is theologically a nonstarter. It is to be opposed in the name of faith and revelation. True theology and so-called natural theology are incompatible.

This is a very radical thesis. Let us pause to hear how Barth states it in his own words.

". . . natural theology" does not exist as an entity capable of becoming a separate subject within what I consider to be real theology—not even for the sake of being rejected. If one occupies oneself with real theology one can pass by so-called natural theology as one would pass by an abyss into which it is unadvisable to step if one does not want to fall. All one can do is turn one's back upon it as upon the great temptation and source of error, by having nothing to do with it and by making it clear to oneself and others from time to time why one acts that way.[3]

Real rejection of natural theology can come about only in the fear of God and hence only by a complete *lack* of interest in this matter. If *this* matter is allowed to become of interest, though but in order to be rejected, then interest is no longer centered in *theology*. For this rejection cannot within theology be made for its own sake. For it is not by this rejection that truth is known, the Gospel is expounded, God is praised and the church is built.[4]

If you really reject natural theology you do not stare at the serpent with the result that it stares back at you, hypnotises you and is ultimately certain to bite you, but you hit it and kill it as soon as you see it.[5]

Why do Barth and others in neo-orthodoxy refuse to show any interest in natural theology? As these quotations indicate, it is not easy to find out why they think as they do, for to take time to say why they are opposed to natural theology is to show an interest in it. It is small wonder, then, that Barth has been accused of dogmatism and irrationalism. By refusing to be drawn on the subject as a matter of principle, he gives the impression of being obscurantist and authoritarian. Barth, however, does have a rationale for his position. He could not speak of reminding himself and others as to why he acts as he does if he did not. Thus there is some hope that his position can be saved from obscurantism and sheer blind irrationalism. Let me try to summarize the main threads of his argument.

The major themes of Barth's theology are the themes of grace and revelation. It is in these that the clue to Barth's rejection of natural theology is to be found. His rejection of natural theology is the negative form of a very positive affirmation of faith. What Barth is positively concerned to do, as John Thompson reminds us, is to affirm the truth of God in Jesus Christ.[6] This positive affirmation and intent explains Barth's lack of interest in natural theology. He has within this affirmation at least three positive theological proposals, which are closely related and which together entail, in his view, the rejection of natural theology.

First, God is known only and known fully in Jesus Christ. Jesus Christ constitutes the sole and sufficient revelation of God to man. Thus, says Barth, the Christian faith does not say that we find God, it says that God in revelation finds us; the Christian faith brings grace and revelation, not human reasoning and discovery. That revelation has been made uniquely in Jesus Christ; in him alone is God known.

[3] Karl Barth, "No!" in *Natural Theology,* trans. Peter Fraenkel (London: Geoffrey Bles, 1946), p. 75.

[4] Ibid., p. 76.

[5] Ibid.

[6] John Thompson, *Christ in Perspective* (Edinburgh: Saint Andrew Press, 1978), p. 120.

Moreover, it has been made fully known in Jesus Christ; he is complete and sufficient as the revelation of God. The corollary of this is that God is not known in nature, in history, in experience, in reason, or in anything save Jesus Christ. Any theology which looks to those is false theology, for true theology has only one source, Jesus Christ. Natural theology is therefore false theology; it seeks to know God apart from Jesus Christ; it construes the Christian religion as a plausible metaphysical construction which is deemed worthy of assent rather than a divine disclosure from God which is to be obeyed in faith. So to affirm the possibility of natural theology is to deny the uniqueness, completeness, and sufficiency of Jesus Christ.

Another way of stating Barth's point here is this: natural theology is unacceptable because it could never lead one to the true God. Barth repeatedly asks whether the "god" of natural theology has anything to do with the God and Father of Jesus Christ. This is an obvious corollary of his claim that God is known only in Jesus Christ rather than a full-fledged independent argument. Any source other than Jesus Christ could not as a matter of principle lead to God, for God is known through him alone. As Barth puts it, ". . . God as our Father, as the Creator, is unknown in so far as He is not made known through Jesus."[7] Barth drew the consequences of this for natural theology in this way:

> If this exclusiveness is taken seriously—then any possibility is barred of conceiving the first article in the creed as an article of natural theology. Jesus' message about God the Father must not be regarded as if Jesus had expressed the familiar truth, that the world must have and really has a creator, and then had ventured to designate this Creator by the familiar human name of "Father"—not as if on his part he intended what all serious philosophy has named as the highest cause, or as the highest good, as *esse a se* or as the *ens perfectissimum,* as the universal, as the ground of meaning and the abyss of meaning, as the unconditioned, as the limit, the critical negation or the origin; intended it and dedicated it by the name of Father, not altogether unknown to religious language, gave it a Christian interpretation and, as it were, baptism. To that we can but say that this entity, the supposed philosophical equivalent of the Creator God, has nothing to do with Jesus' message of God the Father, with or without the name of Father attached.[8]

The second proposal Barth draws on to rule out natural theology speaks of reconciliation rather than revelation. According to Barth, God has reconciled humankind to himself in Jesus Christ. Human beings have not reached up to God by their own efforts or works; God has reached down to them and achieved reconciliation in Christ. To affirm true reconciliation as it really is, is to deny natural theology. Thompson expressed this in this fashion;

> The total deliverance wrought for us by Christ's reconciling act reveals our total inability to lift ourselves up to God or to know him as he is. The denial

[7]Karl Barth, *Church Dogmatics* (Edinburgh: T. and T. Clark, 1960), vol. I, pt. 1, p. 448.
[8]Ibid., pp. 448–49.

of natural theology is but the obverse of a total reconciliation of us by God in Jesus Christ.[9]

As it stands, this exposition does not show exactly why natural theology is wrong. I think the reasoning is that natural theology indirectly involves seeking salvation by works. It makes knowing God a matter of human ability and thus fails to reckon with the doctrine that God is known only because of his reconciling work in Jesus Christ. Natural theology is therefore man centered rather than God centered; it speaks of works not grace; it revolves around natural ability, not divine action. So to affirm reconciliation and grace is to deny the viability of natural theology.

A third element in Barth's position which leads to the same result takes us back to the theme of revelation. According to Barth, the revelation through which God makes himself known and through which he also reconciles the world to himself cannot be subject to the test of human reason. If revelation is really divine in its origin, then it must be ultimate and self-sufficient. Rather than human beings standing in judgment over revelation, revelation stands in judgment over human beings. Were we to judge revelation then we must use some standard to measure and assess it. In that case the standard would be the ultimate criterion. However, it is divine revelation which must be ultimate in matters of faith; to reject this is to deny divine revelation the authority which is its due as divine revelation.

Again let Barth speak for himself on this issue.

> According to Holy Scripture God's revelation is a ground which has no sort of higher or deeper ground above or behind it, but is simply a ground in itself, and therefore as regards man an authority from which no appeal to a higher authority is possible. Its reality and likewise its truth do not rest upon a superior reality and truth, are under no need of an initial actualisation or legitimation as a reality and truth such as might be found at such another point, are not to be compared with such, nor to be judged and regarded as reality and truth in the light of such. On the contrary, God's revelation has its reality and truth wholly and in every respect—i.e., ontically and noetically—within itself. Only by denying it can we wish to ascribe to it a higher or deeper ground different from itself, or regard, adopt, or reject it from the vantage of such a higher or deeper ground. Obviously the adoption of revelation from the point of view of such a ground, differing from it and presumably superior to it—e.g., an affirmation of revelation, in which a man previously set up his conscience to be the judge of it—can only be achieved by denying revelation.[10]

These are the main arguments Barth deploys against any natural theology. However, there are other subsidiary considerations which should also be noted. Two deserve mention. To begin, Barth believed that the natural theologian failed to be entirely honest with the unbeliever. The following quotation makes this very clear.

---

[9] Thompson, *Christ in Perspective,* p. 188.
[10] Barth, *Church Dogmatics,* vol. I, pt. 1, p. 350.

Now suppose the partner in the conversation (i.e., natural theology) discovers that faith is trying to use the well-known artifice of dialectic in relation to him. We are not taking him seriously because we withhold from him what we really want to say and represent. It is only in appearance that we devote ourselves to him, and therefore what we say to him is only an apparent and unreal statement. What will happen then? Well, not without justice—although misconstruing the friendly intention which perhaps motivates us—he will see himself despised and deceived. He will shut himself up and harden himself against the faith which does not speak out frankly, which deserts its own standpoint of unbelief. What use to unbelief is a faith which obviously knows different? And how shocking for unbelief is a faith which only pretends to take up with unbelief a common position.[11]

It is not entirely clear what this objection is. What it appears to mean is that the natural theologian is misrepresenting what the Christian faith involves by omitting any reference to revelation. By appealing to nature, history, experience, or whatever, the crucial matter of revelation in Christ is set aside. Yet revelation is the heart of the Christian faith and is the crucial warrant for the claims of the Christian gospel. Natural theologians can only pretend to argue seriously with the unbeliever when they appeal to some common ground; at the end of the day, however, unbelievers must face up to the demands of the gospel revelation if they are to take the Christian faith seriously. Rather than mask this, Barth is suggesting that it would be more honest to admit it at the outset and work from that standpoint rather than play with working from the standpoint of unbelief.

This leads to a second subsidiary issue which is vital to the whole thrust of Barth's attitude to natural theology. Given that God is made known by revelation and grace, Barth's fear is that in appealing to considerations outside revelation there is a constant danger that the whole theological enterprise will be corrupted or ruined. Natural theologians, therefore, put at risk the unique content and character of theology as a rational discipline.[12] If God is made known in revelation, revelation and revelation alone must determine what the Christian theologian believes. Every doctrine must therefore be grounded in Christ rather than in alien natural or philosophical categories or convictions.

We might illustrate this by reference to the debate about religious language which we have already explored. We noted that logical positivists laid down certain strictures about meaningful discourse.[13] Suppose these become the norm for the theologian. In that case it could well mean that theologians would have to revise very drastically certain central doctrines, as happened, for example, in the case of Braithwaite and van Buren. But that means the gospel revelation is no longer normative. The theologian has to be the slave to the categories and canons of unbelief. For Barth such a position totally undermines the independence and integrity

---

[11] Barth, *Church Dogmatics*, vol. II, pt. 1, p. 93.

[12] This point is made again and again in Thomas F. Torrance, *Theological Science* (Oxford: Oxford University Press, 1969).

[13] See chap. 2.

of the whole theological task. So here is another reason why natural theology must be rejected for religious reasons. It makes theology subservient to canons of thought which lie outside its own unique standpoint. Even if it does not do that, it distracts from the heart of the Christian message.

The alternative to natural theology is revelation. Christian theology should not take its stand on nature or evidence outside faith. Let it stand with God in his revelation and explore the riches of Christ for faith and life. This revelation is a given. It comes from God, who is the norm for all true thinking about the divine. If this seems irrational to unbelief so be it. After all, why should unbelief be considered normative in matters divine?

As we prepare to examine Barth's position it is extremely important that we be fully aware of what he is precluding. In broad terms he is arguing that it is inconsistent to affirm grace and revelation and at the same time raise the classical questions about the rationality of belief in God and special divine revelation in Jesus Christ. Thus Barth precludes our asking the question, What reasons have we for believing that God exists or that he has revealed himself uniquely in Jesus Christ? Reason here is not necessarily identified with the classical proofs for the existence of God or the classical credentials for revelation. The reasons offered could include these if they were satisfactory, but this is neither here nor there. The point at issue is the radical nature of Barth's thesis. It attacks not just any attempt to offer proofs but also any attempt to offer considerations which would, broadly speaking, rationally persuade. What I shall argue is that Barth has not established his case. One can assent without inconsistency both to divine revelation and the pursuit of reasons or rationality. Indeed it is a duty both of faith and logic. Why do I believe this to be so over against Barth? There are several reasons.

REBUTTAL OF BARTH'S MAIN ARGUMENTS

A critical difficulty in Barth's position is that it completely evades the problem posed by the existence of conflicting claims to revelation. Barth insists with great fervor that God is known uniquely and sufficiently in Jesus Christ. Moslems insist with equal fervor that God is known uniquely and sufficiently in the Koran. For Jews it is the Torah, for Mormons it is the Book of Mormon. Let us agree for the present with Barth that we need revelation. But to whom do we turn? Why do we turn to Christ rather than Mohammed? We can always take the first which comes to hand but this course only makes the acceptance of revelation into a religious lottery. And how shall we decide? Are there no reasons, however vague and suggestive, which lead us to turn to one rather than the other? Barth has no answer to this question. Indeed, where we seem to need all the sensitivity we can muster, he would encourage us to look upon the quest for reasons as idolatrous.

That Barth precludes this question should be enough to cast doubt on the whole structure of his position. As it stands, he has handed out a device every sophisticated claimant to revelation can now use to silence those who would critically examine his claims. Revelation is to be believed just because someone says it is revelation. Every peddler of revelation can now take to the streets and be immune from examination. When this happens it is time we asked why we should accept Barth's veto.

Barth's veto is crucially tied to his third main argument. To examine revelation is to make revelation less than ultimate and less than divine. The problem with this argument is that it fails to distinguish two very different sorts of question. It is one thing to question the content of a genuine revelation; it is quite another to question someone's claim to possess a genuine revelation from God. If a particular revelation is a genuine revelation, then it must as a matter of logic stand in judgment over us and our thinking. To pit our fallible, limited, and corrupted reason against God on any matter is ludicrous. It is illogical, unreasonable, and absurd. This is a matter of logic as much as it is of faith. Omniscience does not need human approval for its validity.

It is quite another matter, however, to ask critical questions about someone's claim to possess genuine revelation. In this case one is not questioning God but some human agent who claims to represent God. Here surely we have a right to use our reason, else the danger is that we shall be duped by charlatans, imposters, sincere fools, and the like. The fact is, revelation does not wear its authenticity on its face. We have to live in a situation where various religious traditions equally sincerely and confidently claim to speak definitively for God. Even within the Christian tradition the exact locus of revelation is disputed. This being so, we have to use our minds to decide between the options available. Once we commit ourselves, then revelation acts as a crucial criterion in our theology. How this revelation interacts with other considerations in making theological decisions must be explored elsewhere.[14]

We can speedily dispatch Barth's second main argument in similar fashion. The crux of that argument is that natural theology involves human works seeking to bring us justification before God whereas reconciliation is a matter of divine grace in Jesus Christ. Again two questions are being confused as one. It is one thing to ask how we are reconciled to God. With Paul, Luther, Wesley, and Barth we can reply that it is by God's grace in Jesus Christ and not by works. The doctrine of reconciliation is not therefore in dispute; we can agree for the present on the first-order, religious issue of how people attain salvation. There is, however, a second-order, epistemological question of how we justify this proposal. To answer this question by appeal to grace rather than works is not just wrong but incoherent and irrelevant. At this level one will have to offer some kind of theological rationale. This of course will be a human enterprise, but it need not in itself involve any attempt to justify oneself before God on the basis of one's theological proposals as a human work. On the contrary, the proposal itself rules out that option.

The application of this to the quest of natural theology is obvious. In natural theology one asks whether it is rational to believe in God. This leaves open the issue

---

[14] For the relationship between revelation and moral insight see chap. 11.

of how one is reconciled to God. These two questions are on entirely different levels. The first, according to classical natural theology, will involve the giving of reasons of one sort or another. The second, if Barth is correct (and this is irrelevant to the philosopher) summons one to ask for mercy. There need be no opposition between the two. It is lack of subtlety and sensitivity which would set them in conflict. Belief in justification by faith and the pursuit of reasons in theology as exemplified in natural theology are entirely compatible with one another.

If Barth's last two main arguments fail to rule out natural theology, is there still enough acid left in the first to destroy it? Does the claim that God is known only and known fully in Jesus Christ make impossible the quest for reasons for belief in God?

Prima facie it does look as if Barth has succeeded. Classical natural theology has sought to argue that certain truths about God can be known apart from special revelation in Jesus Christ. If God is known only and known fully in Jesus Christ, it follows as a matter of logic that natural theology thus understood is invalid. However, we can surely ask whether this is the only way to construe natural theology. Once we do so, then the issue takes on entirely new dimensions.

What we need to do is to go behind the classical tradition of natural theology and ask a more general question than that posed by thinkers like Aquinas. Natural theology is a species of a wider genus. We can reject the species of natural theology but retain the genus. The genus issue in the wake of Barth is this: Is it reasonable to believe in the God who is said to be fully known in Jesus Christ? With this question there is genuine continuity with natural theology. With Aquinas we are interested in the rationality of religious belief, but against Barth we note that this rationality is not incompatible with belief in divine revelation. Now the quest for rationality may be complex; it may or may not involve inference from nature, religious experience, moral insight, or whatever; but this quest is not ruled out by Barth's first argument.

Someone may protest that the foregoing is a mere abstract hypothetical reconstruction of natural theology invented *ex nihilo* to counter Barth. We shall see later that this is not the case.[15] Suffice it to note now that many philosophers have come to recognize the artificiality of much classical natural theology. That theology tended to begin from below with nature, then proceeded from the world up to God, and then moved back down again in special revelation. On this view you could take the Christian creed, divide it into atomic units, and then accept or reject these one at a time. But this is not the only way to proceed. Equally well one can begin from above, as it were. One can start off with a developed body of religious belief which already appeals to divine revelation as part of its essence and then proceed to ask why one should accept this particular theological vision. Pursuing this issue sets one in deep continuity with the tradition of natural theology, but it is a different sort of operation and calls for a much wider, but no less genuine, account of rationality than is involved in the narrower proofs.

Once we reformulate and restate the fundamental concern of natural theology in this way we also dispose at one stroke of Barth's protest against the false gods of

[15] See chap. 9.

traditional natural theology. Our interest is not in some vague creator or cosmic architect or abstract ground of being. Our interest is in the God who is said to be uniquely revealed in Jesus Christ. We are not baptizing some pagan god and then asking if it is rational to believe that he exists. We are asking if it is rational to believe in the God and Father of Jesus Christ. Whether we succeed or not in answering may be a matter of dispute. The point is, however, that the question itself is entirely legitimate; it is not precluded by the Barthian veto.

Whether we call this question theological or philosophical is a verbal matter of no great consequence. Barthians may want to exclude it as being outside their job description as theologians. The theologian, they might say, has more positive things to do, his or her job is to expound the Gospel and build up the church. Well and good. The theologian may well want to explore in detail the consequences of divine revelation for every branch of theological science. But this is a dispute about the self-chosen aims of the systematic theologian who has limited time at his or her disposal. It says nothing about the legitimacy of pursuing the quest for natural theology as it has been reformulated. The rationality of religious belief remains a valid question. Perhaps the question should concern both theologians and philosophers as it always has. It is immaterial, however, how we label it. What matters is that we ask it seriously and answer it carefully.

BARTH'S SUBSIDIARY ARGUMENTS

What of the two subsidiary arguments which accompany Barth's central protests? Does natural theology mean that we play games with the unbeliever or corrupt the whole theological enterprise? The answer in both cases is no. The believer can make clear without apology to the unbeliever that the Christian faith should be understood as a rounded whole, prior to settling the question of its rationality. This clarification will involve the Christian faith's claims to possess divine revelation as a decisive warrant for some of its proposals about God. Thus one is not hiding crucial considerations which are produced at the last minute to save the day.

Equally there is no reason why natural theology should necessarily corrupt one's theological proposals. Revelation can still operate as normative in matters of faith and practice. Barth's argument against this rests on his historical evaluation of modern Protestant theology. Torrance expressed this argument as follows:

> ... the danger of natural theology lies in the fact that once its ground has been conceded it becomes the ground on which everything else is absorbed and naturalised, so that even the knowledge of God mediated through his self-revelation in Christ is domesticated and adapted to it until it all becomes a form of natural theology. Barth reached this judgement through extensive examination of the history of German Protestant theology which it is extremely difficult if not impossible to refute. Moreover, he felt this to be reinforced through his analysis of the contemporary situation immediately before and after Hitler's rise to power, for what appeared to lie behind that upsurge of paganism in a Christian country was the domestication and ab-

sorption of Christianity into the romantic depths of German nature and culture.[16]

This statement constitutes a warning the natural theologian should heed; as a veto against natural theology it fails for three reasons. First, there are many examples in the history of theology where even the classical natural theologian remained fully orthodox in his theology and did not allow it to absorb or tame the riches of divine revelation. Anselm, Aquinas, and Wesley might serve as examples. Secondly, purely historical arguments cannot be decisive on this issue. One must ask not just whether natural theology has led to the domestication of divine revelation but whether it must necessarily do so. Where it has, it might still be purged to avoid this consequence. Thirdly, one can legitimately ask whether exclusive attention to divine revelation in Christ is the most healthy course for theology itself to take. Perhaps God has revealed himself elsewhere if only to a lesser degree. If he has then it could be very serious to ignore this fact. Obviously we enter here a whole new nest of issues which we cannot pursue here.

For the present we must conclude that at least one significant version of fideism has failed to satisfy. In the next chapter we shall examine a much more compelling version of fideism, which emanates from the same theological roots as Barth but which offers a much more positive relationship to philosophy. We turn, that is, to examine a fascinating proposal presently being worked out by Alvin Plantinga.

---

[16] T. F. Torrance, "The Problem of Natural Theology in the Thought of Karl Barth," *Religious Studies* VI (1970), 125.

Chapter Eight
Philosophical Fideism

If fideism is to receive the attention it merits as a defense of religious belief, then it is imperative that we avoid those descriptions which dismiss it as irrational by definition. Happily, we can report that in the space of a generation there has been considerable improvement. In 1964 Richard Robinson could argue without difficulty that it was a positive duty to undermine those beliefs held as a matter of faith. This followed very naturally from his account of faith.

> Christian faith is not merely believing that there is a god. It is believing that there is a god no matter what the evidence may be. "Have faith," in the Christian sense, means "make yourself believe that there is a god, without regard to the evidence." Christian faith is a habit of flouting reason in forming and maintaining one's answer to the question whether there is a god. Its essence is the determination to believe that there is a god no matter what the evidence may be.[1]

There is no explicit definition of fideism per se here but one can easily supply it. For Robinson fideism is not far removed from the popular cry that faith is "believing what you know ain't true." In 1979, however, Antony Flew, who shares much of the intellectual hostility to religion exhibited by Robinson, endorsed a much more acceptable account. He accepted the definition of fideism as

---

[1] Richard Robinson, *An Atheist's Values* (Oxford: Clarendon Press, 1964), pp. 119–20.

the view, recurrent throughout religious history, that essential religious doctrines cannot be established by rational means, but only accepted, if at all, by acts of faith. Its extreme form (for example, in St. Augustine or Pascal) reason is not antithetically opposed to faith, but plays an auxiliary role in formulating or elucidating what must first be accepted by faith.[2]

Unfortunately, Robinson's description is still common enough for philosophers to be very wary of the label. Theologians like Barth, who fear philosophy as a distraction or source of corruption in religion, do not worry very much about the issue, for they base their account of religious belief on divine revelation rather than on philosophical argument. This being so we should perhaps distinguish not only between extreme and moderate fideists but also between theological and philosophical fideists. The difference here is one mainly of emphasis. Theological fideists defend their position on religious or theological grounds; philosophical fideists, in contrast to this, seek to offer philosophical arguments in defense of their position.

THE WORK OF ALVIN PLANTINGA

An extremely interesting version of philosophical fideism has been developed of late by Alvin Plantinga. His central thesis is that many of our common beliefs, such as belief in the past or belief in other minds, are held without evidence. Contrary to what we might at first imagine, such beliefs are rational beliefs. Moreover, among the beliefs we may legitimately hold without evidence is belief in God. The primary reason why we hesitate to accept Plantinga's thesis stems from our mistaken commitment to what is known as classical foundationalism. In this chapter we shall outline and evaluate Plantinga's important proposal. In the course of the discussion we shall draw attention to the advantages of Plantinga's position compared to that of other philosophical fideists. We shall also argue that Plantinga's position, contrary to his own understandable protests, can be construed as a very significant expression of the fideistic tradition.

We can begin our exposition by noting that the mainstream of Western thought has assumed that it is rational to believe in God only because there is good evidence for the existence of God. Philosophers, of course, have disagreed on what counts as good evidence and have disputed whether there is good evidence. Generally, however, they agree that if belief in God is to be rational, then good reasons should be available and presented. This is understandable, for we tend to tie rationality to the giving of reasons. It seems strange to say that someone is rational in holding a belief if that person does not have good reasons for that belief.

Not surprisingly, critics of religion have fastened on this question of evidence in their attack on religious belief. In the last century, for example, W. K. Clifford protested vehemently that it was wicked and immoral to accept any belief for which you did not have sufficient evidence. Belief in God fell foul of this law; there-

---

[2] Antony Flew, ed., *A Dictionary of Philosophy* (London: Macmillan, 1979), p. 112.

fore religious believers acted sinfully in believing. Although less extreme in the tone of their criticism, modern sceptics like Bertrand Russell, Antony Flew, and Michael Scriven have agreed with Clifford in his assessment of theistic belief.

Theists who find this position unconvincing can attempt to meet this challenge in a variety of ways. Following the path of natural theology, they can set forth reasons for belief in God and defend them against objection. Alternatively they can ask whether it makes sense to speak of its being wicked or immoral to hold a belief. Perhaps our beliefs are not under our control; they are events rather than actions, hence to hold us morally responsible for our beliefs is wrong. Yet again, theists might accept that we are accountable for our beliefs to some degree but challenge the view that we are always wrong to hold a belief without evidence. Clearly in everyday life much of what we currently believe is held without good evidence. We never had evidence to begin with, or we have forgotten it, or we have not had time to look for any, or maybe we do not need any reasons at all. It is this last option Plantinga has exploited in his defense of theism.

Initially Plantinga simply agreed that there are many respectable beliefs which rational people hold but which are not at all well supported by evidence. Sceptics who argue that we can rationally accept religious beliefs only if we can give reasons and show that the reasons really are reasons are unfair and discriminatory.

> For there are many beliefs we all hold, and hold with no detriment to our rationality, for which we cannot produce both evidence and proof that the evidence really is evidence. Indeed, some of these beliefs are such that to *show* that our reasons for them are good reasons, we should have to provide solutions to certain philosophical problems which (to my mind at least) have not yet been solved.[3]

Among such beliefs are belief in other minds and belief in theoretical entities like atoms and electrons.

It is true, of course, that philosophers have offered reasons for belief in other minds. They have argued, for example, from analogy. We can see a connection between our own mental states and physical states; noting similar physical states in others, we infer mental states in their case similar to our own. It might seem, therefore, that Plantinga's counter example is not very helpful. Perhaps we can, after all, give a good reason for belief in other minds but not for belief in God. A similar strategy could be mounted in the case of our belief in atoms and electrons, thereby isolating belief in God as the only belief we hold without good evidence. If so, then Plantinga's defense of religious belief seems arbitrary and ad hoc.

Plantinga, however, has adopted three moves to rescue his position from danger. The last is by far the most interesting, but we need to be aware of the other two to do full justice to his position.

First, Plantinga has argued at length that there are striking similarities between belief in God and belief in other minds. This was the burden of his argument in *God*

---

[3] Alvin Plantinga, "The Sceptic's Strategy," in *Faith and the Philosophers*, ed. John Hick (London: Macmillan, 1966), p. 227.

and Other Minds. Noting that there are similar problems in the argument to other minds from analogy and the teleological argument for the existence of God, he sums up his position in this fashion. "I conclude that belief in other minds and belief in God are in the same epistemological boat; hence if either is rational, so is the other. But obviously the former *is* rational; so, therefore, is the latter."[4]

Secondly, Plantinga has sought to show that there is at least one good argument that establishes the rational acceptability of belief in God. At this level he has attempted to argue for the validity of the ontological argument.[5] Here Plantinga seeks to pacify the sceptic by resorting to the tradition of classical natural theology, albeit in a qualified sense.

BELIEF IN GOD AS A BASIC BELIEF

Plantinga, however, has in reserve a third alternative, namely, to argue that the sceptic has not at all established the thesis that for a belief to be rational we must have reasons for it.[6] Some of our beliefs are basic beliefs; they are held without evidence; they are the foundations of all our reasoning. Moreover, there is no good reason why belief in God may not be placed in this category. Indeed, it is this insight which has been buried in the Reformed and Calvinistic indifference to natural theology. According to this view, it does not matter that we cannot give reasons for belief in God. Reasons may not be necessary in the first place for our belief in God to be rational.

Why have philosophers and theologians been reluctant to accept this possibility? It stems, in Plantinga's view, from their commitment to classical foundationalism. Classical foundationalists agree that some of our beliefs will be basic beliefs. These beliefs we know immediately, without evidence or reason in their favor. Other beliefs are nonbasic; we know these to be rational only because they are based on other beliefs, some of which may be basic. The essence of classical foundationalism is that only certain of our beliefs may legitimately be considered basic or foundational. Basic beliefs must, in other words, satisfy certain stringent conditions; therefore, a person is rational in believing in God only if he or she has evidence for his existence.

[4] Alvin Plantinga, *God and Other Minds* (Ithaca, N.Y.: Cornell University Press, 1967), p. viii.

[5] For a brief statement of this see Alvin Plantinga, *God, Freedom and Evil* (London: George Allen & Unwin, 1974), pp. 108–12.

[6] Plantinga has laid out his position in the following papers: "Is Belief in God Rational?" in *Rationality and Religious Belief*, ed. C. F. Delaney (Notre Dame: University of Notre Dame Press, 1979); "Is Belief in God Properly Basic?" *Nous* XV (1981); and "The Reformed Objection to Natural Theology," *Christian Scholar's Review* XI (1982). The latter can also be located in *Proceedings of the American Catholic Philosophical Association,* 1980. Plantinga presented his views at the Philosophy Conference at Wheaton College, Wheaton, Illinois, in 1980; the lectures on that occasion, which contain the substance of the above articles, were published in mineographed form as "Reason and Belief in God," October 1981.

What beliefs can legitimately be seen as basic and why? Classical foundational-ists suggest beliefs like the following as properly basic: $2 + 1 = 3$; no person is both married and unmarried; redness is distinct from greenness; the whole is greater than the part. These are accepted as basic because they are self-evident. We simply see them to be true when we understand their meaning. We do not derive them from other beliefs that we hold. Moreover, psychologically we feel compelled to believe them when we think of them; they seem luminously obvious. Another class we ac-cept as basic comprises those which are evident to our senses. For example, as I write now, I see a black pen, I hear a dog bark, I know I am wearing glasses, I feel a numb sensation in my right knee. It does not make sense to speak of proving these propositions to myself; I know them straight off, as it were. At the very least, I do not prove to myself that I seem to see a black pen, or that I seem to hear a dog bark, or that I seem to feel a numb sensation in my right knee. These beliefs are immune from error; they are incorrigible for me. Classical foundationalists suggest that such beliefs as these and only these are properly basic. They must either be self-evident or evident to the senses or be incorrigible. As belief in God does not satisfy these conditions, it cannot be properly basic.

Plantinga's strategy against this thesis is to reject it outright as unacceptable. He gives two reasons for doing so. First, the classical foundationalist position entails that many of our beliefs normally deemed rational now turn out to be irrational. For example, belief in the existence of the external world, or belief in other persons distinct from ourselves, or belief in the past—none of these is self-evident, evident to the senses, or incorrigible, nor are they based on beliefs which satisfy these con-ditions. Even uncomplicated beliefs, like my belief that I took the dog for a walk in the park this afternoon, do not fit the foundationalist's model of rational belief. Yet these beliefs are so clearly rational that it is wise to retain them and reject the claims of classical foundationalism.

A second reason why we should reject classical foundationalism is that by its own standards it is irrational to believe in its central tenets. The classical foun-dationalist says we should accept a belief as properly basic *only* if it is self-evident, evident to the senses, or incorrigible. But what about this thesis itself? Clearly it is not properly basic. Nor have we been given any good reason for adopting this normative belief. Hence we should reject it as irrational. Failing that, it looks as if we have to accept it on the mere say-so of the classical foundationalist.

It is true that someone may attempt to offer a revised account of the con-ditions of proper basicality which would not be open to these objections. At present, however, that is a major statement of faith and hope which is unlikely to be realized. This unlikelihood emerges when we reflect on how conditions of proper basic beliefs should be developed. Rather than proceed by laying down the law about what can or cannot be basic, we should proceed inductively. We should work from a relevant set of examples, that is, those beliefs which are basic for us, and then frame theories as to the correct criterion of proper basic beliefs. Within this set, theists are entirely at liberty to include belief in God. Hence it is highly unlikely that any revised version of foundationalism will pose a threat to construing belief in God as a basic belief, held without any evidence.

Plantinga's strategy, then, is to propose that belief in God be seen as part of the foundations of a theist's system of beliefs. In this case, there is no need to offer positive reasons for theism. Like many other beliefs we hold, belief in God is rational without supportive evidence. Or, at least, it has not been established as ir-rational. He summarizes his position in this way:

> To accept belief in God as basic is clearly not irrational in the sense of being proscribed by reason or in conflict with the deliverances of reason. The dic-tum that belief in God is not basic in a rational noetic structure is neither apparently self-evident nor apparently incorrigible. Nor does it seem to be a deductive consequence of what is self-evident or incorrigible. Is there, then, any reason at all for holding that a noetic structure including belief in God as basic is irrational? If there is, it remains to be specified.[7]

PLANTINGA AS A FIDEIST

Plantinga's strategy to construe belief in God as basic ranks as one of the most interesting proposals in modern philosophy of religion. Before evaluating it, let us pause to see why it should be viewed as a brand of fideism. Plantinga rejects this interpretation for entirely healthy reasons. His dictionary defines fideism as "ex-clusive or basic reliance on faith alone, accompanied by a consequent disparagement of reason and utilised especially in the pursuit of philosophical or religious truth."[8] Obviously, no one with the commitment to logic exhibited by Plantinga will wel-come being called a fideist. Moreover, if he has to choose between treating belief in God as an item of faith or a deliverance of reason, there is no doubt that it is the latter he prefers.[9]

However, others beside myself feel it natural to read Plantinga's recent work as a version of fideism.[10] First, his central claim is that belief in God does not re-quire reasons to be rational. That is surely what most fideists have fundamentally believed. Secondly, Plantinga can very easily use language which clearly echoes prominent fideistic themes. For example, he writes:

> It is worth noting . . . that the mature believer, the mature theist, does not typically accept belief in God tentatively, or hypothetically, or until some-thing better comes along. Nor, I think, does he accept it as a conclusion from other things he believes; he accepts it as basic, as a part of the foundations of his noetic structure. The mature theist *commits* himself to belief in God; this means that he accepts belief in God as basic.[11]

[7] Plantinga, "Is Belief in God Rational?" p. 26.
[8] Plantinga, "Reason and Belief in God," p. 89.
[9] Ibid., p. 94.
[10] Basil Mitchell, "Two Approaches to the Philosophy of Religion," unpublished.
[11] Plantinga, "Is Belief in God Rational?" p. 27.

Thirdly, Plantinga happily associates himself with a version of the Calvinist tradition which has able exponents of fideism in its ranks. Certainly Plantinga is not hostile to Bavinck or Barth or Calvin when he is in a fideistic mood.[12] Lastly, we have argued earlier that there is no need for fideists to disparage reason in any unacceptable sense.[13] Plantinga's fears stem from a definition of fideism which should be cleansed or rejected. On our account of the fideistic tradition he is a moderate fideist, indeed a moderate of moderates, but he is a fideist nonetheless. Perhaps he is one of the best philosophical fideists to appear of late.

We say this because Plantinga's proposals compare very favorably with the standard versions of fideism currently known in philosophy of religion. For example, he has clearly recognized that it is suicidal for the theist to abandon the cognitive status of religious language. Here he differs radically from the school of fideism inspired by the later writings of Wittgenstein.[14] Moreover, his central claims and arguments are luminously clear compared to the ambivalence and dense obscurity of Kierkegaard. Also, he avoids the moral unease evoked by Pascal's famous wager, and he is not committed to the heady voluntarism normally associated with modern existentialism.[15] Thus belief in God does not become the outcome of a lottery, nor does it involve an agonizing effort of will or painful leap in the dark. Plantinga has wisely steered a course which avoids such troubled waters. Has he, however, provided an adequate account and defense of theism?

EVALUATION OF PLANTINGA'S POSITION

Let us accept for the moment that Plantinga's attack on classical foundationalism is essentially correct. Let us agree, that is, that many significant beliefs we have are not proved by inference from other beliefs we hold. They are immediate and basic; they form the foundations of our whole network of beliefs. Let us also agree that there is no definitive account of what beliefs can legitimately be construed as basic and why any belief should be construed as basic. Given this, Plantinga's thesis is technically secure. He can maintain that no one has shown conclusively that it is not irrational to hold belief in God as basic. The wise critic will readily grant all this because criteria of basic beliefs are thoroughly contested; so long as we can entertain doubts about them, then Plantinga can always insist that no one has shown demonstrably that he cannot rationally believe in God without good reason.

We must also agree that Plantinga's proposals do not give us an immediate license to believe anything we like. It might appear, that is, that Plantinga must al-

---

[12] Plantinga, "Reformed Objection to Natural Theology," pp. 187-90.

[13] See pp. 76-77.

[14] I discussed Wittgensteinian fideism briefly on pp. 18-20. For extensive debate on this consult Kai Nielsen, *An Introduction to Philosophy of Religion* (London: Macmillan, 1982); W. D. Hudson, *A Philosophical Approach to Religion* (London: Macmillan, 1974); Paul L. Holmer, *The Grammar of Faith* (New York: Harper and Row, 1978).

[15] An excellent review of fideism can be found in J. L. Mackie, *The Miracle of Theism* (Oxford: Clarendon Press, 1982), chap. 11.

low any belief to be properly basic, so opening the floodgates to irrationalism on a grand scale. Why, for example, should we not believe that the Great Pumpkin returns every Halloween and defend this as basic in the same way as Plantinga has defended belief in God? This does not follow simply because we can often reject a particular claim even though we have no well-formed criteria of what is positively acceptable in the area concerned. Thus we would all reject the sentence, " 'Twas brillig; and the slithy toves did gyre and gymble in the wabe," as meaningless even though we do not possess any comprehensive theory of meaning which is satisfactory. Plantinga has not, therefore, given us a license to believe just anything. Moreover, he is committed enough to epistemology to attempt to work out why we deem some beliefs as properly basic. So some day he may provide a sound theory about basic beliefs which will more positively rule out obvious nonsense from the foundations of our beliefs.

Despite all these concessions, Plantinga's proposal remains unsatisfactory for several reasons. First, Plantinga's argument is of little value to anyone for whom belief in God is not basic. Generally, Plantinga accepts it as a fact of life that there will be many in this position and leaves it at that. At times, however, he gives the impression that for the Christian community belief in God will be basic, and all that needs to be done in this case is to work out a rigorous account of basicality which will accept this as a given fact. As Plantinga, however, notices elsewhere in his discussion, the claim that Christians generally construe belief in God as a basic belief is quite false, for many within and without the Reformed tradition have not construed belief in God as a basic belief. This being so, it is tempting to look upon Plantinga's proposals as thoroughly unhelpful. At present they represent an announcement about the content of his basic beliefs without any reason why we should positively treat them as basic for ourselves. Future prospects look bleak. We are given a promissory note of acceptable criteria of basicality which rests on invalid generalizations about the basic beliefs of the Christian community.

To take this a step further, Plantinga's strategy is relativistic in character. Our basic beliefs on his view are intimately related to the community to which we belong. Thus Christians will have the basic belief that God exists, secularists will have different basic beliefs, other groups will have other basic beliefs, and so on. All we can do is examine empirically what basic beliefs different groups have and then work out the criteria people rely on for judging whether a belief is basic or not. This leaves basic beliefs and their criteria a brute fact, relative to the various communities of the world. In the end all one can do is identify and accept the basic beliefs of the community to which one belongs. This surely leaves one's basic beliefs entirely relative.

Secondly, although Plantinga has wisely guarded against including nonsensical beliefs in the foundations, he has not at all ruled out less obviously silly but equally damaging beliefs from this coveted position. Suppose, for example, a sophisticated dualist who believes that there are two powerful opposing agents eternally at work in the universe, one good and one evil, turns up and masters Plantinga's technical skills. He can surely thank Plantinga for his new-found status as eminently rational so long as he holds his dualism to be basic. Even more relevantly, suppose a sophisticated atheist finds on waking one morning that the belief that God does not exist is basic for him or her. On reading Plantinga, can this atheist not also rejoice on having discovered a splendid new strategy to defend his or her atheism as rational? So long as this belief that God does not exist remains basic, he or she is entirely within his or her rights to claim to be rational. The objection I am urging here is that Plantinga has offered a fascinating defense of theism, but in the end its value is severely limited by its consequences. He has offered the theist the coveted prize of rationality; on closer inspection dualists and atheists can lay equal claim to it without so much as leaving their armchairs; surely one must wonder whether prizes like that are worth coveting.

Thirdly, although we may not be able to say what beliefs should positively be construed as basic, there may still be good reasons why belief in God should *not* be treated as basic. We can think of several reasons why belief in God cannot be a live option as a basic belief for many people. Most of these reasons focus on the clear disanalogies which exist between belief in God and other live candidates for basic beliefs. Let us accept belief in other minds, belief in the external world, and belief in the past as potential basic beliefs for the sake of argument. Belief in God differs significantly from these in the following ways. First, there are several plausible alternatives to theism which are not available in the case of other minds, the external world, and the past. In other words, we can make some sense of the world and its contents without recourse to theism as is witnessed by rival visions of what there is. In the other cases cited, there are very few, if any, compelling alternatives. Secondly, in the case of theism there is good prima facie evidence against it in the existence of widespread evil. Even if the theist succeeds in answering the critics, the very fact that a defense as sophisticated as that offered by Plantinga himself has to be mounted should make us hesitant to treat belief in God as basic. Finally, the fact that even half-plausible accounts of the natural history of religious belief are available should also make us cautious. There are several psychological and sociological accounts of the origins and persistence of religious belief written from a secular perspective which must be taken seriously as plausible objections to theistic belief. There are no such theories in the case of our belief in the existence of other minds, the external world, and the past. Hence it is difficult for the informed theist to look upon belief in God as on a par with such candidates for basic belief.

A further reason for not treating belief in God as basic stems from the complex nature of the Christian God. Philosophers generally have made life relatively easy for themselves at this point by construing belief in God in simple, monotheistic terms. Belief in God is belief in an omnipotent, omniscient, omnipresent, omnibenevolent agent. Christians believe this of course, but equally they hold tenaciously to a trinitarian conception of God. God is three persons in one substance. Once we even begin to think of putting this belief into the foundations, then it becomes a tall order indeed. Unitarians, Moslems, and Jews can ignore this aspect of belief in

God, but Plantinga and those who speak in the name of classical Christian orthodoxy cannot. Once we face up to what the classical tradition proposes, then to speak
of holding to belief in *this* God without evidence sounds thoroughly implausible.

To be sure, one can rebut this argument by suggesting that the Christian theist
proceed by arguing that belief in God be construed as basic but then agreeing that
supplementary argument must be given for belief in a trinitarian God. This might be
grounded, say, in a doctrine of revelation which in turn would be defended on
rational grounds. This way out is certainly open to Plantinga but he has not addressed the issue explicitly. At present this remains a piece of unfinished philosophical business.

AN INTERESTING QUALIFICATION

In conclusion, it is worth noting that Plantinga seems to have qualified his central
claim that belief in God does not require reasons to be rational. Quite generally he
suggests that basic beliefs are properly basic only in certain conditions. These conditions are "the ground of its justification and, by extension, the ground of the belief itself."[16] This applies to belief in God.

> When the Reformers claim that this belief is properly basic, they do not mean
> to say, of course, that there are no justifying circumstances for it, or that it is
> in that sense groundless or gratuitous. Quite the contrary. Calvin holds that
> God "reveals and daily discloses himself in the whole workmanship of the
> universe," and the divine art "reveals itself in the innumerable and yet distinct
> and well ordered variety of the heavenly host." God has so created us that we
> have a tendency or disposition to see his hand in the world about us. More
> precisely, there is in us a disposition to believe propositions of this sort, *this
> flower was created by God* or *this vast and intricate universe was created by
> God* when we contemplate the flower or behold the starry heavens or think
> about the vast reaches of the universe.
>   Calvin recognises, at least implicitly, that other sorts of conditions may
> trigger this disposition. Upon reading the Bible, one may be impressed with a
> deep sense that God is speaking to him. Upon having done what I know is
> cheap, or wrong, or wicked I may feel guilty in God's sight and form the belief
> *God disapproves of what I've done.* Upon confession and repentance, I may
> feel forgiven, forming the belief *God forgives me for what I've done.* A per-
> son in grave danger may turn to God, asking for his protection and help; and
> of course he or she then forms the belief that God is indeed able to hear and
> help if he sees fit. When life is sweet and satisfying, a spontaneous sense of
> gratitude may well up within the soul; someone in this condition may thank
> and praise the Lord for his goodness, and will of course form the accompany-
> ing belief that indeed the Lord is to be thanked and praised.[17]

[16] Plantinga, "Is Belief in God Properly Basic?" p. 46.
[17] Ibid.

This is a tantalizing suggestion. As it stands, it dwells in that twilight zone between the psychology of belief (what triggers our beliefs) and the epistemology of belief (the grounds for our beliefs). Until these are carefully separated out, it is difficult to know how to interpret this claim. Certainly Plantinga and Calvin are correct to point out that there are "many conditions and circumstances that call forth belief in God: guilt, gratitude, danger, a sense of God's presence, a sense that he speaks, perception of various parts of the universe."[18] If we construe these considerations as grounds for belief in God, then two comments impose themselves upon us. First, we are surely no longer treating belief in God as basic in the sense that we do not relate it to specific grounds for it. At the very least, there is an air of paradox in the claim that belief in God is held without evidence or reason, and yet it is not a groundless belief. Surely to speak of grounds or justifying circumstances is *ipso facto* to speak of reasons or evidence, is it not? Secondly, if we are to appeal to such items as guilt, a sense of God's presence, and so on, as grounds for belief in God, then this cries out for careful analysis. It is difficult to construe them as elements in a deductive proof for the existence of God. Perhaps Plantinga is offering us here a distinction between grounds and reasons for belief in God. A reason may be that from which we can logically infer the existence of God; a ground may be that which quite rightly rationally persuades us to believe in God without providing logical demonstration of his existence. Maybe in the neighborhood of this distinction there is hope of making fresh sense of the complex debate that goes on interminably both for and against religious belief.

[18] Ibid.

Chapter Nine
Soft Rationalism

In evaluating arguments for and against the existence of God, we quickly reach an impasse. Proofs in either direction fail. Evidence on one side seems canceled by equally good evidence on the other. We naturally feel attracted to fideism as a way out of this dilemma. In time, however, fideism too runs into difficulty.

DISSATISFACTION WITH FIDEISM

The fideists we have examined offer, in their own distinctive way, a defense of their position. Of course, they no longer offer arguments for the existence of God, although Plantinga clearly wants to keep that option an open one. Instead they offer arguments why arguments for the existence of God are either theologically erroneous or philosophically unnecessary. One lesson to be learnt from this is that those who retreat to fideism do not rely on faith rather than reason to support their fideism. On the contrary, at this level they are ardent rationalists, who quite rightly seek to convince us of the virtues of their position. In other words, fideists throw reason out the front door, but they then slip quietly down the stairs and let her return through a back door. She reigns supreme in the cellar of their faith below the surface.

What do we do if we find it impossible to live in such a construction? What if we find that we can no longer endure this ark of faith and reason? We were driven to it by the storms which assailed us in our tour of arguments for and against religious belief. Now that we have gone on board, we find that the smells coming up from the cellar below threaten to kill us every bit as effectively as those floods we so gladly left behind outside.

In other words, Noah's reassurances have become hollow. He tells us that God has spoken to him and that God stands above our questions. We agree that there is much truth in the view that divine revelation must stand in judgment over us. That is not what troubles us. What troubles us is that Noah was not the only one to build himself an ark in faith. Perhaps we have opted for the wrong ark in the first place. Alternatively Noah explains at great length and with considerable logical skill that we do not need any assurance. We should accept as basic what he tells us; there is no need to give a reason to underwrite what he says. This also fails. We agree that we have basic beliefs, but the belief that Noah possesses divine revelation is not one of these. Nor does he offer us any reason why it should be construed as a basic belief, for he readily acknowledges that there are no agreed criteria of basic beliefs. Fideism has taken us out of one impasse only to bring us to another.

By now we may be wondering if it really was wise to take up philosophy of religion. It promised much light, but we are in darkness still. This is a sad state to have reached. Before we entirely abandon ourselves to it, should we not retrace our steps and make sure we have not been misled somewhere on our journey? Maybe there was no need to go on board the fideist's ark at the outset. Perhaps it captures some insights about the nature of the Christian tradition which are worth preserving, but ultimately it rests on buried assumptions we should never have accepted. In this chapter I shall argue that this is precisely the case. In other words, I shall develop an account of the rationality of religious belief which can absorb much of the protest from the fideist tradition without sacrificing the quest for rational justification which is at the heart of classical natural theology.

THE ENDURING MERITS OF FIDEISM

The chief merit of the fideist tradition is that it seeks to guard both the internal content of the Christian faith and the passion it evokes in the believing heart. To be more specific, fideists like Tertullian and Kierkegaard render invaluable service to truth when they refuse to allow the philosopher to forget the scandal of the Christian Gospel. The Christian religion claims, for example, that God became incarnate in Jesus Christ, and it makes no bones about the foolishness of such a proposal to both the powerful and the intellectual.[1] By concentrating almost exclusively on belief in God, philosophers ignore this crucial element in the Christian heritage and invariably endorse and emphasize canons of rationality which do not face up to the stubborn reality of the faith. A cluster of related problems grow out of this change

[1] See, for example, 1 Cor. 1:18–25.

of focus. In other words, the reduction of the rich heritage of the great theistic traditions to a simple core has consequences which, from a religious point of view, are thoroughly subversive. This is what many fideists suspect, and we need to listen to this protest very sensitively. It is extremely difficult to describe these consequences accurately, but they look something like the following.

Consider what happens when we examine carefully the philosophical focus on theism. The notion of theism haunts classical discussions of the justification of religious belief, as we have already seen. Understandably, in order to justify religious belief we must have a clear and precise account of that which we want to justify. So we isolate what looks most important, namely, belief in God, and then set to work to define the concept of God as minutely as possible. The result is theism. We know already what that is. Let Swinburne remind us that theism affirms

> the existence of a being with one or more of the following properties: being a person without a body (i.e. a spirit), present everywhere, the creator and sustainer of the universe, or free agent, able to do everything (i.e. omnipotent), knowing all things, perfectly good, a source of moral obligation, immutable, eternal, a necessary being, holy, and worthy of worship.[2]

The task now begins in earnest as theist and atheist battle it out to defend or attack whether this is a meaningful belief and whether it is a justified belief. The exercise seems essential if there is to be serious and sustained debate. Be that as it may, the fideist senses that it is far from innocuous.[3]

Note immediately that it involves the invention of a highly formal conception of God, which requires considerable intellectual skill if it is to be understood. Moreover, the debate about God turns on mastery of this concept as the fundamental element in religion. The debate itself requires even more elaborate intellectual skill if it is to be followed. Ordinary believers sit on the sidelines and must await the result before filling in their religious coupons. Unfortunately there is no referee to declare who has scored the most goals, so nobody wins the coveted jackpot. This has far-reaching consequences.

The mystery and complexity of God are eliminated. Finite human beings confidently lay claim to understand his nature in great detail. God becomes the quintessence of simplicity. In the wake of this, talk of God as mysterious trinity must seem ridiculous in the extreme. In time, other philosophers and their theological admirers grow dissatisfied with this conceptual invention. Theism becomes a problem to them, so the hunt begins for better conceptions of God. The divine is now to be construed as the Absolute, or the Ground of Being, or Being Itself, or something even more difficult to fathom. Thus theism gives philosophers and theologians their cue to develop grandiose, metaphysical speculations, which quickly become the essence of the faith. Once again finite human beings confidently, if not proudly, claim to capture the inexhaustible mystery of God.

[2] Richard Swinburne, *The Coherence of Theism* (Oxford: Clarendon Press, 1977), p. 2.

[3] In what follows I am indebted to Paul Holmer, *The Grammar of Faith* (New York: Harper and Row, 1978), p. 162.

As a result, ordinary believers become second-class citizens in the kingdom of faith. They become dependent on philosophical theologians to explain to them the "true" meaning of religious concepts and doctrines. They feel they have to master some vast hermeneutical apparatus to make sense of the texts which first brought them to faith in God. Official teachers of the tradition consider it profoundly religious to come up with ingenious new conceptions of God and sense it their duty in the modern world to explain these to the faithful in order to initiate them properly into the tradition. The meaning of religion, therefore, becomes more and more remote from ordinary believers.

So too does the justification of their cherished convictions. Justification means mastering elaborate philosophical arguments developed by experts. Unfortunately the experts disagree. Even if the experts sound convincing, believers seem to be dependent on works of great genius before they have any right to believe. The ordinary believer seems thoroughly naive when compared with such brilliant defenders of the faith.

Worse still, it appears that true piety depends on the experts. After all, if religious action must spring from faith, and faith involves grasping the truth and being justified in so doing, the expert has to be on hand to make sure that all this is in order. Once again we have a deep cleavage between the ordinary believer who naively or partially participates in the faith and the sophisticated believer who really and fully participates in the faith. Such a division within the household of faith very naturally arouses concern; fideists have every right to protest that it is religiously unacceptable. Three further issues absorb their attention.

First, they protest against the gratuitous and ethereal nature of the divine being as developed within philosophical versions of the faith. There is a gap between those divinities cherished by the philosophically inclined and the God who is worshipped and adored. Somehow the concepts of the philosopher are far removed from the concept of God mediated by scripture, prayers, hymns, confessions, sacraments, and sermons. Moreover, the anecdotal, informal, occasional texts of transmission do a fine job as they stand in nurturing religious belief and practice. By contrast, the philosophical material seems rather bogus; it has life only in those restricted circles where it was first invented; it is artificial and unrelated to the real world the believer inhabits; and at the end of the day, no one really knows if it is true or not.

Secondly, fideists protest against the transformation of Christian values which so easily follows a lasting interest in theism and its defense. Paul Holmer expresses this protest forthrightly.

> Through the centuries, it has become a very complicated matter either to defend or to attack, for example, Christianity. For the theistic contention is that the concepts making up theism are the essence of Christianity. Until one isolates theism and positively countermands it, one cannot even be a respectable critic of the Christian religion. On both sides, the attack and the defense, the task becomes terribly abstract. There is something absurd about this. Crucifying Jesus, living faithlessly, and loving the world with all one's heart, soul, mind, and strength tend then to become trivialities compared to denying

theism. It is almost as if the academics have made crucial what was not so initially. Nonetheless, the theist will have us believe that to deny God's existence and the things said about him somehow are profoundly involved in doing all the above things, just as he will have us believe that in following Jesus, behaving faithfully, and obeying the first commandment are contained the theistic concepts.[4]

Thirdly, and most important, the whole drive to develop a formal justification of religious belief can act as a stimulus to unbelief. Given certain stubborn facts about the average spiritual pilgrimage, rationality becomes exceedingly difficult to attain. For a start, the believer's assurance does not rise and fall with the evidence. Objections may well be acknowledged, but they do not seem to make much difference because the believer holds tenaciously to his or her convictions. For example, Sarah may end up in the hospital and become rudely awakened to the dreadful suffering which is the lot of many. Yet she does not abandon her faith. On the contrary, she may now say that what she believes is absurd under such circumstances, but she nevertheless believes, prays, and goes on about her religious business unchanged. How can this be considered rational?

Moreover, the lives of the great saints and martyrs exhibit a heroic and profound sense of assurance about God. No matter how carefully the theologian develops a case for the justification of his or her position, somehow the deep commitment held by the heroes of the tradition involves a sense of certainty which goes far beyond that warranted by the evidence. How can this be defended by the normal canons of rationality?

Lastly, standard attempts to justify religious belief are deeply suspicious of those elements which often matter most in conversion. Thus people often become believers because of a profound sense of God speaking to them; or because of a sense that he loves them unconditionally; or because they know in their hearts they will only find rest when they follow his word. They find that the gospel story with all its loose ends rings true. They find their faith makes sense of their fragility and sin. Such factors are inward and subjective. How can they ever be captured in the rigorous, formal kind of deliberation which is the hallmark of standard philosophical discussion?

Is it not to be expected, then, that believers who go in search of justification will end up in disbelief? The gap between faith and reason is too wide to be bridged. When this is carefully weighed, it seems more honest to confess that faith really is irrational and live with the consequences.

THE ULTIMATE IMPLAUSIBILITY OF FIDEISM

I suggest, however, that there are several factors buried here which shake this conclusion in its foundations. As we explore them briefly, we shall soon discover that there is a much better option open to us.

[4]Ibid., p. 162.

First, fideists cannot eradicate the fact that there is a cognitive dimension to religion. There is an element of theory no matter how poorly it may have been captured by philosophers. Secondly, this element of theory is claimed to be true, and believers are deeply committed to its truth. It is central to their integrity; it underlies their commitment to mission, moral action, and theological reflection. Thirdly, as we have seen, fideists find it difficult to avoid all talk of justification or reasons for belief. Plantinga speaks of *justifying* circumstances.[5] Pascal speaks of *reasons* of the heart.[6] Kierkegaard even dares to speak of *proof.*

> There is only one proof of the birth of Christianity and that, quite rightly, is from the emotions, when the dread of sin and a heavy conscience torture a man into crossing the narrow line between despair bordering upon madness and Christianity.[7]

Fideists, therefore, are interested in reasons for religious belief despite polemic and protest to the contrary.

The problem is that they all too easily commit themselves to unfounded assumptions about the nature of arguments for and against religious belief. This hidden element invariably fuels their fideism. They protest vehemently that religious belief will not fit the standard canons of argument which we use to establish whether our beliefs are rational, but they rarely stop to ask whether those standards themselves exhaust the canons of rationality. Consider again what happens. Fideists note that religious belief cannot be demonstrably proved; they note that it is not decided by experiment, as scientific hypotheses were once thought to be decided; they note that it is not the result of a probability calculus; they note that it is not evident to the senses, as is belief in tables, chairs, and the like. Not satisfying any standard or formal procedure, they conclude that there can be no rational assessment of religious belief. One believes or disbelieves as a matter of faith; one treats belief in God as a basic belief, or one makes a stark existential choice for or against theism. But is this analysis of the options at all adequate?

Two points can be made immediately. First, it is far from obvious that one chooses neatly between, say, atheism and theism *tout court.* For instance suppose I choose atheism. At first glance it looks like a simple choice. I opt for the belief that God does not exist. What could be more simple? But is it so simple? Surely not, for in opting for atheism I still have to decide between a whole range of belief systems all of which can claim to be atheistic. My troubles have just begun, for now I have to choose among, say, humanism, Marxism, and Buddhism. Likewise, if I choose theism, I have to choose among say, Judaism, Christianity, and Islam. And even if I choose Christianity I still have to choose between many rival Christian schemes of belief, which are by no means compatible with one another. Once we grasp this, we are less sure that it can, as a matter of principle, be a question of blind existential

---

[5] See p. 96.

[6] Blaise Pascal, *Pensées,* trans. A. J. Krailsheimer (London: Penguin, 1966), sec. 110.

[7] Quoted in J. Heywood Thomas, *Subjectivity and Paradox* (Oxford: Basil Blackwell, 1957), p. 166.

choice. It turns out that we are forever making existential leaps of faith or treating complex beliefs as basic beliefs, and this just does not ring true to our experience. If as atheists we choose liberal humanism, we somehow want to claim that there is good sense in doing so. It is likewise if as theists we choose to become classical pietists, Roman Catholics or old-fashioned modernists like H. E. Fosdick. To talk of momentous existential choices or basic beliefs at this level sounds portentous, inflated, and inaccurate.

Secondly, it is equally obvious that the general principle about arguments which underpins so much fideism is questionable. Why should arguments for and against religious belief take the form either of a demonstration or of strict probability or any other such formal procedure? How do we know that there is not another possibility that should be explored before we flee in eagerness to the ghettos of faith and revelation?

THE SOFT-RATIONALIST ALTERNATIVE

That there is an alternative is the view of those who embrace *soft rationalism*. This term is a new one, which is now beginning to find its way into the literature. It is used to describe a middle way between classical natural theology and fideism. The word *soft* in the name does not suggest woolly-mindedness or shallow thinking on the part of its proponents; it simply denotes that the position is a middle option between certain extremes: it softens the extreme positions to find a third alternative.

Soft rationalism is essentially a claim about the kind of argument that should take place in debates about significant religious beliefs. It attempts to lay bare the general character of the arguments which really make sense of the kind of disputes which take place between believers and unbelievers. The central tenets of soft rationalism can be laid out as follows.

There are three main points. First, religious belief should be assessed as a rounded whole rather than taken in stark isolation. Christianity, for example, like other world faiths, is a complex, large-scale system of belief which must be seen as a whole before it is assessed. To break it up into disconnected parts is to mutilate and distort its true character. We can, of course, distinguish certain elements in the Christian faith, but we must still stand back and see it as a complex interaction of these elements. We need to see it as a metaphysical system, as a world view, that is total in its scope and range. We can develop this viewpoint by briefly schematizing the content of the Christian religion. Consider the following minimal outline of the Christian faith.

Christians believe that the whole universe is created and sustained by God, a transcendent, invisible, personal agent who is omnipotent, omniscient, and all good. Thus it attempts to say why the world exists and why it is partly as it is by saying that it is the effect of the action of God. Along with these beliefs about the natural world, Christians hold certain beliefs about human beings. Human beings are made in the image of God, and their fate depends on their relationship with God. They are free to respond to or reject God and they will be judged in accordance with how they respond to him. This judgment begins now but finally takes place beyond death in a life to come. Christians furthermore offer a diagnosis of what is wrong with the world. Fundamentally, they say, our problems are spiritual: we need to be made anew by God. Human beings have misused their freedom; they are in a state of rebellion against God; they are sinners. These conclusions lead to a set of solutions to this ill. As one might expect, the fundamental solution is again spiritual: in Israel and in Jesus of Nazareth God has intervened to save and remake mankind. Each individual needs to respond to this and become part of Christ's body, the church, where they are to grow in grace and become more like Christ. This in turn generates a certain vision of the future. In the coming of Jesus, God has inaugurated his kingdom, but it will be consummated at some unspecified time in the future when Christ returns and becomes all in all. All of these elements taken together generate a characteristically Christian ethic, which differs in key respects from other rival systems of morality.

We see here an overall theory about life with several dimensions which can be isolated but need to be seen as a whole. Christianity is one such theory. It offers an account of the world as a whole; a theory of human nature; a diagnosis of the world's ills; a prescription for those ills; a vision of the future; and a vision of morality which is intimately connected with these elements taken as a whole.[8]

It might, of course, be questioned whether this is a fair account of the Christian faith. Clearly it is ridiculously brief, and it is much tidier than the rich vision which is passed on in the media of transmission within Christianity. However, if this account is rejected, some other account will have to be substituted. Otherwise we invite the charge of being obscurantist. Religion is inescapably a creedal affair, and fideists exaggerate if they insist it is impossible to summarize the faith. After all, that is what a creed is: it is a summary of the faith intended to fix its central reference points so that believers know what they believe. Fideists also exaggerate if they insist that such summaries become remote and lifeless. That can happen but it need not. Moreover, there is no objection in principle to articulating as clearly as possible the central concepts of religion. Clarity is not enough, nor is it essential to holiness of life; but neither are the pure in heart given special grace to become muddle-headed. Therefore soft rationalists are right to insist that the Christian tradition does offer an overall theory about life as a whole.

Much could be said about such overall theories. To begin with, there are many on the market. Marxism, humanism, existentialism are but three examples. Moreover, no one can avoid having some such theory. Here we vote with our feet; we may move from one to another, or live in accordance with elements of one one day and elements of another the next, but choice is inescapable. Therefore the only issue facing us is not, Shall we choose a theory of life as a whole?, but, Shall we choose as wisely as possible between the various options? With this we arrive at the second tenet of soft rationalism.

[8]This analysis of different theories has been evoked by Leslie Stephenson, *Seven Theories of Human Nature* (Oxford: Oxford University Press, 1974), chap. 1.

Assessment of such global theories is never a matter of simple demonstration or strict probabilistic reasoning. On the contrary, one appeals to various considerations which taken together lead one to say that one is true and another false. One develops what Basil Mitchell calls a cumulative case.[9] The different pieces of evidence taken in isolation are defective, but taken together they reinforce one another and add up to a substantial case. What is vital to realize is that there is no formal calculus into which all the evidence can be fitted and assessed. There is an irreducible element of personal judgment, which weighs up the evidence taken as a whole. Moreover, there is no agreed starting point, and there may well be dispute about what is to count as evidence, but this does not vitiate the process. What matters is not where you start but the total case you make out. Dispute about what is to count as evidence is to be weighed by sensitive personal judgment.

Philosophers and some theologians tend to become uneasy at this point. They fear a lurking subjectivism behind this appeal to personal judgment. They want hard evidence that is beyond doubt and dispute. It is precisely this that the soft rationalist rejects as irrational. Hard rationalists set the standards for rationality far too high for the subject matter. By so doing they pave the way for fideistic brands of theists and atheists. Fideistic theists are just hard rationalists who opt for theism. Hard rationalists appear the more rational because they seem tough-minded and are always insisting on clear, precise evidence which will fit into some sort of formal calculus. But this appearance of being more rational is an illusion, for hard rationalism is open to the following objection: hard rationalism cannot make sense of a whole range of debates which depend for their existence on cumulative case arguments. This objection constitutes a *reductio ad absurdum* of the position of hard rationalism. We can develop this objection into a third positive thesis of soft rationalism.

The kind of assessment proposed by soft rationalism is a genuine rational assessment because cumulative-case arguments are generally accepted as reliable. Without such arguments we could make no sense of the disputes that go on in fields as diverse as jurisprudence, literary exegesis, history, philosophy, and science. Some of these may involve strict demonstration and strict probability arguments, but that is not the whole story. All of these arguments often involve what we might call informal reasoning. They require judgments of plausibility. They involve an irreducible element of personal judgment, which cannot be measured by a formal calculus but which can be trained and rendered more sensitive. Hard rationalism would eliminate this, which is one reason why it needs to be attacked with a fair degree of vigor. It destroys the sensitivity for dialectic and dialogue; it inhibits the commitment to fair and sympathetic understanding to both sides in the argument.

That such arguments as soft rationalists appeal to exist is surely obvious. Theologians should be the first to recognize them, for work in exegesis, in the history of Israel, and in the history of the church depends crucially on such arguments. Consider, for example, the question of the priority of Mark. Was Mark the

[9] Basil Mitchell, *The Justification of Religious Belief* (London: Macmillan, 1973), pp. 39–57. By permission of Macmillan, London and Basingstoke.

first gospel to be written? On this issue there is no demonstration and there is no strict probability argument. Yet there is surely a rational discussion; it is not a matter of blind opting; and the arguments are typically cumulative case arguments. So there can be no denying that they do exist and that they are a genuine expression of rationality.

What might be denied is that this type of reasoning can apply to global metaphysical systems. Thus it might be thought that cumulative-case arguments have a restricted role and only work in the field, say, of history or literary criticism but do not apply outside such areas. This, however, cannot be assumed in advance. We have to look and see if this type of reasoning does apply to disputes about metaphysical or religious systems. Let us explore this further and see if it is a fruitful way to consider the rationality of the Christian faith. We can helpfully approach this by sketching an imaginary intellectual pilgrimage from unbelief to belief.

SOFT RATIONALISM ILLUSTRATED

Rachel has been brought up on the edge of the Christian tradition. She knows enough about it to reject it as lacking credibility. Then one day a close friend is converted and begins taking the Christian faith in earnest. Initially Rachel accepts this as entirely normal; through time, however, she notices a profound change in her friend's life. What especially impresses her is the love which has come to characterize her friend. Casting around for an explanation of this change, she asks her friend what has happened. Her friend's reply is that any change for the better is due entirely to the grace of God in her life. When she explores this further, she understands it to mean that God has acted in her friend's life, giving her a deep sense of forgiveness and self-acceptance and filling her with love. In other words the change is due to the activity of God in her life. At first, Rachel was tempted to dismiss this as pious rambling, but somehow the explanation had a faint ring of truth about it. For a while she thought that the change could best be explained psychologically. However, these alternative explanations tended to be as debatable as the theistic alternative or were more on the level of hypothetical possibilities lacking specific backing for the case in hand. Thus the faint ring of truth in her friend's initial explanation remained, and she decided to explore the matter further.

She went to the library and began delving into the lives of such figures as Augustine, Luther, and Mother Teresa. Here she found her friend's experience vividly confirmed to a degree that amazed her. Those whose lives exhibited conspicuous sanctity invariably insisted that this was entirely due to the grace of God. In addition, she found that Augustine, for example, laid bare, in his *Confessions,* an incisive and penetrating analysis of evil and temptation which spoke very powerfully to her own condition, illuminating and exposing concealed corridors which she would have preferred remain closed. In other words, he presented an account of human nature and a diagnosis of its fragile and broken condition which found a very clear echo in her own experience.

That diagnosis was matched by a proposed solution which involved two distinct dimensions. On the one side, it involved a complex story of what God had done in Israel, in Jesus Christ, and in the church to bring liberation and new life to those caught in a web of self-service and spiritual indifference. In other words, Rachel found substantial claims about special revelation which fitted and illuminated her reading of the Christian scriptures and the historical events which lay behind them. The Christian creed, that is, made intelligible events and experiences which otherwise were puzzling and inexplicable. The other dimension to the solution was human. It called for a change of heart, a radical openness to God's Spirit, and a total trust in God for one's life and future. Rachel found this disturbing and shattering, yet attractive and adventurous. She found, for example, that the gospel story of God's sacrificial love deeply enriched her natural moral sense and inspired a measure of concern for others in herself which surprised and delighted her.

These experiences, in turn, led her to raise some old cosmic questions which had been hibernating since adolescence. She found herself at times overwhelmed by a sense of finitude and contingency. It puzzled her why there should be a world at all. Moreover, she found herself in pursuit of an explanation which would render intelligible the existence of order, beauty, and seeming design in nature. As she pondered these questions, in some detail, she sensed a fresh ring of truth in the overall vision proposed by the Christian tradition. That vision had immense explanatory power, as it made intelligible the fact and nature of the world by viewing these as effects of the activity of God.

All this led Rachel to embark on her own personal search for God. She continued reading in the Christian scriptures and attendant literature. She began participating in a local Christian community. She haltingly began to pray and make use of other means of grace. She found herself vividly aware of God in nature and at worship. She sensed God speaking intimately to her as she listened to the Gospel story and the call to commitment. She eventually gave herself over to God in faith and found a peace of soul which was profoundly authentic and long lasting.

At no point in this process is there any deductive proof nor is there any argument which could be formally set in a probability calculus. Rather a whole series of considerations come together over time to provide a cumulative case for the Christian creed. At every step objections of a rational character can arise. However, when examined they do not prove to be decisive, and the various elements provide mutual support and give credibility to commitment and faith.

This point has been succinctly made in a parable by Basil Mitchell.

Two explorers find a hole in the ground, little more, perhaps than a slight depression. One of them says, "There is something funny about that hole; it doesn't look natural to me." The other says, "It's just an ordinary hole, and can be explained in a hundred and one different ways." Shortly afterwards they come upon a number of smaller holes in the same area as the first. The first explorer thinks they must be related to it: indeed he fancies that they have the same *sort* of oddness about them. The other pooh-poohs the idea. He sees nothing in any way remarkable about the holes—anything could have caused them, they are probably just natural depressions. Later, to their surprise, they find in a neighbouring cave a papyrus containing fragments of the plan of a building. "Ah," says the first explorer, "now I see what was odd about those holes; the big one was made to take the centre post of a wooden building, the smaller ones took the other posts."

"All right," says the other, "we can soon test your theory. Let us take the fragments of your plan and piece them together on the site. If they fit, well and good, but they probably won't." So they take them to the site. The first explorer says he can see how the plan fits the site, and arranges the fragments accordingly, with what might be the centre of the roof over the largest hole. Then he sketches his reconstruction out on paper and shows it to his companion. "This is all very well," says the latter, "but you haven't accounted for all the holes or all the features shown in the fragments. The way the remainder fit is purely coincidental." The first explorer replies that he doesn't claim to know precisely what the original building was like, or how all the details fitted in. Moreover he thinks he can explain why some of the features mentioned in the plan should be missing in what remains on the site. If his impression of the character of the complete building is right, then these would be the first to be stolen or to disintegrate. "But," says the other, "the facts as we have them are compatible with a number of quite different interpretations. Each of them taken by itself can be explained away without much difficulty. And as for the fragmentary plan in the papyrus, of which you make such extensive use, it could well be an imaginative construction with no reference to the real world at all."

In the parable the original large hole represents the intellectual demand for ultimate explanation to which natural theology appeals. The smaller holes represent private religious experiences of sin, grace, etc. The fragmentary plan represents the concepts of the Christian revelation.[10]

THE VIRTUES OF SOFT RATIONALISM

This approach to the rationality of religious belief shows considerable promise. To begin, it would seem to capture and articulate the kind of reasoning which has a clear place in disputes between different belief systems. Thus it shows how interminable religious disputes can be, for they range over a whole network of phenomena and thus require great patience if they are to be understood and resolved. Moreover, it brings out the self-involving nature of religious belief by highlighting the crucial place of a person's religious experience in the total set of considerations which convince the believer. It also explains why becoming a believer is often a matter of conversion. Radical changes in one's metaphysical and religious commitments may have been brewing for a long time, but the actual change may take place quite quickly and dramatically. Exposure to revelation or a vivid awareness of the presence of God may be enough to lead one to reassess all the other strands in the case. One comes to organize one's world in a wholly new way and to develop a completely different perspective on life.

Furthermore, it does justice to the internal content of the Christian faith. The God in whom one comes to trust is not some idol invented by a philosopher; he is

[10] Ibid., pp. 43–44.

the God and father of Jesus Christ. The evidence which has been accumulating undergirds the total theistic vision rather than some isolated element within it. To be sure, that comprehensive vision is never static, for there are rival accounts of what the Christian faith is. But the tradition in its classical form, at least, has sufficient stability to bear adequate scrutiny. Also this account of the rationality of faith is entirely compatible with the emphasis on proclamation and call to repentance which is such a central feature of the Christian Gospel. Indeed these are elements which have to be weighed and taken into account in the deeply personal judgment which must ultimately be made.

This approach also attempts to do justice to those subjective elements which matter so much to religious believers. Clearly not just any experience leads to Christian commitment, but some characteristically do, and I have sought to acknowledge their proper epistemic significance. Note that this means that there is no question of the believer's relying on abstract philosophical evidence. The philosopher's task is more modest. He or she seeks to clarify the informal logic which operates in the life of faith. Some philosophers may well want to attempt to quantify the whole process and thus bring the matter within the domain of inductive logic. This is entirely laudatory so long as it is recognized that it is not essential to the rationality of informal reasoning. In recent years Richard Swinburne has attempted to a limited degree to achieve this end.[11]

Another feature of soft rationalism which commends it is its ability to make sense both of tenacity in believing and the certainty which often accompanies it. The latter stems from the believer's vivid sense of divine love commonly described as the witness of the Spirit. The former derives from the need to exercise patience in order to allow all the evidence to play its part. Equally it derives from the fact that, once believers commit themselves, they need to examine any counterevidence very carefully before concluding that it requires modification of their beliefs. Well-established convictions about matters of religious significance should not be abandoned at the first sign of trouble but should be weighed sensitively over time.

RESOLVING PROBLEMS IN SOFT RATIONALISM

Whatever the virtues in soft rationalism there are several problems within it that have to be faced.

First, when the soft rationalist speaks of, say, Marxism or traditional Christian theism as a metaphysical system or world view, it is clear that these terms are not simply descriptive in character. In fact it is very difficult to specify what they mean. World views are complex, dynamic traditions which interact with their intellectual environments, hence even to specify their content is to enter into a heated debate about what they actually embody. They tend to be elusive and subject to interpretation and reinterpretation in the light of new knowledge. This means that it is

---

[11] Richard Swinburne, *The Existence of God* (Oxford: Clarendon Press, 1979).

extremely difficult to pin them down and then proceed to determine whether they are rationally acceptable or not by appeal to a cumulative case argument. If this is so it becomes difficult to judge on the merits of a particular world view. For if understanding their claims is elusive and difficult, so too must their rationality, for until they are properly understood, they cannot be properly judged to be rational or irrational.

Secondly, there are several problems related to the crucial notion of personal judgment which need to be resolved. We can agree that the soft rationalist has drawn attention to something very important. In everyday disputes and scholarly debate, we do speak of a piece of evidence or a body of accumulated evidence as being beyond reasonable doubt, reasonable, persuasive, plausible, convincing, possessing rational force, intuitively compelling, and the like. However it is worth asking what kind of necessity such informal judgment has in rational evaluation. Is it logical or psychological necessity? Rod Sykes has raised the issue pointedly in this way.

> The epistemic Scrooge can admit that informal judgement is a psychological reality, that as a matter of fact we do usually depend on intuition and rarely consciously apply rules of thought. It is heuristically necessary, since adequate rules of good reasoning would be tediously complex to use: efficiency favours the use of intuition. Flying by feel is usually preferable to flying by the book, and the reason for this is that the former is more flexible and thus better able to meet sudden changes in conditions. But it must also be noted that flying by feel can quickly degenerate into flying by the seat of our pants, and that is where the book is the only thing that saves us. Similarly, intuition is useful in matters of rationality, even suggestive perhaps, but theoretically—and when things go wrong, pragmatically—dispensable. The difference must be noticed between a description of the psychology of an evaluative judgement (or its phenomenology—what it feels like to make such a judgement) and a description of its logical structure, which is to say of the justificational relations among propositions that underpin it. Soft Rationalism must argue that intuitive judgement is adequate as such a *logical* description.[12]

A legitimate worry behind Sykes's challenge is the fear that a person's judgment is liable to serious error. There is the danger of personal whim, bias, emotional involvement, and other non-rational factors adversely influencing the weighing of evidence. This is less likely where the canons or rules of critical thinking are objectively specified and deliberately followed. To rebut this the soft rationalist can reply that there is such a danger but it can be offset by an appeal not just to personal judgment but to *trained* personal judgment. Thus, as Mitchell points out, the ability to exercise rationality depends on having "appropriate intellectual, moral, and spiritual values."[13] One must be well educated in the relevant fields, be committed to the search for truth, be sensitive to any relevant moral, aesthetic, or spiritual possibilities, and the like. This is surely correct but it generates its own problems.

[12] Rod Sykes, "Soft Rationalism," *International Journal for Philosophy of Religion* XI (1980), pp. 60–1.
[13] Mitchell, *The Justification of Religious Belief*, p. 126.

To begin it is not clear where or how one can receive such training to develop the appropriate skill to judge between world views. Such training is available, say, for debates about the meaning of disputed texts, the strength of a particular case presented in a court of law, the elegance of a particular scientific theory, and so on. However such training is not available for deciding between competing metaphysical interpretations of the universe.

Moreover, mastering all the relevant data and warrants needed to exercise the required personal judgment seems remote and impractical. For example, to arrive at a proper historical estimate of the scriptures of the world religions is a matter of heated debate between rival schools of experts. Yet this cannot be ignored if considerations from putative revelation are to be weighed as part of a cumulative case. Matters only become more elusive when one is invited to add up considerations derived from religious experience, classical natural theology, the existence of moral and natural evil, the existence of conspicuous sanctity, and so on. This is surely beyond the capabilities of most ordinary mortals.

Lastly, there is the danger that the process of weighing the rationality of world views is thoroughly circular. Training in personal judgment would seem to involve training in a tradition. One is initiated into a way of life where skills, virtues, and dispositions which enable one to judge correctly are inculcated. But a way of life, in the soft rationalist's view, is itself intimately related to a world or metaphysical system. Hence the appeal to personal judgment presupposes commitment to a deeper vision of things and cannot be used to test the rationality of that deeper vision. If one does appeal to personal judgment to support the metaphysical system that helped to create it then that appeal is patently circular.

It is open to the soft rationalist to attempt to rebut these objections, if necessary modifying the details of his or her position yet without abandoning its essential elements. Thus one could fully accept that the articulating of a world view and the weighing of all the revelant data and warrants is an elusive affair. From a practical standpoint one will have to rely to some extent on the intellectual labors of others both in the interpretation of the pertinent metaphysical system and its justification by appeal to a cumulative case. But this is not something that the soft rationalist has ever denied. It is admitted that the process of justification is difficult and must be done over time. For a time much may have to be taken on faith. Moreover, the appeal to personal judgment is not necessarily circular. All the soft rationalist requests is that all sides be open to their opponents, competing ontological claims and explanations. Thus religious believers, for example, must seriously consider the possibility that alternative, secular explanations can be given of what they take to be the experiences of the divine. Equally non-believers must explore sensitively the possibility of genuine experience of the divine. Such openness, although it is clearly intellectually demanding, does not necessarily depend on initiation into a particular metaphysical tradition. Therefore the appeal to personal judgment is not circular.

Furthermore, even though there is no simple way to acquire training in the exercise of personal judgment in metaphysical disputes, this is not a decisive consideration. Learning to judge and weigh evidence is a general skill which can be informally developed. For example, in voting in an election one has to exercise personal judgment in weighing up the merits of competing candidates even though it is difficult to receive formal training in this area. One simply has to proceed, often in an ad hoc fashion, and work through the issues as honestly and rigorously as possible. Finally, it seems difficult to eliminate an element of personal judgment or intuition from many rational procedures. For example, even the foundations of logic depend upon an intuitive grasp of the truth of certain basic premises. Codifying such intuitions does not establish the rationality of such judgments; it simply describes them more clearly and conveniently. If this is the case then the appeal to personal judgment is not in itself epistemically reprehensible.

It is clear by now that the soft rationalist must admit that the actual justification of religious and metaphysical beliefs is in practice a very elusive affair. Much is taken on faith in the articulation of the metaphysical position under review, in the gathering and weighing of the relevant evidence, and in the use of personal judgment. So soft rationalism could perhaps be equally well described as soft fideism. What label we use at this point is a matter of verbal convenience. What really matters is to emphasize the relevance of various considerations in the debate about the merits of rival interpretive systems. The soft rationalist wants to insist that, *logically* speaking, there are relevant data and warrants. That data and warrants may be contested and elusive does not destroy this fact. Equally the soft rationalist wants to insist that there is little point in craving more rigorous standards of rationality in this domain. Arguments may at times appear elusive when compared to what is available in science, mathematics, or some other favored paradigm. But if such standards are not available, the best course is to examine the relevant evidence as best one can, learning in the process to cultivate as much wisdom as one can muster.

Nonetheless many will still remain unhappy. They might suggest an alternative way to respond to the objections against soft rationalism. Rather than move further towards fideism, why not move in the other direction towards hard rationalism? Why not avoid all reference to world views and return to assessing the truth or falsehood of simple theism? And why not eradicate reliance on personal judgment by quantifying formally a cumulative case argument for such theism? To that we now turn.

Chapter Ten
Hard Rationalism

Every serious student of philosophy of religion must offer some account of the truth or falsehood of religious belief. That account must be clear about two issues. First, it must declare what the status of religious belief is. That is, it must ultimately come clean on whether religious belief is true or false or not known to be true or false. Secondly, it must make clear how the proposed conclusion has been reached. That is, it must show what kind of epistemology is to be applied to sensitive and appropriate debate about the status of religious belief. Clearly for the philosopher it is this latter issue which is of greater importance, for philosophers typically are preoccupied with questions about the pattern and standards of appropriate argument. In fact, it is widespread disagreement about the status of significant beliefs which fuels this abiding concern. The hope is that by going beneath the surface of the actual issue to the kind of arguments deployed we may be able to arrive at more warranted conclusions. So it is that first-order disputes about, say, belief in God, generates second-order disputes about canons of argument and good judgment.

REVIEWING THE OPTIONS

The debate has been with us for centuries. For most of the twentieth century, philosophers have been so preoccupied with the cognitive status of religious language that little attention has been given to the rationality of religious belief. Even yet, introductory textbooks in philosophy of religion can be written which take the issue of religious language as the exclusive topic for consideration.[1] In the last ten years this situation has changed dramatically. On the one hand, the debate about language has become somewhat sterile. Thus J. L. Mackie, one of the leading philosophers of the last generation, treats the issue as more or less settled. For him the central assertions of theism are literally meaningful.[2] I have argued for the same conclusion in an earlier part of our discussion. On the other hand, it is strikingly obvious that the debate about the rationality of theism is currently one of the more important questions in philosophy.

Certainly in philosophy of religion there has been a dramatic revival of interest in the topic. I have no doubt but that this is the crucial question which confronts the discipline in the immediate future. Many others await attention, as we shall see, but the weight of past tradition and the vitality of recent writings combine to make the issue of rationality of religious belief inescapable.

One powerful alternative is philosophical fideism. In this tradition belief in God is to be construed as a basic belief requiring no argument in its favor for it to be considered rational. A second alternative is soft rationalism. In this tradition religious belief is to be construed as one among many competing, complex metaphysical visions, which are to be defended or attacked by a cumulative case argument that makes an irreducible appeal to intuitive, personal judgment. The third alternative is hard rationalism. In this tradition belief in God is to be defended by a rigorous appeal to the canons of normal logic. This latter position has been developed of late by Richard Swinburne.[3] To some extent these divisions are artificial, for there can be much overlapping in what they maintain. However, there are distinctive trends of thought on the rationality of religious belief, and it is useful to chart what they are. I want now to outline and examine the third option.

SWINBURNE'S GENERAL PROPOSALS

Swinburne's writings in the philosophy of religion constitute an exceedingly significant option in modern philosophy of religion. No one can ignore them. For one thing, Swinburne has worked out a position which seeks to deal comprehensively with all the key issues related to the rationality of belief in God. Thus he has left few, if any, philosophical stones uncovered in his quest to settle this issue. Secondly, he develops his position with a clarity and vigor which is rare. In fact, Swinburne examines belief in God in a thoroughly cool and calculating manner. His whole style expresses a cold-blooded rationalism. One is tempted to protest that this approach

[1] Kai Nielsen, *An Introduction to the Philosophy of Religion* (London: Macmillan, 1982).

[2] J. L. Mackie, *The Miracle of Theism* (Oxford: Clarendon Press, 1982), pp. 1–4.

[3] Swinburne has laid out his position in a trilogy: *The Coherence of Theism* (Oxford: Clarendon Press, 1977); *The Existence of God* (Oxford: Clarendon Press, 1979); *Faith and Reason* (Oxford: Clarendon Press, 1981).

is theologically insensitive. However, even if it is, we should not make too much of it, for Swinburne is writing as a philosopher discussing the issue vigorously and dispassionately. Certainly no one can complain that his method formally lacks standard philosophical acumen and expertise.

Placing it in historical context, Swinburne, without saying so explicitly, seems to offer a formidable project indeed. On the philosophical side, he intends to undermine the consensus which has been with us for well over a century. That consensus states that Hume and Kant have basically demolished any rigorous argument for belief in God. Swinburne plans to show that this is not so. On the theological side, he aims to challenge the influence of Barth. Although Swinburne does not discuss Barth in any detail, I think it accurate to report that he finds the Barthian approach to religious belief thoroughly unsatisfactory. Against Barth, Swinburne therefore intends to show that theology can be built on solidly rational foundations. A project with such intentions cannot but be of significance.

What are the essential elements in Swinburne's project? One way to understand it is to read it as a massive restatement of classical natural theology. Its focus is theism, or belief in God. Thus at the outset Swinburne isolates this as the fundamental proposition under consideration. All else seems to be formally set aside until the truth or falsity of this claim is established. Only then can other issues, such as belief in divine revelation, be taken up and assessed.

Furthermore, this issue is to be formally decided by the canons of logic. If it is to be shown to be true, that must be done by appeal to evidence and logic. Thus the proposition to be considered, that is, belief in God, must be set out clearly and definitively so that there is no ambiguity or vagueness. Moreover, it must be defended as a coherent proposition.[4] Secondly, the evidence must be laid out systematically and rigorously. Thirdly, the conclusion must be shown to follow by normal canons of logic. Clearly this represents substantial continuity with the tradition of classical natural theology. It is because of this that I have chosen to classify Swinburne's position as that of a hard rationalist.

The crucial discontinuity with natural theology lies in the kind of logic Swinburne utilizes. Swinburne rejects the classical attempt to prove the existence of God. He does not believe that one can deductively prove that God exists. His claim is that one can establish that the existence of God is more probable than not. He appeals therefore not to deductive but to inductive logic, and his argument is that, given the total evidence available, the canons of inductive logic make belief in God rational.

Another way to see what Swinburne is arguing is to compare and contrast it with soft rationalism as I expounded it in the previous chapter. Both agree that there is no proof for the existence of God. Both agree that the evidence for religious belief is to be taken as a complex cumulative case. Moreover, both agree that the task of the philosopher is to articulate an account of the reasons for religious belief which captures what some believers at least want to say. Thus the philosopher seeks

[4] This is set out in *The Coherence of Theism.*

to knock into shape arguments which believers themselves can identify as relevant to the genesis of belief. In other words, both Swinburne and the soft rationalist hope to offer an account of rationality which not only is compatible with faith but actually illuminates the life of faith. They hope to lay out in a disciplined, philosophical manner the loose and often disorganized insights which believers in their more rational moments seek to express. This means that although the ordinary believer may find it difficult to follow the detailed outline of the argument of the philosopher, the difference between the two is one of degree and not of kind.

There are, however, significant areas of disagreement between Swinburne and the soft rationalist. To begin, the soft rationalist is more sympathetic to fideism than is Swinburne. Swinburne concedes that fideists like Tertullian may be on to something important. Thus they may be saying that claims of deep significance may seem absurd at first glance.[5] But generally he does not linger with other concerns of the fideist. The soft rationalist, in contrast, will be more patient, seeking to understand and accommodate more of the fideistic protest.[6] Furthermore, Swinburne and the soft rationalist disagree on whether the cumulative case for religious belief can be quantified or codified. Swinburne argues that it can be laid out according to the formal calculus of confirmation theory. The soft rationalist rejects this, holding that the evidence has to be weighed in the scales of informal, personal judgment. They also disagree on the locus of the debate. Extending the forensic metaphor, we might say that they disagree on the motion before the house. Swinburne insists it should be whether or not God exists; the soft rationalist holds that it should be the truth or falsehood of a summary account of the Christian vision taken as a whole. This means, in turn, that for the soft rationalist the nature and role of revelation plays a much earlier and much more decisive role than Swinburne seems to allow.

THEISM AND PROBABILITY

Let us explore now in greater detail what Swinburne is claiming. His central claims are laid out very cogently in *The Existence of God.* His conclusion is quite simple. When all the relevant evidence is considered, belief in God is an explanatory hypothesis which is more probable than not. How does he reach this goal? It is quite impossible in a brief summary to do justice to the details of his argument, but the general strategy adopted is very clear. It is helpful to identify four essential steps in the development of his case.

The first phase is a ground-clearing exercise. In it Swinburne argues that there are ultimately two ways of explaining any phenomenon which puzzles us. If we do not leave the phenomenon (P) as a sheer brute fact without explanation, we can explain it either by means of a scientific explanation or by means of a personal explanation. Speaking very loosely, a scientific explanation is one where we explain P by

[5] Swinburne, *Faith and Reason,* p. 24.
[6] I have consciously sought to do this in chap. 9.

showing that P will take place given certain initial conditions and general laws related to those initial conditions. To take an example, "We explain a particular explosion by the ignition of a particular volume of gunpowder in certain conditions of temperature, pressure, and humidity, and the generalisation that under such circumstances ignited gunpowder explodes."[7] By contrast, a personal explanation is one where we explain P by showing that P was brought about by some rational agent doing some action intentionally. To take an example, we explain the movement of Smith's feet by showing that Smith himself intentionally moved his feet.

In the course of our relations with the world we again and again offer explanations for events. We propose hypotheses as to why certain events occur. Moreover, we judge some hypotheses to be true explanations or to be more probable than other explanations. How do we make such judgments? According to Swinburne, we rely on the criteria of prior probability and explanatory power. Prior probability is the probability of the hypothesis independent of the observations or evidence cited in its favor. This in turn breaks down into its simplicity, fit with background knowledge, and scope. The explanatory power of a theory or hypothesis is basically its ability to predict the phenomena which we observe. Both of these criteria can, says Swinburne, be codified by means of a theorem of confirmation theory known as Bayes's theorem.[8] This theorem represents the element of hard rationalism in Swinburne's position.

The second phase in Swinburne's analysis is the application of this theorem to the hypothesis that God exists. It should be noted that Swinburne is quite serious when he treats the assertion that God exists as a hypothesis. For obvious reasons religious believers and theologians do not find this a natural way to construe belief in God in modern times. Swinburne at this point overturns the conventional way of thinking about religion. Theism for him is fundamentally an explanatory hypothesis. As such it is to be judged by the general criteria we apply to explanatory hypotheses. In other words, we should seek to determine the prior probability and explanatory power of theism.

How do we judge the prior probability of theism? In this case the issue turns fundamentally on the simplicity of the hypothesis on offer. Background knowledge is not relevant because all our empirical data are among the things to be explained; fit with known data does not therefore apply. As to the other factor in prior probability, that is, scope, the situation is somewhat ambiguous. Theism is narrow in scope, for it postulates one entity as the explanatory agent; on the other hand, its scope is wide in that God is said to have control and knowledge of all other agents. However, this ambiguity should not worry us, for by far the most important factor is simplicity. On this score theism scores exceptionally well.

This is so because the entity it postulates, i.e., God, is omnipotent, omniscient, and perfectly free. These properties God possesses externally by nature rather than by choice. Given these properties, others follow by inference; hence

---

[7] Swinburne, *Existence of God,* pp. 25–26.

[8] Swinburne explains Bayes's theorem in *Existence of God,* pp. 64–66. In order to keep the exposition to manageable proportions, I omit it here.

God is also omnipresent, creator of all things and perfectly good. Such an agent is an agent of a very simple kind, for we do not have to reckon with inelegant properties. We would have to were we to posit an agent who was less than omnipotent, omniscient, perfectly free. Wherever we would draw the line on any of these attributes it would be arbitrary and awkward. Moreover, theism has great simplicity in that it reduces all explanations in the end to personal explanation. It explains all events as due to the action of personal agents and thus avoids any kind of ultimate dualism in the fundamentals of our explanations of what happens. All in all, then, "the intrinsic probability of theism is, relative to other hypotheses about what there is, very high, because of the great simplicity of the hypothesis of theism."[9]

How then do we judge the explanatory power of theism? The task at this level is a formidable one. What one must do is determine how far one can predict the phenomena we observe from the hypothesis of theism. Swinburne explores this question with regard to a wide range of occurrent phenomena ranging from the physical universe to reported miracles such as the resurrection of Jesus. With regard to each of these phenomena, he urges that they are more to be expected and therefore more probable if there is a God than if there is not. This represents Swinburne's way of laying out the cumulative-case argument for theism. He summarizes the data and the conclusion in this way:

> The existence of the universe, its conformity to order, the existence of animals and men, men having great opportunities for co-operation in acquiring knowledge and moulding the universe, the pattern of history and the existence of some evidence of miracles, and finally the occurrence of religious experiences, are all such as we have reason to expect if there is a God, and less reason to expect otherwise.[10]

There is no substitute at this point to working through the details of each argument in the total case for theism. For our purposes we content ourselves with some general comments on what Swinburne says and how he proceeds. Several points deserve mention.

First, as one expects, much energy is given to stating the weight of evidence to be assigned to those phenomena which originally were used as proofs for the existence of God. Using confirmation theory, Swinburne skillfully articulates his own version of, for example, the cosmological and teleological arguments for the existence of God. Secondly, Swinburne rejects some considerations which have often been thought of as relevant to establishing the existence of God. Most conspicuously, he does not make much of the appeal to morality. In his view, morality as an institution in society can be adequately explained on utilitarian grounds. Morality as a set of moral truths is a set of analytical principles and therefore cannot provide an argument for the existence of God. In contrast to this Swinburne devotes considerable time to developing an argument from consciousness. As part of the argu-

---

[9] Swinburne, *Existence of God,* p. 106.
[10] Ibid., p. 277.

ment he tries to show that materialist theories of the mind are very unlikely to succeed. What all this reveals is that the details of Swinburne's case for theism depend at crucial points on thoroughly contested philosophical argument in both moral philosophy and philosophy of mind.

Thirdly, in considering arguments against the existence of God, Swinburne limits himself to an examination of the problem of evil. Outside this problem the atheist's arguments have been largely in the form of criticisms of the theist's arguments. According to Swinburne, the existence of evil does not constitute a good inductive case against theism. Put very simply, the existence of evil does not count against the existence of God. Finally, there is a fascinating and significant change of method when Swinburne evaluates the evidence from religious experience. Rather than ask how well religious experience supports the hypothesis of theism, he treats it as a perceptual claim arguing that, on the principle of credulity, religious experience should be treated as veridical unless it is shown otherwise. This has an important bearing on the ultimate conclusion Swinburne reaches about the probability of theism. With that we arrive at the fourth and last phase of our exposition of his position.

What final conclusion then does Swinburne reach on the probability of theism? The answer he gives comes in two stages. First, leaving aside religious experience but taking into account all the relevant evidence which can be codified by Bayes's theorem, he concludes that theism is neither overwhelmingly probable nor overwhelmingly improbable. He sums it up this way:

> I now suggest that it is reasonable to come to the following qualitative judgement about the force of the evidence *so far* considered (i.e. all the evidence apart from the evidence of religious experience). Theism does not have a probability close to 1 or to 0, that is, on the evidence considered so far, theism is neither very probable nor very improbable. It does not have a probability close to 1 because it does not have high predictive power. . . . It is compatible with too much. There are too many different possible worlds which a God might bring about. . . . On the other hand, theism is a very simple hypothesis with a remarkable ability to make sense of what otherwise is extremely puzzling. . . . For this reason the probability of it is not too close to 0.[11]

We can construe this conclusion as one where the scales are evenly balanced so that the rational agent does not know whether to come down on one side or the other. Theism is neither probable nor improbable. When, however, we add in the evidence from religious experience the situation changes drastically. When this evidence is weighed it comes down heavily on the side of the probability of theism. Theism must then be construed as more probable than not. This constitutes the second stage of Swinburne's conclusion. He summarizes both stages as follows:

> My conclusion so far has been that the probability of theism is none too close to 1 or 0 on the evidence so far considered. However, so far in this chapter I

[11] Ibid., p. 289. I have omitted the symbols used in the last sentence.

have ignored one crucial piece of evidence, the evidence from religious experience. . . . I concluded the last chapter . . . with the claim that unless the probability of theism on other evidence is very low indeed, the testimony of many
witnesses to experience apparently of God suffices to make many of those
experiences probably veridical. That is, the evidence of religious experience is
in that case sufficient to make theism over all probable. The argument of
Chapter 13 was that the testimony of many witnesses to experiences apparently of God makes the existence of God probable if it is not already on other
evidence very improbable. I believe that I have shown this in this chapter that
that condition is well satisfied and hence the conclusion of Chapter 13 applies.
On our total evidence theism is more probable than not.[12]

HARD RATIONALISM AND RELIGIOUS ADEQUACY

How should we evaluate Swinburne's position? Much could be said about the details
of his various arguments. We shall concentrate here on the main structure of his
position, attempting to focus on crucial aspects of his proposals. Before we raise
any questions it is important to acknowledge that complaints about Swinburne's
dry and seemingly insensitive style are irrelevant to any serious evaluation of his
work. We can raise questions about whether his position is religiously satisfactory,
but if we do so they should be cast in a recognizably philosophical manner. In my
view careful reflection on much of what Swinburne says can enrich one's religious
perception of the world. But this is neither here nor there. Nor should the matter of
style distract us. The relation between philosophy and literature is a contingent one.
One can judge a writer's philosophical contribution as invaluable while remaining
dissatisfied with the way his or her position is expressed. We might well say this, for
example, in the case of Aquinas or Kant. Equally perhaps with Swinburne.

Actually it is very useful to begin by raising questions about the religious adequacy of his position, for this leads into some critical philosophical considerations.
It is vital to realize that the point here is not whether Swinburne believes any particular religious creed and thus satisfies some sort of theological test. In fact, like
many philosophers who are religiously committed, Swinburne is remarkably orthodox in his beliefs. The issue is whether his account of the rationality of religious belief is compatible with the kind of certainty not necessarily required but definitely
often associated with paradigm cases of religious devotion. *Prima facie* there is an
obvious tension between the two. Many ordinary believers and most saints do not
treat their religious beliefs as simply more probable than not. They claim a certainty which is much deeper than this. Clearly this needs detailed attention, and I do
not think Swinburne's analysis can resolve this problem.[13] Related to this issue is
the role of the passions and will in arriving at one's religious beliefs. As it stands,
Swinburne's model believer seems more like an ingenious calculating machine automatically matching hypotheses and evidence than a person whose life may be shaken
to the foundations by exposure to a religious tradition.

[12] Ibid., p. 291.
[13] I discuss the relation between philosophy and commitment in chap. 20.

A second kind of tension is located in the relation between Swinburne's emphasis on simplicity as a mark of prior probability and the Christian conception of God. Swinburne makes much of the simplicity of theism, and given his definition of theism, his conclusions on that score are secure. The problem is that Christian theism works with a far more difficult and complex notion of God, as Swinburne himself must acknowledge. How Swinburne can have any room for the trinity, and the mystery surrounding such a notion is far from clear. As it stands, acceptance of such a concept would radically alter the probability status of theism. This in turn would affect how far one can rely on the argument from religious experience. Hence this issue has significant consequences for the final account of probability that we can offer.

SIMPLICITY, COMPLEXITY, AND TRUTH

A related question is the logically prior one of the role of simplicity in evaluating the epistemic value of a theory. We can agree that it plays an important role in our decisions in science. But whether simplicity is a genuine mark of truth is another matter entirely. It is arguable that we prefer simplicity because it is much more convenient; we can cope more easily with simple theories than complex ones. Thus the attraction of simplicity could be entirely psychological. If that is the case, then the relation between truth and simplicity may be more complex than Swinburne allows.

This seems especially so in some areas. In some kinds of investigation we may intuitively begin from the assumption that whatever the truth is, it is far from simple. This applies especially in historical study. For example, suppose someone offered a historical explanation of the present troubles in Ireland. What role does simplicity have in establishing the truth of the proposed theory? I suspect very little. Indeed, the most simple theories I have encountered are invariably wrong. So complexity may not at all be a serious flaw in a satisfactory explanation.

Moreover, explanatory power is far from easy to determine in such cases. How can we tell in any detailed way what is more likely than not in history? If the theory is going to have any predictive power it must be given in some detail. Hence it will be relatively complex. Furthermore, we are unlikely to have any detailed theory without considerable knowledge of what is to be explained. Thus our historical explanations have to be retrospective. We seek to account for what has happened by telling the most coherent and illuminating story we can, and we do so after the events, when talk of predictive power seems lame and unnecessary. Certainly explanatory power, coherence, scope, accuracy, plausibility, and the like, matter enormously in our evaluation of historical explanations. My discomfort with Swinburne's analysis at this point is that he focuses too exclusively on explanatory power and expounds it in a way which is difficult to apply to live options on disputed issues in historical investigation. In other words, ability to predict what is likely to occur, a factor Swinburne sees as a crucial index of explanatory power, seems artificial and only marginally helpful.

What I am arguing here is that testing historical explanations of events in the past is more complex than Swinburne suggests. The criteria of truth in this domain are not just a matter of simplicity and explanatory power. Also, our choices between various options may depend upon judgments which are impossible to quantify. Even good theories may have some loose ends and be quite complex internally. Hence Swinburne has oversimplified the actual kind of rational justification we have to deploy. This move itself stems from his desire to achieve simplicity in the domain of epistemology. He is seeking to offer one uniform theory of rationality which will cover all kinds of explanation both within and without science. Presumably simplicity will be a mark of truth for such theories. I am contesting this claim, suggesting that such a uniform theory of rationality is not available and that simplicity is less important than Swinburne has argued.

Confirmation for this can be derived from Swinburne's final conclusions on the probability of theism. What is conspicuously invaluable is his attempt to quantify a cumulative-case argument for theism. Yet the results are disappointing. To begin, the actual codification of the argument is limited. Not only is there an enormous contribution from personal judgment in reckoning the weight of each piece of evidence, the actual final conclusion is very much a matter of personal judgment. In actual fact Bayes's theorem is not equipped to deal with the crucial contribution from religious experience, for the latter comes into the reckoning *after* the theorem has done its work. Hence the attempt to codify breaks down in the last analysis, and we have to rely on our own judgment as to the final balance of probability.

SOME QUESTIONS ABOUT MATERIAL CONTENT

What I have questioned just now is the way in which Swinburne lays out the argument. In particular I am challenging the possibility of making the kind of codified argument he deploys. But we can also raise questions about the material content of the cumulative case he presents. For reasons already given, I do not think that Swinburne has shown that evil does not count seriously against Christian theism.[14] Moreover, I am not convinced that Swinburne has fully reckoned with the case against theism. He does not acknowledge the force of the arguments deployed by sceptics like Freud or Marx, for he believes that the atheist's case rests just on the argument from evil and the failure of positive arguments for theism. Thus though I do not think that the sceptical case has been made successfully, the evaluation of that case is important in our final assessment of the rationality of any theistic option. Swinburne omits this evaluation from his calculations.

Another point at which his position is difficult to support is in the argument from consciousness. Swinburne's contribution at this juncture is highly original; we might even say it constitutes a new species of natural theology. The claim is that in explaining the existence of consciousness there are basically three options. We can

[14] See chap. 5.

accept a materialist theory of the mind, seeking to provide a scientific explanation for mental properties or events. For various philosophical reasons this program fails. We can accept some kind of dualism, admitting two radically different kinds of things in the world which happen, as a matter of brute fact, to interact and coexist side by side. This, however, leaves us with a very messy world view. The only other alternative is to look for a personal explanation of the correlations which exist between minds and bodies. Such an explanation is furnished by theism.

> The theist claims that an explanation of why brain-event of kind B_1 is correlated with mental events of kind M_1, brain-event of kind B_2 with mental event of kind M_2, and so on is that God has chosen that these kinds of events be so correlated; an explanation in so far as there is one of why I have the thoughts, feelings, etc. that I have is that my having thoughts, feelings, etc. of these kinds is correlated with certain kinds of brain-states and that God has chosen that these kinds of thoughts, feelings, etc. be so correlated; it follows from God's omnipotence that his choice will be executed.[15]

Such an explanation would be more natural than that provided by a materialist because there is a natural connection between an agent's intention to bring about a state of affairs and the occurrence of that state of affairs.

There are two difficulties in this proposal. First, it is very obscure how divine action is going to bring about the correlation between brain-events and mental events. At one point Swinburne speaks of divine intervention.

> I argue that, even given the existence of an orderly inanimate universe, the prior probability of the existence of embodied agents, conscious beings who bring about effects through intentions . . . is very low, unless a God *intervenes in the natural order* to bring about their existence.[16]

Yet Swinburne also has no wish to deny that "there is a story of the gradual evolution of conscious beings out of inorganic matter."[17]

> I do not wish to deny that there is a satisfactory scientific explanation given by the biological theory of evolution of the evolution of more and more complex beings which interact in increasingly complex ways. But there is not, I have argued, a scientific explanation of their increasing complexity of physiological organisation and behavioural response giving rise to the particular conscious life to which it does give rise and which subsequently in part determines what happens in and through the body.[18]

The question surely arises, Where does God intervene and act in this process? What does God actually do? At best we have only a formal possibility of some kind of

[15] Swinburne, *Existence of God,* pp. 172–73.
[16] Ibid., p. 161. Emphasis mine.
[17] Ibid., p. 172.
[18] Ibid.

divine action. As such it remains too obscure to explain anything and thus resolve one of the most perplexing problems in the whole of philosophy.

There is another problem too. Even if we knew what God actually did in intervening, we would still need to know why he acted or worked in this way. Otherwise the explanation remains partial and incomplete. It would be like knowing that the general went to war but not knowing the exact reasons why he went to war. In other words, why does God correlate mental events with brain-events rather than with, say, feet-events? Mackie raises this pointedly in this way.

> . . . if, as Locke puts it, omnipotency has given to some systems of matter fitly disposed a power to perceive and think, why is it only to fitly disposed ones? Could not *omnipotency* superadd a faculty of thinking as easily to a block of wood as to a brain? If materialism has difficulty in explaining how even the most elaborate neural structures can give rise to consciousness, theism, with its personal explanations and direct intention-fulfilments, has at least as great a difficulty in explaining why consciousness is found *only* in them.[19]

TENSION BETWEEN REASON AND REVELATION

This leads into a more general problem in Swinburne's whole approach to the rationality of religious belief. It is one which theologians in particular may want to press. Swinburne writes very confidently of what reason can conclude about God and his intentions. Thus he thinks that the omnipotence, omniscience, and freedom of God can be grounded independently of religious experience and revelation. From these he then deduces that God is omnipresent, creator of all things, and perfectly good. More than that, he attempts to deduce what reasons God might have for bringing about the phenomena which constitute the evidence for the explanatory power of theism. He recognizes, of course, that such an exercise is tentative and cautious. It is worth quoting Swinburne's general remarks on this in some detail.

> It is the fact that a God will be a completely rational being, and so a perfectly good being, which gives us some ability to predict what he will do. Only some ability of course, for clearly all too often there are reasons for bringing about states of affairs and reasons for not bringing them about, where neither override the other. But sometimes there are overriding reasons for doing things, and we with our limited understanding can recognize these. Of course, as ignorant and morally corrupt human beings, we may have very inadequate ideas of which actions God has reason to do and which actions he has overriding reason to do (which actions are good, and which actions are good over all). Yet clearly most of us have some understanding of this matter, for we have some understanding of what is morally good and what is morally bad (e.g., when we judge that torturing children just for fun is morally bad, we make a true moral judgment) and the capacity to grow in such under-

---

[19] Mackie, *Miracle of Theism*, p. 131. Emphasis as in original.

standing. And clearly too our understanding of most other things discussed in this book, and in most books about most things, is very limited and prone to error, but is such that we can grow in it. We have to make tentative judgments in the light of our understanding at the time of our investigation—in this matter as in all matters—bearing in mind the possibility of future revision. With this caveat, we will move on.[20]

But can we move on so confidently? Deists of an earlier generation thought so; yet many theists have not shared their optimism about what we can say about what God might or might not do. The point is succinctly made by Gary Gutting.

> . . . it is hard to see how we could have reason to think that God will have any specific intentions or will act in any specific way. We can, of course, say that he will always intend the best goal and act for this in a maximally effective way. But precisely because we lack his omniscience, we have no way of judging what specifically he would be likely to do. Any such judgments must be ultimately based on what we (or a moral idealization of ourselves) would do (if we could), given our understanding of the situation. But our understanding of anything will at best be only a dim reflection of God's, and so there is no reason to think that our judgment would coincide with his. We know how far wrong we would go by inferring the likely behaviour of a wise adult from the judgments of even the best-intentioned child as to what ought to be done; and the distance between God and man is immeasurably greater than that between a child and even the wisest adult.[21]

This issue is especially acute for Swinburne, for not only does he believe in divine revelation, he also recognizes why divine revelation may be extremely important to the theist. That reason stems from the possibility that "the human race gets into a really bad mess."[22] Due to the abuse of their freedom, human beings "do not altogether know which actions are right and which are wrong, and they conceal from themselves even what they do know."[23] Elsewhere Swinburne draws attention to human stupidity in religious matters and readily acknowledges the role sin may play in moulding belief.[24] The more this is emphasized, then the more precarious becomes Swinburne's brand of rationalism. The more we need revelation, then the more difficult does it become to speculate what God is likely to do and why he is likely to do it. Hence there is considerable internal strain in the way Swinburne seeks to determine the explanatory power of theism.

That strain emerges at key points where Swinburne has to appeal to much more than his simple theism in order to offer a plausible rendering of the evidence. Thus in order to appeal to the argument from history and miracle, he has to make mention of moral and metaphysical assumptions which space does not allow him to

---

[20] Swinburne, *Existence of God,* pp. 110–11.

[21] Gary Gutting, *Religious Belief and Religious Skepticism* (Notre Dame, Indiana: University of Notre Dame Press, 1982), pp. 129–30.

[22] Swinburne, *Existence of God,* p. 239.

[23] Ibid., p. 239.

[24] Swinburne, *Faith and Reason,* pp. 180–81.

expound.[25] More conspicuously, in his treatment of the problem of evil, Swinburne has to articulate one particular way of construing the doctrine of creation. We might say that he prefers an Irenaean to an Augustinian account of creation.[26] In other words, Swinburne indirectly relies on considerations which are derived in part not from theism as he defines it but from Christian theism. As has happened again and again in the history of philosophy, material really drawn from divine revelation is smuggled in under the patronage of pure reason.

If this criticism has merit, then the consequence for any cumulative-case argument for theism is far-reaching. It means that Swinburne's version collapses into the kind of position I attributed in the previous chapter to the soft rationalist. According to the soft rationalist, the theory to be attacked or defended is not the simple hypothesis of theism set out by Swinburne but a collection of "hypotheses" brought together to form a significant metaphysical or theological vision of life as a whole. To be sure, various elements can be isolated and scrutinized for their truth value. But we need also to see such single beliefs as part of an intricate network of beliefs which must be assessed as a whole. Quine and Ullian have reminded us economically of this point:

> Often in assessing beliefs we do best to assess several in combination. A very accomplished mechanic might be able to tell something about an automobile's engine by examining its parts one by one, each in complete isolation from the others, but it would surely serve his purpose better to see the engine as a whole with all its parts functioning together. So with what we believe. It is in the light of the full body of our beliefs that candidates gain acceptance or rejection; any independent merits of a candidate tend to be less decisive.[27]

This means that laying out the evidence will be more difficult to codify than Swinburne allows. Yet this is no excuse for obscurantism. If a case is to be made out at all it needs to be articulated in detail. Thus the particular cosmological, religious, moral, and personal considerations appealed to as evidence need to be carefully spelled out. Also, all of these must in the end be taken together as essential to the case to be argued.

VARIETIES OF CUMULATIVE-CASE ARGUMENTS

This point might seem obvious but it is easily overlooked. Thus Gary Gutting, while highly critical of Swinburne's position, himself offers a cumulative argument for religious belief which ignores this policy. He can do this because he thinks that there are two different ways of deploying such an argument.

[25] Swinburne, *Existence of God,* p. 241.
[26] Ibid., pp. 192–93.
[27] W. V. Quine and J. S. Ullian, *The Web of Belief* (New York: Random House, 1970), p. 8.

One is based on the apparent power of a theistic framework to explain diverse features of our world and lives; the other on the claim of many to have experienced the immediate presence of a divine being. Both arguments . . . present cumulative cases for belief that do not stand or fall with any one premiss. They present belief as legitimated not by a single chain of argument but by many independent threads. Further, evaluating these arguments does not require the resolution of any esoteric philosophical disputes, but only the sort of judgement that we all employ in countless everyday matters.[28]

Gutting rejects the former possibility as represented by Swinburne but defends the latter as a viable account of the justification of religious belief.

What is surprising here is that Gutting should want to split the evidence to form two different cumulative-case arguments. This is surely artificial. Indeed Gutting elsewhere acknowledges the importance of taking all the evidence into account at once. In other words, he notes that a cumulative case involves an appeal to both religious facts and cosmological, moral, and personal facts.[29] But he seems to forget this when he offers his own cumulative case for theism. As a result, all he really offers is a carefully qualified appeal to religious experience. It seems odd to treat the brief arguments he deploys as a rigorous statement of the total argument which can be made out for religious belief. What he has really offered are good reasons for taking religious experience seriously.[30] However, relying on religious experience alone will, in turn, as Gutting quite rightly recognizes, lead to rather meager conclusions. As he points out in a summary of his conclusion:

> The heart of true religious belief is a realisation that we can have *access* to God but only minimal reliable *accounts* of his nature and relations to us. This realisation undermines the claims of both believers and non-believers who think they have essentially adequate pictures of the overall meaning and values of our lives. As a result, true religious faith is in fact a religious scepticism that deflates the pretensions of both belief and non-belief.[31]

Gutting is correct to argue that his version of the cumulative-case argument cannot in the end say very much about God. He is wrong to hoist this into a religious virtue. True religious belief does involve substantive claims about the overall meaning and value of our lives. That has been vital to religious sensibility, to spirituality, and to moral action, religiously conceived. Such claims have invariably appealed to a particular historical revelation in order to establish their plausibility. Whatever the difficulties this situation may evoke, it means that divine revelation must be taken much more seriously by those who seek to defend the rationality of religious belief. Cumulative case arguments which, as in the case of Swinburne, bring it in *after* the fundamental religious beliefs have been established or, as in the

---

[28] Gutting, *Religious Belief,* p. 8.
[29] Ibid., p. 128.
[30] Ibid., p. 152.
[31] Ibid., p. 9.

case of Gutting, construe it as part of an outer belt which is adopted on purely pragmatic grounds are inadequate.

CONCLUSION

To put it sharply, if one is to remain a theist one develops the kind of cumulative case offered by the soft rationalist and evaluates a complex web of religious belief by appeal to several independent threads of evidence taken together, using informal, sensitive, personal judgment to weigh its validity, or one converts to some version of fideism. Neither a hard rationalism which seeks to quantify the argument nor a cumulative case which leaves out revelation will work. This is the conclusion to which the discussion in this chapter ineluctably drives us. Equally should one reject the various religious alternatives and embrace some kind of secular vision of the world, hard choices will have to be made. If one cannot establish the truth of one's position in a strict sense along hard rationalist lines, then one must either develop some kind of soft rationalist position or else maintain one's secular beliefs on fideistic grounds. In other words one still has to decide what to believe about the world as a whole and its contents, and one has to decide what kind of epistemology to use in defense of it.

On the epistemological issue soft rationalism has much to commend it. In the final analysis fideists and hard rationalists both look for standards of argument that seem inherently inapplicable to the complex data and warrants that are relevant to the debate between adherents of rival metaphysical systems. According to the soft rationalist, adherents of such systems have a duty both to spell out in some detail the intricate body of beliefs to which they are committed and to test such beliefs against the relevant body of contested evidence as best they can. In the end we are all left to weigh the available evidence for ourselves.

We have now brought to a conclusion our discussion of the rationality of religious beliefs. We turn therefore to examine a wide range of diverse topics which commonly crop up in the philosophy of religion. Some of these arise because of the relation that exists between religion and other fields of thought and action. Some of them arise because of the nature of particular doctrines held by religious believers. We shall begin by looking at the relation between religion and morality.

Chapter Eleven
Religion And Morality

Religious belief and practice are interesting and important for a variety of reasons; we are wise to examine them with sympathy and critical care. They are important because of their universal appeal through space and time. They are urgent because they seek to express and embody significant claims about the way things are. They also matter because they seek to embody and preserve the essence of morality. Certainly religious believers generally show considerable interest in morality, sometimes to the point where they claim a monopoly of interest in it and thus argue that they are its exclusive guardians. Why does this interest arise? Should it arise at all? Is there a significant connection between religion and morality? These are the kinds of questions which will occupy us in this chapter.

RELIGION AND MORALITY DISTINCT

Most contemporary philosophers are convinced that religion and morality are entirely distinct operations with no vital relation to one another. Many religious believers are shocked at such a position and construe it as one more reason to distrust philosophy. It runs counter to their experience when they sometimes find that religion does seem to make a difference to how people behave and what they believe in moral matters. It also clashes with their fleeting and awesome sense that if there is no God, then anything goes. Somehow religious belief is the foundation of moral belief. If there is no God, then everybody does what is right in his or her own eyes, and that means moral chaos. Hence a radical break between religion and morality seems *prima facie* wrong and even dangerous. There are cogent reasons, however, why philosophers tend to read this as an expression of panic rather than a statement of good sense. Let us explore this point in some detail.

To begin, let us note that philosophers in insisting on a distinction between religion and morality are not denying the obvious. They do not deny, for example, the fact that religions characteristically set forth an ethic for their adherents. Religious leaders and officials expect adherents of their faith to act in certain distinctive ways and make this a necessary feature of belonging to their community. Some of these acts will be liturgical, e.g., praying, attending religious meetings, participating in sacraments, but some will be clearly moral, e.g., abstaining from murder, parenting, loving one's neighbor, helping the destitute and needy. The latter will not be accidental; they will be constitutive of sincerely belonging to the faith in question. Philosophers cannot and do not deny this truism.

Nor do they deny that religious believers will be moral persons in the sense that they will try to conform to the moral rules of the religion they profess to follow. They expect religious people to be morally earnest, for this is usually part of the very definition of religious commitment. Part of what it is to be a Moslem is to seek to follow sincerely the ethical outlook of Islam. The same applies to Judaism and Christianity.

What many philosophers deny is that there is any *necessary* connection between religion and morality. Expressed briefly, they claim that one can be moral without being religious and that one can have morally correct convictions without relying on religious conviction. In other words, morality is both empirically and logically distinct from religion. This is a radical thesis which has much in its favor. Consider more fully what it means and how it can be supported.

NO EMPIRICAL RELATION

Suppose we claim that there is a necessary empirical relation between religion and morality. What does this mean? It is relatively clear what we normally signify when we speak of an empirical relation between two entities. Take the case where swallowing a certain dosage of aspirin relieves me of my headache. If we claim a necessary empirical relation between swallowing aspirin and relief of pain, then we establish this claim inductively, by experience. Presumably chemists and other experts have performed the necessary tests to show that aspirin relieves headaches. They have established a law relating the two, relying on careful scientific procedures to make sure that aspirin really does work. That is why we take it when we have a headache. Is this what is at stake when we speak of an empirical relation between religion and morality? Surely it is a plausible way to construe the claim. If it is, then it is open to the fatal objection that those who make this claim have not shown much interest in providing the necessary scientific evidence. It is not enough for zealous officials and evangelists to say that religious decline causes moral decline or that religious revival leads to moral renewal. They must actually show that this is the case by means of standard scientific procedure. That has not been done. If anything, such evidence as we possess counts against this thesis. Everyday experience and common-sense generalization show that there are many moral atheists and not a few immoral religious believers. Northern Ireland, for example, is conspicuously religious as indicated by widespread religious practice, but it is not conspicuously moral as indicated by the level of violence. Moreover, social anthropology suggests great variation in the relation between morality and religion in so-called primitive societies.[1] Hence it has not been shown that there is any necessary connection between religion and morality on the empirical level.

A MISLEADING ISSUE

What are we to make of this claim and the arguments against it? We can agree that no scientific evidence has been given for a lawlike relation between religion and morality. We can also agree that there are good atheists and evil theists. However, we need to question the terms of reference in which the discussion has been set. The discussion assumes that the believer is claiming a direct causal relation between religious affiliation and moral belief. It also assumes that religious believers are to be identified in terms of external participation in religious acts of one sort or another. These assumptions are inadequate. Religious affiliation is often a very poor guide to a genuine religious life. The Old Testament prophets bear eloquent witness to this, reserving some of their fiercest denunciation for those who delight in solemn assemblies and external ritual.[2] If this is the case, then sociological evidence is of little use in deciding any possible causal relation between religion and morality. On the contrary, it may positively mislead by making religion identical with joining a particular social organization.

It may also mislead in a far more significant way by masking the claim that religious believers actually want to make. What they may want to say is that God's grace makes a difference to the way one behaves. In other words, it concerns the effects of one's relationship with God in one's moral life. This claim as to God's grace is a factual claim, analogous to the impact a close friend may have upon one for good. Yet it is not a scientific claim which can be tested by sociological surveys. Some may want to reject it for precisely this reason; evidence must be scientific in a narrow sense, or it does not count as evidence at all. The latter claim, however, is a piece of philosophical dogmatism which echoes the hard rationalism we have seen good reason to reject. Moreover, we are not entirely at a loss to weigh up the impact of human agents in our lives. In our own cases, we know their effects first-hand,

---

[1] See A. M. Macbeath, *Experiments in Living* (London: Macmillan, 1952).
[2] See, for example, Amos 5:21–24.

and in the case of others we attend critically to their testimony. Similar considerations are clearly relevant in claims about the impact of divine grace. The possibility of a causal relation between divine grace and moral endeavor remains a live option.

NO LOGICAL RELATION

Many philosophers would be happy to concede this possibility but dismiss it as of secondary significance. What really matters, they might say, is whether religion is logically related to morality. The case this time is that religious assertions are logically distinct from moral assertions, and one does not have to believe the former in order to assent to the latter. Moral concepts and arguments are autonomous. To understand them one does not need to rely on significant religious concepts or convictions. In other words, moral language and debate do not require the learning or adopting of religious discourse. Why have so many philosophers accepted this conclusion? The argument runs something like this.

Let us take seriously the possibility that religion and morality are *not* logically distinct. Let us say, for example, that moral concepts must be defined in terms of religious categories if they are to be adequately understood. This is, in fact, the view embraced by several theologians. They suggest, for example, that good and evil are to be defined in terms of God's will. Good is simply what God wills and does; evil is what is done contrary to the will of God. Carl F. H. Henry expresses this view in this way:

> Biblical ethics discredits an autonomous morality. It gives theonomous ethics its classic form—the identification of the moral law with the divine will. In Hebrew-Christian revelation, distinctions reduce to what is good or what is pleasing, and what is wicked or displeasing to the Creator-God alone.[3]
>
> Hebrew-Christian ethics centres in the divine revelation of the statutes, commandments and precepts of the Living God. Its whole orientation of the moral life may be summarised by what the Holy Lord commands and what he forbids. What accords with his edicts is right, what opposes his holy will is wicked.[4]

If this view is correct, ethics is a subsection of systematic theology; it is not a discipline with its own fundamental concepts and logic; on the contrary, it relies on theology as a matter of strict logic.

What is wrong with such a view? At first sight it might seem odd to challenge it, for that appears as if you are against God, surely an embarrassing position for anyone. However, to question it is not to challenge God, it is simply to query

---

[3]Carl F. H. Henry, *Christian Ethics and Personal Morality* (Grand Rapids, Mich.: Eerdmans, 1975), p. 210.
[4]Ibid., p. 217.

Henry's conception of the relation between religion and morality. One might object to this conception on theological grounds by asking if it does justice to the biblical material on morality. If it fails in this respect, then it cannot stand as an adequate biblical account of morality. Philosophers attack it, however, on very different grounds. The chief argument deployed is as old as philosophy itself, for it goes back to Plato in the *Euthyphro*.[5] Plato sets out in embryonic form an argument whose logic seems unassailable. Its essence lies in posing a dilemma for those committed to a logical relation between religion and morality. Suppose we define goodness in terms of God's will, and suppose God's will is made known in certain commands given by God. We can then ask a critical question about these commands. Does God give them because they are good, or are they good because God commands them? No matter which answer we give, there is a serious problem for theologians like Henry.

If we take the first alternative and say that God gives certain commands because they are good then goodness is clearly independent of God's commands. The two are not identical in meaning or content. Indeed if we treat them as identical in meaning the claim that God commands *x* because *x* is good is reduced to the tautology "God commands *x* because God commands *x*." The first alternative rejects this because it wants to claim something substantial about God's commands; it wants to say that God chooses the commands He gives because they are good commands. It keeps the goodness of God's commands logically distinct from His merely giving them. In this case morality is logically distinct from religion. In making proper moral choices we should only follow divine commands insofar as we know that these commands are given for good reasons. These reasons are distinct from the divine commands. Presumably we have to rely on our own moral judgment to decide what such reasons might be.

The other alternative is equally unattractive for the position under review. If we say that the commands are good merely because God commands them, then, as God might command anything, the fundamentals of our morality become purely arbitrary. If, for example, God commanded us to kill innocent children or rob the local bank, we would have a duty to do so. Anything God might command would be by definition good, and we cannot set moral limits in advance to what God might command.

Believers quickly respond to this option by insisting that God would, of course, never command such wicked acts. He just does not command such dreadful deeds, and it is wrong to say that he might. This, however, is thoroughly unsatisfactory. It smuggles in crucial moral constraints on what a good God can or cannot command. On the basis of one's own moral insight, one is not allowing certain commands to count as divine commands because they fail some standard of goodness. Hence God is not the ultimate criterion of goodness, and we have fallen back into the first alternative. Moreover, this response ignores the fact that religious canons like the book of Genesis attribute to God the command to kill an innocent child,

---

[5] Plato, *Euthyphro,* secs. 10a–d.

for it tells how Abraham was commanded to sacrifice Isaac.[6] This story highlights the dilemma afresh. On the one hand, if the story so offends our moral judgment that we seek a morally acceptable interpretation of it, then it is our moral judgment which is the ultimate foundation of our moral choices rather than divine commands. On the other hand, if we accept it as it stands, anything can count as being good, and morality is entirely arbitrary. If God commands us to cheat, torture, murder, then it becomes our moral duty to perform these acts.

The dominant trend in contemporary philosophy and theology is to reject the second alternative and accept the first. Theologians accept that morality is distinct from religion and happily hand morality over to philosophy. Theologians have no more to contribute to ethics than biologists or police officers. This trend can easily be construed as a great gain, for it has pastoral and political significance. On the pastoral side, it gives resources for dealing with the religious rebel who is tempted to ditch morality in ditching the faith. People may feel that if they abandon religion in adolescence or in a crisis, they can then do what they like from a moral point of view. However, if religion and morality are distinct, then this does not follow at all. A moral appeal can still therefore be directed at the religious rebel. On the political side, this solution is also beneficial. Religious believers may join with secular moralists in attempts to reform society or bolster morality against attack from those who would seek to discredit its claims or to undermine its importance. So Plato's argument turns out to be a considerable practical blessing as well as a philosophical imperative.

There are several other arguments as to why people have accepted that religion and morality are best construed as logically distinct.[7] I shall mention two here. First, it is argued that a religious morality commits the naturalistic fallacy by attempting to derive an *ought* from an *is*. Richard Robinson sets out such a view helpfully as follows:

> There could be a man who said: "There is one and only one moral law, and it is that we ought to do whatever God commands." If this man believed it possible to discover what his god did command, he could then go on to discover it and do it; and he would then be acting morally because he would be acting under a moral law, a sentence with an "ought" in it. There could be another man who said: "I am determined to devote myself utterly to God, and to do whatever he commands." If he also believed that it was possible to find out what his god commanded, he, like the former man, could go on to discover it and do it. But unlike the former man he would not be acting morally, because he would be acting from a principle which contained no "ought" and no "thou shalt," but merely said "I will." His procedure would be like that of a man who gives up trying to do right and tries instead to please his mistress. He would simply have taken a god for his mistress. To devote oneself utterly to a divine being, and decide to do everything he ordered, would not be to

[6]Genesis 22.

[7]Philip L. Quinn provides a comprehensive review in *Divine Commands of Moral Requirements* (Oxford: Clarendon Press, 1978), chap. 2.

base ethics, but to abandon it and substitute another way of living. We get an entailing religious basis for ethics only if we adopt the moral law that we ought to do whatever our god commands.[8]

The second argument has been splendidly laid out by P. H. Nowell-Smith.[9] His central thesis is that religious morality is infantile. To establish this he draws on Piaget's research on development in children. Consider the attitude of children in regard to playing with marbles. Very small children can play with marbles but they cannot play games with them. At this stage they cannot grasp what a rule is, so no game is possible. Here there is a premoral attitude to rules. Later on they can grasp rules and can now play games with marbles, but their attitude to the rules is absolutist. They regard the rules as sacred and as being imposed from outside. They take up a heteronomous attitude to them. Later, at a third stage, children become autonomous. Here they see the point of the rules and become responsible themselves as to whether they should follow them as they are or adapt them.

According to Nowell-Smith, religious morality is infantile because it involves attitudes which are appropriate to the young child but not to an adult. Thus Christian ethics, according to Nowell-Smith, emphasizes obedience to God as fundamental to the moral life, calls for total surrender of will such as in the case of Abraham's sacrifice of Isaac, and focuses exclusively on the relationship of the soul to God as the crucial factor in moral action over against any interest in others for their own sake. Such attitudes bear clear affinity to those identified in the heteronomous stage of childhood development. There is not that autonomy, freedom, and responsibility which are the marks of an adult. Clearly if this is correct then, it is crucial that morality and religion be seen as distinct. Those who wish to reach moral maturity had better abandon their religious commitments as swiftly as possible.

QUESTIONING CONVENTIONAL WISDOM

We need to ask, however, how sound this conventional wisdom really is. Can we so easily cut morality loose from religious moorings and send it happily out to sea without shedding any theological or philosophical tears? The situation is far more complex than the conventional wisdom will admit. I shall be content if I can make this clear, creating space in the process for a viable version of Christian ethics. Let me prepare the ground by noting two assumptions that are fundamental to the arguments I have outlined.

First, it is all too readily assumed that a religious morality will be exclusively a morality of divine commands. This may well be part of a religious morality, but it need not be the whole of it. Even scripture does not confine its moral expression to

---

[8] Richard Robinson, *An Atheist's Values* (Oxford: Clarendon Press, 1964), p. 131.

[9] P. H. Nowell-Smith, "Morality: Religious and Secular," in *Christian Ethics and Contemporary Society,* ed. Ian T. Ramsey (London: SCM, 1966), pp. 95–112.

this category, for it also includes moral advice and suggestion, appeal to conscience and personal judgment, the call to follow and imitate Christ, suggestive parables and stories, and much else besides. This settles nothing, but it questions the adequacy of the standard terms of reference in which the recent debate has been set.

Secondly, it is too quickly assumed that religion and morality if they are to relate intellectually must relate directly at the level of meaning. On this view religion must entirely determine the meaning of moral concepts, or it cannot affect them at all. Somehow the relation between religion and morality must be an all-or-nothing affair. Either it fully determines one's moral views or it contributes nothing to one's moral views. This seems hasty and suspicious, to say the least. Perhaps there is a third alternative, which would seek to show that the relation is more subtle and partial but no less significant.

CONSTRUCTING AN ALTERNATIVE

Let us attempt to construct such an option.[10] We can agree that many moral terms can be adequately understood without reference to religious concepts. This fits our experience, for unbelievers can talk perfectly coherently to each other and to believers on moral issues without there being a complete wall of incomprehension between them. Moreover, moral language can clearly be learned in atheistic homes and cultures. The same can apply to the logic of moral argument insofar as we can discern and formulate it. We can agree, further, that moral arguments need not necessarily appeal to religious premises. They can involve appeal to certain facts about the case, or to ultimate moral principles, or whatever, and be none the worse for that. Let us even agree that we have to rely on our own moral insight to decide whether a putative command from God is really from God. Thus if someone claims to have a command from God which says he is to roast our children alive for fun at three o'clock in the morning on the front lawn, we do not accept it without exercising our critical judgment. Indeed we would reject it immediately and say that it does not even count as a divine command in the first place.[11] So let us accept some level of autonomy in making moral judgments. In other words, there is much truth in the protest against identifying morality with divine commands. However, that protest does not at all show that religion is entirely irrelevant to morality. Religion can still have a profound and legitimate role to play in moral decision.

We can approach this by noting how paradoxical it is to speak of human beings telling God what to command if his commands are to be morally acceptable. This paradox is implied by the way the first alternative in the *Euthyphro* dilemma is described. The standard of good and evil is independent of God; we can, therefore, relying on our moral standards, assess God's commands and let him know how

---

[10] I am indebted for some of what follows to Basil Mitchell, *Morality: Religious and Secular* (Oxford: Clarendon Press, 1980), chap. 10.

[11] It would take me too far afield to discuss the famous case of Abraham and the command to sacrifice Isaac.

well he is doing. So if there is a day of judgment we arrive at the day, armed with our moral calculators, and score God on his performance as he attempts to separate the sheep from the goats. This whole scenario is both theologically and logically absurd. We do not tell God how to do his moral sums; he, if he sovereignly so chooses, tells us. We do not assess omniscience; omniscience assesses us and surely shakes our moral insensitivity and blindness in the process. God, being good, necessarily does not utter morally arbitrary commands.

The relevance of these considerations to the relation between religion and morality is considerable. First, religious believers have good warrant for trusting and exercising their critical moral sense. This moral sense is a gift from God given in creation and hence to be cultivated with diligence. Traditional reference to conscience as the "voice of God" bears eloquent witness to the importance of native moral insight. At this level the believer may gladly seek the help of the philosopher as to how best to give a formal analysis of this phenomenon. Theories of conscience, natural law, intuition, utilitarianism, naturalism, or whatever, may be drawn on at this stage. Perhaps even the notion of moral sense has more philosophical mileage in it than is commonly believed. However we proceed, the believer offers an account of the human agent which gives warrant for relying on one's moral insight.

Secondly, divine commands and divine revelation may well deepen and transform one's moral insight. Thus exposure to God in religious experience and in divine revelation may greatly enrich one's capacity to make good moral judgments. This is very similar to what happens in everyday life, so let us begin there in order to portray what is in view.

Suppose we love watching soccer. In time we develop certain standards of what counts as a good player. If asked to, we might well supply a formal account of these standards, but we might well insist that some of these elude explicit analysis. Suppose, further, that we go to the World Cup. It is very likely that when we do so we will encounter teams and players who enrich and change our conception of good soccer playing. Likewise with learning something as difficult as philosophy. When we begin we may not have a clue as to what constitutes a good philosopher. Through time we pick up insights here and there, and we soon proceed far enough to pick out someone in the field as a model of good philosophy. As we explore their work, we find our genuine but rudimentary insight refined and enriched. Even the very standards we rely on to pick out our model may alter considerably in the process.

Intellectually the logic of this confounds the hard rationalist, who typically wants to avoid error by laying down secure norms in advance. We can see how complex the logic of development is by recourse to recent developments in ice skating. Recently standards used to judge ice skating changed rather drastically. This happened not because the international judges got together and drew up a new set out of thin air but because skaters like John Curry and Toller Cranston added dimensions to skating which simply shattered the old ones. Initially the artistic element they introduced was rejected, and skaters who expressed it in their routine got low scores. In the end, the new performance showed up the inadequacy of the old standards and an enrichment in judgment was agreed to have taken place.

As with much learning, there is a paradox here which demands sensitive treatment if we are to do justice to all the facts involved. This paradox was well known to the Greeks when they queried how we could ever learn anything. In learning, either we know what we seek to discover or we do not. In neither case is learning possible. In the first case it is impossible because we know already; in the second case it is impossible because we do not know what we are seeking. If we hit upon the answer by chance, we cannot identify it as the answer because we do not know the answer. When we think about this we realize that the dilemma is a false one. It makes no room for coming to know in the actual process of learning. As we actually learn, exercising such judgment as we possess, we develop the ability to identify correct answers even though it may be difficult to formalize precisely what counts as a correct answer.

RELIGION AND MORAL DISCERNMENT

This is very relevant to morality. Again let us work with a nonreligious example to make the point. Let us accept as a moral platitude that parents should love their children. Clearly we need not appeal to revelation to show that this is so. Let us grant, therefore, that people have a minimal moral sense which tells them that taking care of their children is a good thing. It is something all parents ought to do if they can. It is obvious that one's conception of this care can be deeply enriched by experience. Perhaps one comes across a parent who has a severely handicapped child. Exposure to such a parent may have a profound effect on one's conception of what true parental love really is. Such a case is recorded in the experience of a man, Archie Hill, who married a woman who has such a son. The son is severely handicapped both mentally and physically. He is twenty-six years old and cannot walk or talk or feed himself or toilet himself. He has to be cared for like a baby, for his wasted neck muscles give him no more than thirty degrees of head turn. The doctors told his mother to put him away in an institution when he was a baby. Her husband writes:

> She did not "put him away" but took him away to her secret places of motherhood and womanhood. She took him away and kept him and in the keeping, relinquished most of her own life. She gave her own life as an extension of her son's. She even plans the planting of the garden each year so that she can take him around it when the flowers bloom. She plants them so that they are the right height for him to see them from his chair.[12]

Then comes this significant comment:

> I never met love like this before. My ideas of love had been so shallow. What privileged few amongst us really know what love is? We know self love, pride love, power love, money love, comfort love, dependent love. We know shal-

[12] Archie Hill, "Life Within a Prison of Flesh," *The Listener*, 19 February 1978, p. 206.

low love and glitter love. These are good and rich loves, most of them. But there are different loves, levels of love, and the deepest depths of all is this closed world of love between a mother and a useless creature which was the child drawn in pain from her body into the poisoned light of day.[13]

The saints, and indeed the ordinary believer, testify to similar experience in their exposure to the love of God in Christ. They can well begin with an incipient awareness of love as a virtue. This love, however, can be, and is, radically transformed by their experience of God's love through the cross of Christ.[14] New concepts have to be found if necessary to capture this experience, and one reason for sacraments and other means of grace is to fathom the full length, height, depth, and breadth of the ocean of God's love. To explore the full intellectual ramifications of this is beyond our purpose here, but enough has been said to indicate the route to follow. On this route clear space can be found for the role of divine commands.

Clearly one such role they can play is to prevent us from straying too far from the path of moral truth. At this point we part company with the optimism of humanists like Nowell-Smith. As J. R. Lucas points out:

> Christians are . . . a good deal readier to recognise the necessity of having rules than Professor Nowell-Smith would be himself. This is because Christians take a much lower view of themselves than do humanists. They do not think that because they choose to do something, therefore it is right. On the contrary, the Christian believes that most of his unaided choices would have been likely to land him in chaos. The Christian differs from the humanist, therefore, in having a much livelier sense of the difficulty of leading the good life or coming to the knowledge of the truth.[15]

Relying on divine commands as a guide to moral decision does not, as Nowell-Smith suggests, entail an infantile morality. Reasons are given for such reliance; it is not a matter of blind obedience. Moreover, the hope is that spiritual growth and maturity will bring the freedom Nowell-Smith considers constitutive of the final stage of mature moral development. Lucas makes this point succinctly.

> The Old Testament element in Christian morality reflects . . . the fact of man's being imperfect. We need the Moral Law, St. Paul can be roughly rendered (Gal. 3:23), because we are not adult enough to take our decisions correctly. But when, and if, we come to a full knowledge of God's love, then we shall be emancipated from the shackles of the Law, and shall be able to enter into the full freedom of the Christian who takes all his decisions for himself, and being filled with the spirit of love takes them all correctly.[16]

We can thus dispose of Nowell-Smith's claim that a religious morality must necessarily be infantile. Can we as neatly dispose of Robinson's claim that it ille-

---

[13] Ibid., p. 107.

[14] For biblical warrant for this see 1 John 3:11–18.

[15] J. R. Lucas, "Discussion," in *Christian Ethics and Contemporary Society,* p. 132.

[16] Ibid., pp. 128–29.

gitimately attempts to derive an ought-statement from an is-statement? The literature on this topic is abundant, so whatever one says will sound hasty and inadequate.[17] Suffice it to say that believers can make one of three moves. Either they can challenge the view that it is a fallacy to derive an ought-statement from an is-statement; or they can argue that some is-statements provide good nonentailing reasons for an ought-statement;[18] or they can develop a moral vision which includes ought-statements as part of its developed structure.[19] In any case it should be remembered that Robinson's objection rests on a very simplistic version of a religious ethic which construes it rather crudely as obedience to divine commands. It is not obvious that the view sketched above falls foul of his stricture. Fully developed it can accommodate Robinson's objection.

Why is it important to develop such a religious ethic? Clearly it is important for theology. Believers need to explore in some detail and with some care what their moral vision involves. Exploring the relation between religion and morality encourages such exploration. There is a more general reason too. It was a common belief in the Victorian era that one could maintain the traditional moral convictions of the Western world without the underlying vision of life out of which they emerged. The latter was a fundamentally religious vision deeply informed by the Judaic-Christian heritage. This vision, it was said, could be discarded without loss. This claim, a century later, seems much less secure than it once was. Secular moralities have not been wholly successful in providing adequate warrant for even such a basic principle as the sanctity of life. This is a controversial claim, which often offends the secular mind, but it can be argued with considerable plausibility.[20] If it is at all true, then it would be a great pity if the full resources of a religious ethic remained hidden from sight. Philosophers of religion have a contribution to make in exploring afresh the option of a religious morality however modest that contribution may be.

---

[17] See, for example, W. D. Hudson, *The Is/Ought Question* (London: Macmillan, 1969).

[18] Robinson himself suggests this possibility. See *An Atheist's Values*, pp. 131–32.

[19] This option is briefly discussed in Philip L. Quinn, *Divine Commands and Moral Requirement*, pp. 45–46.

[20] See Mitchell, *Morality*. Cf. Alasdair MacIntyre, *After Virtue* (Notre Dame: University of Notre Dame, 1981).

Chapter Twelve
Grace And Freedom

In recent years philosophers have not given much attention to particular religious doctrines. This is understandable. On the one hand, philosophers prefer to remain in their own specialist domain and thus not run the risk of treading inelegantly on theological toes. On the other hand, they have recently been preoccupied with the meaning of religious discourse. Linguistic analysis and attention to religious doctrine meet, however, when we examine the relation between grace and freedom. The waters which swirl around this issue are deep, but they need not be muddy.

TENSION BETWEEN GRACE AND FREEDOM

It is a cardinal element in classical accounts of the Christian life that people are saved not by human effort but by divine grace. Salvation is ascribed to God's grace, hence God receives the praise and glory. Equally it has been a cardinal element in classical Christian thought that human beings are in some sense free when they enter into a personal relationship with God. If we are free, then salvation is impossible without our agreeing to it. Hence human beings do have a role, however minimal, in salvation. There is, therefore, a place for human beings to receive credit and glory for their salvation. Thus grace and freedom are incompatible; one or the other must be sacrificed if there is to be consistency.

Christian theologians have battled over this issue for centuries. The list of protagonists is impressive: Augustine versus Pelagius, Luther versus Erasmus, Calvin versus Pighius, Whitefield versus Wesley. One of the most interesting attempts to resolve the issue was offered by John Calvin (1509-64) and his followers. Much of this chapter will be taken up with his ideas. We begin with his account of human nature.

CALVIN'S SOLUTION

Human beings cannot save themselves because they are deeply enmeshed in sin. Without grace they are dead, unable to do anything to get out of their bondage. If a person becomes a Christian, it is entirely a matter of divine decision and action. Now experience shows that not everybody becomes a Christian. Why is this? Calvin offers a theological explanation for this state of affairs. Some people become Christians because God has given them saving grace; the rest remain as they are because God has not given them saving grace. God simply chooses that one group of people will receive grace and that the rest will not. In other words, God predestines some to eternal life and the rest to eternal death. Here is how Calvin explains this concept:

> We call predestination God's eternal decree by which he compacted with himself what he willed to become of each man. For all are not created in equal condition; rather eternal life is fore-ordained for some, eternal damnation for others. Therefore, as any man has been created to one or other of these ends, we speak of him as predestined to life or to death.[1]

Calvin is very clear about the ramifications of this doctrine of predestination. Predestination is clearly double in its scope: the reprobate or damned are not an incidental by-product; God quite literally chooses that they be so. Predestination is related specifically to individuals; it does not apply merely to groups. It is unconditional in its intention; God looks to nothing as the basis of his choices but his own inscrutable will for which no reason can be given. Moreover, predestination is the basis of God's foreknowledge. God knows what will take place in the future because he has decreed what will take place, and nothing can thwart his intentions. Indeed all that takes place is a matter of necessity, including the fall of Adam into sin. Adam had no free choice in the matter.

> They say that he had free choice that he might shape his own fortune, and that God ordaineth nothing except to treat a man according to his own deserts. If such a barren invention is accepted, where will that omnipotence of God be whereby he regulates all things according to his secret plan, which depends solely upon itself?[2]

[1] John Calvin, *Institutes of the Christian Religion,* ed. John T. McNeill, trans. Ford Lewis Battles (Philadelphia: Westminster Press, 1960), p. 926.
[2] Ibid., p. 955.

He concludes elsewhere:

> I shall not hesitate, then, simply to confess with Augustine that "the will of God is the necessity of things," and that which he has willed will of necessity come to pass, as those things which he has foreseen will truly come to pass.[3]

Clearly in this scheme of things there is no problem in ascribing salvation to God. It is all of God from beginning to end, and the Calvinist tradition has over time worked out the process of salvation in intimate detail. But where in the process is there any space for human freedom? And if there is no human freedom, how can God be considered just for condemning the reprobate for what he, God, has ordained should take place?

Calvin was somewhat impatient with these queries. He offered a two-fold answer. First, whatever God does is necessarily just even though we may not be able to show that it is just. Indeed we are not really in a position to question if it is just. He is very blunt about this. "For God's will is so much the highest rule of righteousness that whatever he wills, by the very fact that he wills it, must be considered righteous."[4] "Monstrous indeed is the madness of men, who desire thus to subject the immeasurable to the puny measure of their own reason."[5] This is a bold but hopeless way out. God indeed is just, and it may be difficult for human beings always to discern how his justice operates, but this is not what is at issue. At issue is Calvin's account of God's activity and whether that account embodies elementary moral insight about justice. Calvin too easily makes questioning his view of God look like questioning God. Fortunately, there is nothing monstrous about questioning Calvin's view of God; it is a duty both of faith and logic.

Happily, Calvin has a second and much more compelling line of defense. God is not unjust to damn the reprobate because the evil they do is brought about by causes that lie within them. ". . . man falls according as God's providence ordains, but he falls by his own fault."[6] When people sin, there is a kind of double agency in operation. When evil persons are damned, "their perdition depends on the predestination of God in such a way that the cause and the occasion of it are formed in themselves."[7] If this baffles us, Calvin urges us to

> contemplate the evident cause of condemnation in the corrupt nature of humanity—which is closer to us—rather than seek a hidden and utterly incomprehensible cause in God's predestination. And let us not be ashamed to submit our understanding to God's boundless wisdom so far as to yield before its many secrets. For of those things which it is neither given nor lawful to know, ignorance is learned; the craving to know a kind of madness.[8]

[3] Ibid., p. 956.
[4] Ibid., p. 949.
[5] Ibid., p. 952.
[6] Ibid., p. 957.
[7] Ibid.
[8] Ibid.

Calvin is sliding into dogmatism again, but his second argument is a powerful one. Calvin offers here an informal expression of a formal position which was worked out by later Calvinists like Jonathan Edwards. The latter is quite happy to speak of freedom and free will.[9] Indeed, the genius of his position is to offer an account of human freedom which is logically compatible with determinism. Proponents of this view generally refer to their position as soft determinism. Its essence is that free actions are those actions which are performed voluntarily. Voluntary acts are those acts an agent wants or wishes to do; they proceed from within the agent. Such acts are contrasted with involuntary acts; in this case the agent acts against his or her will; the acts are forced upon the agent externally, by constraint. In both cases there is determinism; both voluntary and involuntary actions have causes; only the former, however, are free, and they are the foundation for our ordinary conceptions of responsibility.

Applying this analysis to the problem in hand, we see how the Calvinist can retain a consistent account of divine grace, divine justice, and human freedom. God decrees everything that happens including the internal events in the life of an individual. In the case of the elect, God by giving them grace brings them to salvation. This is entirely of God, so there is no question of pride or credit accruing to human beings. In the case of the reprobate, God passes over them, deliberately decreeing them to perdition. They do not receive grace, so they are not saved. God, however, is not unjust, for they have voluntarily followed their evil inclinations and desires. The causes of their actions lie within; therefore they are free; therefore they merit divine judgment. Grace, justice, and freedom coexist in logical unison.

The appeal of this position over the years has been formidable. Aside from its internal coherence and theocentricity, proponents have welcomed its explanatory power and the comfort it gives. Its explanatory power rests in its explaining all events as the effects of divine decree. The simplicity of such an explanation is staggering. Just as the arrangement of all my books on my bookshelves before me is explained by my having placed them there in order to fulfill my purposes, so all events are really acts of God which fulfill his purposes. Further explanatory power derives from the way this theory accounts for the phenomenology of conversion. Converts like Augustine insist that they did not become Christians as a result of their choice. They were pursued relentlessly by God, who ultimately overcame their opposition by the power of irresistible grace. If Augustine, for example, had had his way, he would never have become a believer.

The comfort Calvin's position affords is also considerable. On the one hand, it provides a profound sense of divine providence. The most trivial event can be fraught with divine significance. Even the worst that happens is an act of God performed at his behest and therefore has some purpose in his sight. Also, the perils of contingency have been eliminated. If God's ultimate purposes depend in any way on free human choice, then it is logically possible for God's purposes to remain unfulfilled. In this case how can we be certain about the future? And if we cannot be

---

[9] Jonathan Edwards, *Freedom of the Will*, ed. A. S. Kaufman and W. K. Frankena (Indianapolis: Bobbs-Merrill, 1969).

certain of what will happen, how can we have any hope that God's plans will prevail? Moreover, if our salvation depends on our free choices, how can we have any assurance? If we know our true condition and its inevitable corruption devoid of divine grace, then any process which involves even the slightest effort of will has a crucially weak link in the chain of cause and effect. That link, apart from grace, is bound to break; hence assurance can be found only when God is entirely responsible for the whole process of salvation, stretching from eternity to eternity.

DIFFICULTIES IN CALVIN'S POSITION

This account of the relation between grace and freedom has always had its critics. It is not easy to be dispassionate in evaluating its claims. Historically it has evoked much moral outrage and personal despair. Many exposed to it have been haunted by the possibility that they have been damned from all eternity. This fear has been exacerbated by Calvin's claim that sometimes God gives all the basic marks of grace to the reprobate so that believers can never really be sure whether they are temporary believers or true believers.[10] This doctrine of temporary faith arises as an attempt to reconcile Calvin's views with key passages of scripture, and it too has evoked considerable controversy. I do not myself believe that Calvin's position can be squared with the demands of the canonical writings. However, this is irrelevant to our concern. What is at issue here is the internal coherence of Calvin's position.

It is highly questionable whether it is internally coherent. Everything hangs at this point on its account of human freedom. Without this, God becomes accountable for all moral evil, and he also seems unjust for punishing the reprobate. Two objections arise. First, it is not at all clear that human beings as seen in this tradition really are free, even in the soft-determinist sense. Certainly the actions of the reprobate come from within, but the antecedents of those actions are ultimately controlled from without, by God. The wishes, desires, beliefs, wants, and so on, which cause the actions of the reprobate are internal to them, but they are given and entirely controlled by divine providence. Compare a situation where we are hypnotized or given certain drugs. The acts of the hypnotist or the effects of the drugs produce within us certain beliefs, wishes, wants, and so on, which cause us to perform certain acts. Those acts stem from within, but we would not generally look upon them as free. They are caused by external agents and are therefore coerced or compelled in a strong sense. God, of course, in the Calvinist view, is not a hypnotist or a drug, but he is causally efficient in the same sense as hypnotists and drugs are, so the objection is entirely appropriate.

This objection can be expressed in a different way. Suppose we accept the Calvinist version of accountability, then consider what follows when we apply its canons to the true believer. The true believer performs some good acts, good that is,

---

[10]This issue is discussed at length in R. T. Kendall, *Calvin and English Calvinism to 1649* (Oxford: Oxford University Press, 1979).

to some degree, for Calvinists see all acts, even those of the redeemed, as tainted by sin. These acts have internal causes. They are brought about by wishes, wants, desires, beliefs, and the like. It is true, of course, that these are given by grace, for God rules them by particular providence, just as God rules the internal operations of the reprobate. Now if the reprobate must take the credit for the evil actions, so the elect must take the credit for the good acts. Good acts stem from within; therefore the elect are responsible for them; therefore they can have pride in them, boast about them, and claim merit for them. Rather than safeguard divine glory, the Calvinist tradition, therefore, destroys it at its foundations.

There is another objection to the Calvinist position. It is very questionable whether the conception of freedom on offer is at all adequate to render human agents responsible. Calvin's conception of freedom consists in agents doing what they want to do or choose to do. How adequate is this? Imagine you find yourself in a train carriage and you stop at your home station.[11] You stay on board because you want to travel on down the line to the next station to visit a friend. No one forces you against your will to stay; you voluntarily stay on board. Suppose, however, that five minutes before you arrive in your home station all exits from your carriage were automatically closed. The locking mechanism has failed and now shuts you in, but you are unaware of this. You sit on and get out at the next station, by which time the exits are open. Were you really free or were you just fortunate? On a more radical view of freedom, you were not free because you could not do otherwise. Freedom is not just a matter of doing what you want to, it is also a matter of being able to do otherwise. Even though you wanted to travel on, you could not do otherwise; hence you were not truly free. It was simply your good fortune that what you wanted to do coincided with what you had to do. You could certainly not be blamed for not getting out at your home station because you could not do otherwise.

The objection to Calvin's position based on this analysis is obvious. The reprobate do what they want; they sin and rebel to their hearts' content. They cannot, however, do otherwise. Given the desires, beliefs, wants, and so forth, that God has allotted them by his providence, they must act as they do. Hence they are not free or morally culpable for their actions. When they appear before God and are held accountable for not being honest, loving, patient, they can honestly say they could not do otherwise. Given the way God controls the inner operations of their lives, they had to act as they did.

Given these serious problems, it is not surprising that those who follow the Augustinian tradition have been thoroughly ambivalent in their commitment to freedom. Luther rejected it outright;[12] Calvin was uneasy with talk of free choice; modern popular Calvinists like J. I. Packer confess that the relation between pre-

---

[11] This example is prompted by a similar one borrowed from Locke by William L. Rowe, *Philosophy of Religion* (Belmont, Calif.: Wadsworth, 1978), p. 156.

[12] Martin Luther, *On the Bondage of the Will,* trans. J. I. Packer and O. R. Johnston (Westwood, N.J.: Fleming H. Revell, 1957).

destination and human action is a mystery or antimony which cannot be resolved.[13] We can, however, avoid such remedies when we take note of a suggestion made recently by J. R. Lucas.[14] Let us approach it by posing two critical questions. First, does the ascription of salvation to God entail that genuine human action is excluded? Secondly, does allowing for genuine human action in the total process of salvation entail giving credit to human agents for salvation? The answer to both questions is no.

Augustine, Calvin, and others were wrong to argue that ascribing salvation to God excluded human action because they failed to grasp the complex logic of causal explanation. When we use causal language, as when we say that God saves human beings from sin, that language is under tension. As Lucas points out, "Part of its sense is straining towards the ideal of complete cause, part towards the most significant cause."[15] In other words we use causal language in both a broad and a narrow way. Thus we use it, in the broad sense, to mean a complete specification of the antecedent, sufficient conditions of an event. For example, suppose a house catches fire and is burnt to the ground. A full causal explanation will call for a full account, say, of weather conditions, failure of the fire department to arrive in time, striking of matches, state of the wood, and laws governing combustion. With such descriptions the outcome is inevitable: given the preceding causes, the event must happen. However, we also use causal language, in the narrow sense, to pick out the most significant cause. Thus we say that the cause of the fire was the action of the arsonist, who deliberately ignited it with matches in order to make life more adventurous for himself and more difficult for the fire department. The arsonist's action, under this description, was the cause of the fire, and we take him to court to get compensation. In this case there is no inevitability. What we have done is pick out what is most significant from a legal point of view and refer to that as the cause.

Calvin ignores this crucial point. He conflates both senses of cause in his analysis of divine causality. Noting that believers ascribe salvation to God, he drew the consequences which only follow when it is used in the broader sense. He insists that the outcome is determined and inevitable. Hence he has enormous difficulty finding any place for human freedom or genuine human action. This is compounded when God is construed as the sole agent at work in the process. God is the agent of salvation; therefore there can be no other agency involved anywhere in the process. What we need to see is that language ascribing salvation to God is indeed causal language, but it should be interpreted in the narrow sense. When believers say that it is God alone who saves, they are simply picking out the most crucial agent at work in the whole process of salvation. This does not rule the activity of other agents, nor does it preclude genuine human freedom. Causal language used in the narrow sense has no such entailments. Calvin and his followers have been misled by the surface grammar of the language. We can allow logical space for human action without thereby excluding a sincere ascription of salvation to God.

[13] J. I. Packer, *Evangelism and the Sovereignty of God* (Downers Grove, Ill.: Inter-Varsity Press, 1961).

[14] Lucas, *Freedom and Grace* (London: SPCK, 1976).

[15] Ibid., p. 2.

HELM'S COUNTERPROPOSALS

Does this not open the door to human pride and credit? If human agents are involved, however minimally, are they not allowed a measure of pride and glory, however minimal? Paul Helm rightly raises this question.[16] He is worried that such an option is not excluded by non-Calvinist alternatives of the kind Lucas embraces. Helm approaches this issue from two directions. First, he wants to know why God should be construed as the crucial factor in salvation.

> Mr. Lucas claims, as part of his argument, that God is the most important causal factor in a man's salvation. No Christian is likely to demur. According to our changing interests we could count now this factor, now that, as the cause. But how could we establish in a more objective sense than this that God is the most important causal factor in a man's salvation? And in particular how could we establish this when, according to Mr. Lucas, there are other independent causal factors? Given that there is more than one contributory causal factor how does one ascribe to one of them more importance than the others? How can our judgment that one factor is more important than another factor in the production of some state of affairs be more than impressionistic when, as with God and his grace, no arithmetical measure of the size of the various causal factors is available? Suppose that someone was disposed to dispute the idea that the activity of God was the most important factor in a man becoming a Christian. How might he be convinced otherwise?[17]

Secondly, Helm argues that there is nothing in the logic of personal relations to exclude our taking pride in or credit for any action we have taken related to our salvation. His argument is ingenious. He sets it out as follows:

> A person's relation to God is based upon an act of free will. Every result brought about by A's free will is pride-allowing for A. Therefore, A's relation to God is pride-allowing.

He then asks what is wrong with this argument.

> Given that an action based on free will is pride-allowing, that a person's relationship with God is very desirable, why should one's relationship with God not be a matter of pride? Perhaps it is possible to argue that a person may be so impressed with God making his grace available that he will not think of expressing pride, even though both logically and morally he could. But what Mr. Lucas would say is that the possibility of someone being morally justifiably proud of his relationship to God, and *a fortiori* actual causes of such pride, could disfigure and perhaps ruin a person's relation with God. But why? If pride is allowable for acts of free will, then presumably God, being just, will recognise the facts of the situation, and recognise the propriety and legitimacy of one's taking pride in a freely chosen relationship with him. If credit is due, then a perfectly just being will give the credit.[18]

[16] Paul Helm, "Grace and Causation," *The Scottish Journal of Theology* XXXII (1979), 101–12. Published by Scottish Academic Press, Edinburgh.

[17] Ibid., pp. 102–3.

[18] Ibid., p. 108.

Helm refuses, therefore, to accept free will. Given free will, good manners might prevent us expressing our pride, but morality does not prevent us taking pride in our achievement.[19] The moral phenomenology of the Christian religion excludes the latter; hence we must reject free will as a logically necessary condition of a personal relation with God.[20] What shall we make of these arguments?

EVALUATION OF HELM'S ARGUMENTS

We should note that Helm has not offered an account of personal relations which excludes free will; he has merely suggested this as a way out for the Christian theologian. Certainly Helm has not proved that this possibility is available, and *prima facie* it is very odd to speak of a genuine personal relation without free will. This, however, is a controversial issue, and it is unlikely to be settled beyond dispute. At present Helm can rest his case by saying that the possibility of his alternative has not been disproved. He has every right to do so.

He is also right to argue that personal relations, logically speaking, are not pride excluding. We can certainly think of examples where people do take pride in those acts which initiated and sustained an important personal relationship. Many relationships require strenuous effort on our part and would collapse without that effort. But the issue is not simply one of logic. As Helm acknowledges, it is also a question of whether morality warrants taking pride. At this level Helm's objections display extraordinary theological insensitivity. It emerges in two ways.

First, he posits the need for some kind of arithmetical measure of the size of the causal factors in operation in salvation. Without this measure, claiming that God is the most significant agent in salvation remains for him vague and impressionistic. This is a typical expression of hard rationalism, which has only to be exposed to be rejected. Perfectly satisfactory theological arguments can be given why God must be construed as the utterly crucial agent in salvation without using the measuring rod imposed on the discussion by Helm. This takes us to the second level in insensitivity.

Helm is unaware of the obvious cogency of such arguments to rule out taking pride in those human actions related to salvation. Those arguments would involve factors such as an analysis of the human condition, the objective work of God in past history, the subjective activity of the Holy Spirit, and the role of external means of grace. Given these factors, it is not a matter of good manners that the believer does not take credit; it is a matter of sober theological reality, elementary moral insight, and personal religious experience.

An analogy will help make the point. Compare salvation to the recovery of an alcoholic from drunkenness. The alcoholic cannot cure himself; indeed admission of this is essential to a cure. The alcoholic must admit his need and then submit himself to a rigorous program of self-analysis, motivation, social support, and medication. The alcoholic cannot cure himself, yet his problem did not arise without the

---

[19] Ibid., p. 110.
[20] Helm hints at this. I have made the argument quite explicit.

exercise of his free will, nor can it be removed without that either. For him to claim pride in his cure ignores the complexity of his problem and makes moral nonsense of the facts of the situation. The phenomenology of Christian experience is much more complex than this analogy would suggest, but even a rudimentary analysis of the factors involved morally excludes any taking of credit or pride.

An accurate phenomenology of Christian experience will also incorporate two further considerations. First, it will not exaggerate the role of divine grace to the point where it becomes completely irresistible. At this point abstract talk about divine grace can be thoroughly misleading. We too readily picture divine grace as a kind of fluid to be poured into the machinery of human life to make it work. The machinery is inactive or works improperly until it receives the requisite supply of grace. Once the grace is poured in, it works automatically; the fluid's activity is irresistible. God indeed pursues, woos, and even overwhelms converts, so that in some moods they want to speak of irresistible grace. But this is not the whole story and should not be treated as the whole truth. Converts also know that they can and do resist God's love and grace.

Secondly, an accurate account of Christian experience will be aware of the pitfalls of causal language. As Lucas points out, there are subtle pressures at work which would bring in merit through the back door again.[21] As was noted, when we pick out something as the most significant cause, we normally accompany it with an ascription of praise. That this is so in the case of God goes without saying. There are circumstances where we may want to insist, however, on human decision as a crucial ingredient in the whole process of salvation. We might do so in a philosophical discussion on the nature of persons, in a religious context where people are spiritually asleep, or in an evangelistic context, and so on. Given our normal tendency to ascribe praise when we use causal language to pick out the most important factor in the total process, the door is open for merit to creep in unnoticed. At this point our fat egos seize on the subtleties of language to deceive and delude us. Sound linguistic analysis can keep us humble in such circumstances.

The conclusion we have reached is that grace and freedom are compatible. We can hold to both without committing ourselves to the dubious analysis of freedom presented by the Calvinist tradition. In rejecting this element in the Calvinist position we will also need to reject several other tenets. In other words, we will need to reject Calvin's account of predestination, divine foreknowledge, divine providence, personal assurance, and future hope. This does not mean that such concepts are excluded from our theological vocabulary. All it means is that they will be given either different meanings or different warrants in a rival theological vision of God and salvation. The construction of such a vision lies within the field of systematic theology, so it shall not detain us here. Suffice it to say that the ingredients of such a vision have been long available in the history of Christian thought and that the philosopher can have a modest but genuine role to play in its articulation in our own day.

---

[21] Lucas, *Freedom and Grace*, p. 11.

Chapter Thirteen
Miracles

Outside the classical arguments for the existence of God, few religious issues have excited as much philosophical interest as that of miracles. Its discussion is virtually mandatory in philosophy of religion. Thankfully it is not a question which has grown stale with the years, for it is a delight to explore it in detail. Yet many have remained thoroughly dissatisfied with the standard philosophical discussions. More particularly, many theologians have felt that the classical definition of miracle much beloved by philosophers has been both inadequate and subversive. It has been inadequate because it imported into religion a conception of miracle which was not there in the first place. It has been subversive because it has evoked or inspired a conception of divine action which has virtually banished God from the universe. What makes this protest especially interesting is that it cuts across some of the great divides within theology. Both conservatives and liberals have felt ill at ease with what philosophers have written. In what follows I plan to mediate the classical discussion of miracles while remaining sensitive to the concerns of the modern theologian. Let us begin by sorting out the many questions which arise from the topic of miracle.

QUESTIONS RAISED BY MIRACLES

The theme of miracles covers a multitude of issues. For the sake of convenience it is worth dividing them into three broad classes. There are, first, those questions which relate to an adequate definition of miracle. What is a miracle? Is the concept of miracle coherent? Does it do justice to those events in the Bible commonly referred to as miracles? Are miracles something God alone does, or can other agents conceivably perform them? Is the concept of miracle inevitably elusive, covering events of different magnitude? How do we distinguish miracles from marvels? Are miracles necessarily public and visible in their nature?

The second class of questions focuses on the issue of evidence for or against miracles. Are miracles necessarily improbable? Are there occasions when they are more likely to occur than not to occur? What kind of evidence is relevant in deciding for or against the truth of the report of a miracle? Are there particular passions or dispositions which make us prone to either believe or disbelieve? Is there a special kind of evidence relevant to evaluating reports of miracles? Is it possible for the sceptic to hold out indefinitely against accepting a reported miracle as a miracle? Is it ever rational to believe in miracles?

The third class of questions hangs on the significance of miracle. How central are miracles to the great religions of the world? Can one dispense with miracles without shedding any theological tears? How should miracles stories be appropriated in the life of faith today? Does God perform miracles in the present? Do miracles provide any evidence for belief in God? Can they function as warrants for a divine revelation in history? Are miracles necessarily an embarrassment or stumbling block for modern religious belief?

Philosophical interest in miracle covers all three types of questions enumerated. Thus philosophers have sought to develop an adequate conception of miracle, have reflected at length on the nature of relevant evidence, and have been interested in the apologetic significance of miracles. The discussion here will remain loyal to the full range of the classical philosophical discussion. Let us proceed in the order outlined.

THE CLASSICAL DEFINITION

Clearly we need at the outset a relatively stable definition of what a miracle is. The classical definition is an excellent point at which to begin. Miracles, on this view, are events which violate a law of nature and which are brought about by God or some other invisible agent. This definition has two elements. First, it contrasts miracles with ordinary events in nature by saying that they are contrary to what usually or naturally happens. So much so that they violate laws of nature. Secondly, this definition attributes miracles to the activity of some invisible, supernatural, personal agent. It is thus strictly speaking a deliberate act; it is an event brought about by a personal agent for certain intentions or purposes.

Why have so many people been unhappy with this conception of the miraculous? Samuel M. Thompson provides a useful summary of some of the key protests.

> The notion of *miracle* as something which happens in nature and is contrary to the laws of nature is a curiously confused concept. In the first place, no such conception can be found in the Biblical sources of the Hebrew-Christian tradition, for those sources did not have the conception of natural law. To call an event a *miracle* is to call it a "marvel," and to say that it evokes wonder and awe. It is to say that the event is inexplicable apart from its supernatural significance. Even if direct intervention by God occurs in nature only ignorance can make it appear capricious. Whatever it is, it has its explanation and it fits the rational order of being. If we cannot account for it in terms of the natural order it is because the natural order is not the whole of the rational order of being. We have to assume that complete knowledge would show us the absolute harmony of divine and natural causation in every event.[1]

Thompson is claiming here at least three things. First, he claims that the classical conception of miracle is incompatible with the Bible. Secondly, that unless we are careful it makes miracles appear capricious. Thirdly, that it contradicts the assured theological claim that God always acts through natural causes. Consequently, the standard notion of miracle is unhelpful and confused. Unfortunately for Thompson, however, none of his claims are very convincing.

To begin, those who want to retain it need not worry if this definition is not found in the Bible. It is simply naive and irrationally restrictive to lock ourselves in to Biblical concepts in either theology or philosophy of religion. This scarcely needs to be argued. We are duty bound to find those concepts which are most useful to do justice to all the relevant data. Within the data the biblical sources constitute one element of vital importance, but it is not the only consideration relevant to an adequate definition of miracle. Even as it stands, Thompson's use of the biblical sources is inadequate. Although the biblical writers do not technically have a conception of natural law, some of them clearly have a kind of common-sense idea of natural law. They have a very definite conception of events which are contrary to what is normal.[2] What matters here is not whether we restrict ourselves to the biblical material but whether, given what we now believe, we need to use the classical notion of miracle to do justice to what the biblical writers at times report as happening.

When we bear this in mind, Thompson's alternative is not as attractive as it might initially appear. We can agree that miracles and marvels both evoke awe and wonder for they are events of religious significance to the believer. But does the concept of marvel do justice to what is involved in events like the virgin birth or the resurrection of Jesus? Note that we are not at this point asking whether these events happened; our concern is how best to describe them. It seems much more sensible

---

[1] Samuel M. Thompson, *A Modern Philosophy of Religion* (Chicago: Henry Regnery, 1955), pp. 454–55.
[2] John 9:32; Matt. 1:19.

to look for something stronger than a marvel to do justice to their extraordinary nature. Indeed the reason why they make us stop and wonder is that they seem to be clean contrary to what we normally experience. In other words, they violate a law of nature. Therefore, if the biblical writers were alive today, they might well be tempted, if not wholly persuaded, to accept this as an accurate portrayal of their claims. Hence I do not believe that the classical conception of miracle is incompatible with the Bible.

Of course, miracles fundamentally evoke awe and wonder because they are held to be deliberate acts of God. It is this which guarantees their religious significance. It also undermines Thompson's second argument. Miracles as classically understood are not at all capricious, nor need they even appear to be so. On the contrary, they are fully and adequately explicable as acts of God brought about to achieve his intentions and purposes. They are not, therefore, bolts from the blue but events causally related to the personal agency of God, who acts as he deems appropriate. Thompson was misled, at this point, very understandably and naturally because he ignored the second crucial element in the classical notion of miracle. He half realizes that what makes miracles explicable is precisely their relation to the divine, but he does not explore this in any depth. He thinks that an event contrary to nature may appear to be capricious. But this is false. If God brings that event about, it is not at all capricious but entirely rational given his intentions and purposes. Whether God on any particular occasion violates a law of nature is not under our control. Hence Thompson has no right to assume that complete knowledge would show us the absolute harmony of divine and natural causation in every event. We cannot decide in advance of actual investigation if God always acts through natural causes. Therefore, Thompson's third argument also collapses.

Thompson's third argument may well reflect a strong desire to provide a uniform theory of divine action. On this view, whenever God acts he always operates in, with, and through natural agents and causes. This has considerable attraction. It attempts to provide one simple, comprehensive account of all divine action. Moreover, it avoids any clash with science, for it suggests that naturalistic explanations of events will always be compatible with theistic explanations of events. In addition, it sees God at work in everything which happens, thus bringing God into the heart and soul of all of life. By contrast, belief in miracles seems to relegate divine action to the gaps in our knowledge of the world.

This alluring vision, however, has its obvious defects. It certainly does justice to some divine action, notably that divine action commonly known as providence. In this case God acts in, with, and through events of nature and history without directly intervening in the natural order of events. But this is only one class of divine action. We cannot presume that it is the only type of divine action, treating divine providential activity as the paradigm case for all divine action. Clearly creation *ex nihilo,* a central tenet of classical theism, does not fit this account of divine action, so as a general theory of divine action it fails at the first fence in the race for success. What has misled us here is the quest for the wrong kind of general theory. I see no reason to suppose that divine action must somehow satisfy some general pattern of the kind proposed. God can act in many and varied ways. General theories of how he acts must proceed inductively, working with the full range of acts which prima facie have been attributed to God. Paradigm cases of divine action must cover the case of divine creation, cases of providence, and cases of miracle. There may also be cases of divine intervention which do not involve miracle.[3]

Whether reports of particular divine acts or classes of divine acts are incompatible with scientific explanations of the same events must be taken on a case-by-case basis. I shall argue later that, in itself, failure to be scientifically explicable is not something which should worry us.[4] Moreover, the believer in miracles does not at all banish God from the heart and soul of creation. That only happens when all divine action is conceived as miraculous and this idea we have already rejected. Curiously, this is another point where the quest for generality can so easily mislead. Suffice it to note that the wary will not limit divine action to the case of miracles. God has created and continually sustains the universe. He may also have intervened and performed miracles. Asserting the latter in no way entails the denial of the former so long as the diversity of divine action is kept in mind.

Up to this point I have argued that those who hold to the classical conception of miracles can be thoroughly sensitive to the Bible and to both the complexity and the religious significance of divine action in the world. This, however, is not enough to settle the issue. There are two further arguments which deserve attention. The first I shall call the relativity of science arguments, the second, the ordinary language argument.

The former argument makes much of the fact that our knowledge of laws of nature is always relative to the scientific beliefs of the day. When we come across an event which appears miraculous, it may simply be that we have an inadequate account of nature. Reports of miracles call for a revision of our understanding of nature which accommodates the described events according to hitherto unknown laws of nature. Thus so long as we can conceive of revising laws of nature, then miracles will always turn out to be non-miracles.

We can illustrate this by means of an example. Suppose we had a time machine, and we could speak directly to our ancestors. Suppose we told them about traveling to outer-space or about talking to one another through wires or watching athletic games on glass screens. They would almost certainly think of such events as miracles. We, however, given what we know, could never agree with them, for our account of the actual laws of nature is so much richer than theirs. Extend this into the future, and we can imagine how what we now might think of as miraculous could turn out in time to be an entirely natural occurrence.

This argument fails because it exaggerates the extent to which we can *practically* expect accounts of laws of nature to be revised. Abstract, logical possibilities are not enough at this point. If we are to take science seriously as a form of knowl-

---

[3] This could be the case of divine speaking. See William J. Abraham, *Divine Revelation and the Limits of Historical Criticism* (Oxford: Oxford University Press, 1982), chap. 1.

[4] See chap. 15.

edge, then we must grant that some laws of nature really are known. Further revisions in them are not seriously countenanced, not even in those cases where we have to resort to statistical probability, as has happened at the microscopic level of explanation. Much common sense captures this fact. We expect water to boil at certain temperatures relative to height above sea level; we expect those who have had their throats cut to die; we expect corpses to stay dead and plan our lives accordingly; we allow doctors to perform operations only because we are certain that they can predict what will happen next. Not all laws of science are open to revision in the way envisaged in the relativity-of-science argument. Scientists, for all their humility and openness to future counterevidence, are less in the dark than this argument insists. Hence a violation of a law of nature—a miracle—is perfectly conceivable.[5]

What of the ordinary-language argument? The claim in this case is that our usage of the term *miracle* is much less restrictive than the classical account will allow. It is used to cover almost anything which evokes awe and wonder. Even theism, as J. L. Mackie points out, can count as a miracle on this view.[6] Within this general usage, it especially refers to extraordinary coincidences of a beneficial nature, as R. F. Holland has argued.[7]

Proponents of the classical definition of miracle can choose between two entirely satisfactory strategies to answer this objection. First, they can offer to revise ordinary usage on the grounds that the concept of miracle loses its value when, like money, it is allowed to become too inflated. Somehow something is lost if miracles become too commonplace. Secondly, they can offer to distinguish between stronger and weaker conceptions of miracle. Thus we might treat violations of laws of nature as satisfying the stronger criterion; all the rest can be construed as satisfying the weaker criterion. As we turn to the question of evidence, it is the stronger conception which will detain us here.

HUME'S OBJECTIONS TO MIRACLES

One of the most interesting discussions of the nature of relevant evidence is that furnished by David Hume. Hume may have developed his ideas somewhat tongue in cheek, but it is very profitable to peruse in some detail the main points of his argument. Hume held that it was thoroughly irrational to believe in miracles. He reached that conclusion by deploying one central, philosophical argument backed up by four subsidiary, historical arguments. His philosophical point is pivotal to his whole case and can be summarized as follows.

When confronted with the story of a miracle, we have to make up our minds as to whether we shall believe it or not. This is especially so if the story has any kind

---

[5] I discuss this argument at some length in *Divine Revelation*, pp. 32–36.

[6] J. L. Mackie, *The Miracle of Theism* (Oxford: Clarendon Press, 1982), p. 12.

[7] R. F. Holland, "The Miraculous," *American Philosophical Quarterly* II (1965), 43–51.

of universal and therefore personal religious significance. How, however, are we to evaluate the story? What canons of thought lead us to accept it or reject it? Clearly where events in the past are concerned we rely very fundamentally on testimony. Someone reports what has happened and we believe it. But this is not always the case. Although initially we might believe what is reported, on balance we might come to reject what is reported as false. According to Hume, this rests on the fact that our believing testimony to past events rests on inductive evidence about the relation between testimony and its conformity to fact. It is general experience which establishes testimony as a source of truth about the past. In any particular case we may come therefore to reject the testimony because it falls foul of our general experience. As Hume puts it, "A man delirious, or noted for falsehood and villainy, has no authority over us."[8]

Consider now the case of a miracle. This by definition is an event which violates a law of nature. It runs counter to all our past experience. No matter how good the testimony may seem, it will be counterweighed by all our experience. The rational person will weigh one against the other and attempt to strike a balance. In this process the evidence against miracle will always outweigh that produced by testimony. Hence it will never be rational to believe in miracles. Proportioning the evidence to belief, the wise person will always come down against miracles. Hume summed it up admirably as follows:

> A miracle is a violation of the laws of nature; and as a firm and unalterable experience has established these laws, the proof against a miracle, from the very nature of the fact, is as entire as any argument from experience can possibly be imagined. Why is it more than probable, that all men must die; that lead cannot, of itself, remain suspended in the air; that fire consumes wood, and is extinguished by water; unless it be, that these events are found agreeable to the laws of nature, and there is required a violation of these laws, or in other words, a miracle to prevent them? Nothing is esteemed a miracle, if it ever happen in the common course of nature. It is no miracle that a man, seemingly in good health, should die on a sudden: because such a kind of death, though more unusual than any other, has yet been frequently observed to happen. But it is a miracle, that a dead man should come to life; because that has never been observed in any age or country. There must, therefore, be a uniform experience against every miraculous event, otherwise the event would not merit that appellation. And as a uniform experience amounts to a proof, there is here a direct and full proof, from the nature of the fact, against the existence of any miracle; nor can such a proof be destroyed, or the miracle rendered credible, but by an opposite proof, which is superior.[9]

Hume drives home this conclusion by deploying four subsidiary arguments which are mostly historical in nature. Thus when Hume gets down to examine particular claims about miracles, he claims to show that "there never was a miraculous event established."[10] His reasons are these.

[8] David Hume, *Enquiries* (Oxford: Oxford University Press, 1975), p. 112.
[9] Ibid., pp. 114–15.
[10] Ibid., p. 116.

First, the number, education, integrity, and reputation of those who report a miracle leave much to be desired.

> For first, there is not to be found, in all history, any miracle attested by a sufficient number of men, of such unquestioned good-sense, education, and learning, as to secure us against all delusion in themselves; of such undoubted integrity, as to place them beyond all suspicion of any design to deceive others; of such credit and reputation in the eyes of mankind, as to have a great deal to lose in case of their being detected in any falsehood; and at the same time, attesting facts performed in such a public manner and in so cele-brated a part of the world, as to render the detection unavoidable. All which circumstances are requisite to give us a full assurance in the testimony of men.[11]

Secondly, people generally have a tendency to love stories of surprise and wonder, especially so in the case of religious believers as they are subject to fanati-cism, vanity, self-interest and impudence.

> With what greediness are the miraculous accounts of travellers received, their descriptions of sea and land monsters, their relations of wonderful adventures, strange men, and uncouth manners? But if the spirit of religion join itself to the love of wonder, there is an end of common sense; and human testimony, in those circumstances, loses all pretensions to authority.[12]

Thirdly, reports of miracles invariably come to us from primitive and un-civilized societies.

> It forms a strong presumption against all supernatural and miraculous re-lations, that they are observed chiefly to abound among ignorant and barba-rous nations; or if a civilized people has ever given admission to any of them, that people will be found to have received them from ignorant and barba-rous ancestors, who transmitted them with that inviolable sanction and authority, which always attend received opinion.[13]

Fourthly, when we take seriously the claims to miracles found within the various religious traditions of the world, then they indirectly undermine each other. If certain miracles are the foundation of a particular religion, then they indirectly disconfirm the truth of a rival religion together with its miracles. But if we start with the rival religion and take its miracles seriously, they indirectly disconfirm the claims of the first religion we encountered, together with its miracles. Either way, the testimony to one set of miracles cancels out the testimony to the other.

> To make this the better understood, let us consider, that, in matters of re-ligion, whatever is different is contrary; and that it is impossible the religions of ancient Rome, of Turkey, of Siam, and of China should, all of them, be

[11] Ibid., pp. 116–17.
[12] Ibid., p. 117.
[13] Ibid., p. 119.

established on any solid foundation. Every miracle, therefore, pretended to have been wrought in any of these religions (and all of them abound in miracles) as its direct scope is to establish the particular system to which it is attributed; so has it the same force, though more indirectly, to overthrow every other system. In destroying a rival system, it likewise destroys the credit of those miracles, on which that system has established; so that all the prodigies of different religions are to be regarded as contrary facts, and the evidences of these prodigies, whether weak or strong, as opposite to each other.[14]

ASSESSMENT OF HUME'S SUBSIDIARY POINTS

Hume's discussion of miracles is a model of lucid philosophical prose. Yet one can easily wonder if he was really giving miracles the kind of serious attention they deserve. For one thing, Hume's central philosophical argument does not integrate altogether naturally with his own earlier account of causality.[15] Hume argued that our belief in the uniformity of nature was a matter of habit and association rather than reason. But when he comes to discuss miracles, he treats the uniformity of nature as a proof against the possibility of miracle. These two claims clearly conflict. If the uniformity nature is not established by *reason* it cannot be a *proof* against miracle. Moreover, Hume at the end of his discussion suggests that really his arguments are a splendid defense of miracles, offering them as a way of confounding the enemies of the Christian religion. But this undermines his earlier self-congratulation at having discovered "an everlasting check to all kinds of superstitious delusion."[16] One such delusion in his view is belief in miracle. Also, in Hume's subsidiary arguments one has a distinct sense that there is an air of unreality about them. They constitute a very clever piece of writing, but Hume never really comes to grips with a particular and significant case of miracle. He works in a historical vacuum. Indeed, throughout the discussion one feels that Hume has already made up his mind in advance and that he is skillfully casting around for any argument which will be useful in confirming his initial prejudices. It rather looks as if reason has been the slave of his passions.

Arguments, however, are not in themselves discredited by their tone or their psychological origin. Hence Hume's position deserves to be examined seriously. Certainly Hume's influence has been phenomenal, and it is tempting to look upon subsequent opposition to miracles as little more than learned footnotes to Hume. Let us begin with his subsidiary points.

Hume's first and third arguments make the same general point. They impugn the intellectual ability of those who report miracles either because of their ancient setting or because of their lack of education, integrity, and the like. Hume must be careful here if he is not to beg the question. He must not use belief in miracle as a sign of intellectual credulity and then rely on intellectual credulity as an argument

[14] Ibid., pp. 121–22.
[15] Ibid., sec. iv.
[16] Ibid., p. 110.

against miracle. Hume does not do this explicitly, so we should give him the benefit of the doubt. Our suspicions are aroused simply because he offers no substantial evidence for his generalization. Even if he did, it would be of limited value, for generalizations of the kind Hume offers are rather dubious. At best they make us cautious and suggest that we be on guard. As an argument against a particular miracle story, they do not help much either way.

Hume's second argument is even less helpful. On this occasion Hume appeals to the tendency in human nature to believe what is marvelous and unusual. Hume's observation clearly carries weight, but it completely overlooks one salient fact which cancels it out in the debate about miracle. It should not escape our notice that our passions can also easily lead us to reject miracles uncritically. First, the touch of arrogance in the self-congratulation which would see ourselves, without belief in miracle, as enlightened and our ancestors, with belief in miracle, as barbaric and uncivilized, certainly boosts our ego. In other words, there is considerable personal and social pressure in some circles against belief in miracles which makes it prone for those influenced by such pressure to dismiss them out of hand without serious examination. Secondly, Hume never looks beyond the bare assertion of a miracle to see the penetrating and drastic upheaval belief in miracle may initiate in a person's life. If one claims to believe in, say, the resurrection of Jesus, the implications, when this belief is taken seriously, are profound and costly, involving radical reversals in one's life-style and moral behavior. When this is realized, the passion against belief in miracle can be considerable.[17] In the New Testament miracles are intended to bring us to radical repentance.[18] People do not welcome such a prospect with manifest enthusiasm. Once we realize this, Hume's third argument collapses. Perhaps unbelief is our more natural reaction to miracles when we really see what they involve. Certainly, if bare assent to propositions about miracle does not begin to touch what real belief involves in religion, Hume's account of the role of our passions is extraordinarily superficial.

His account of the relation between rival religious traditions as enshrined in his fourth subsidiary argument is also superficial. The issues here are far more complex than Hume or his Christian contemporaries could allow. Suffice it to report Richard Swinburne's verdict.

> ...evidence for a miracle "wrought in one religion" is an only evidence against the occurrence of a miracle "wrought in another religion" if the two miracles, if they occurred, would be evidence for propositions of the two religious systems incompatible with each other. It is hard to think of alleged miracles of this type.[19]

Hume does not begin to take his very general argument close to this requirement.

I conclude, therefore, that Hume's subsidiary arguments are unsuccessful. The first and third are based on a weak generalization, which at best bids us be cautious.

[17]This is clearly seen in the reaction to the miracle in John 9.

[18]See Luke 10:13–15.

[19]Richard Swinburne, *The Concept of Miracle* (London: Macmillan, 1970), p. 60.

The second ignores contrary considerations about the role of passion in unbelief. The fourth is simplistic and inconclusive. This is important because it is tempting to fall back on these arguments when Hume's central argument runs into difficulty. J. L. Mackie hints at this possibility in a carefully developed assessment of Hume's discussion. Mackie gives Hume's subsidiary arguments a double twist. First, he extracts a fifth subsidiary argument from Hume. He suggests that religious believers have added reason to the credulous because "credulity is often thought to be meritorious, while doubt or critical caution is felt to be sinful."[20] This is really a variation on Hume's second argument. As such it is one more generalization, which vastly oversimplifies the complex relation between faith and reason within responsible religious communities. Clearly it ignores those injunctions which urge great caution when confronted with signs and wonders.[21]

Mackie's second twist is to suggest that Hume's points, though of unequal force when taken in isolation, when taken together "provide grounds for a high degree of initial scepticism about every alleged miracle."[22] Mackie is deploying a classical cumulative-case argument, so formally he is entirely correct. Materially, however, Hume's subsidiary points reduce in the end to three, and of these only one counts for much. We do well to bear in mind at this juncture the advice of another admirer of Hume, Antony Flew.

> We have here to insist upon a sometimes tricky distinction: between, on the one hand, the valid principle of the accumulation of evidence, where every item has at least some weight in its own right; and, on the other hand, the Ten-leaky-buckets-Tactic, applied to arguments none of which hold water at all.[23]

EVALUATION OF HUME'S MAIN ARGUMENT

We turn now to an assessment of Hume's main philosophical argument against miracle. According to Hume, miracles, because they are clean contrary to our general experience as expressed in our belief in laws of nature, are intrinsically improbable. What shall we make of this claim and the argument Hume advances in its favor?

Hume is on to something here which is extremely interesting. We can make this point by a simple thought experience. Suppose I were to meet you in the street and tell you that my grandmother had just come back from the dead. You would hesitate before believing me. Because of the principle of initial credulity you would listen, but you would be puzzled and would almost certainly treat my remarks as a joke or as a misobservation or even a lie. Why is this? Surely the answer lies within sight of Hume's central argument. It is because this occurrence goes against our

[20] Mackie, *Miracle of Theism,* pp. 15–16.
[21] Mark 13:21–23.
[22] Mackie, *Miracle of Theism,* p. 16.
[23] Antony Flew, *God and Philosophy* (London: Hutchinson, 1966), p. 141.

general experience of death and its aftermath. Compare your reaction to hearing of the death of my grandmother. In this case initial credulity would go through without any obstacle. Hume, therefore, is entirely correct to insist that there is something intrinsically improbable about miracle. He is wrong, however, to take this point to its logical limit and say that it will always be wrong to believe in a miracle. This is so for several reasons.

First, Hume underestimates the place of testimony in determining our beliefs. When confronted with good, independent witnesses who have nothing to gain, we may have to grant that a law of nature has to be abandoned, thus showing that general experience does not have conclusive weight every time. This point is well made by C. D. Broad.

> Clearly many propositions have been accounted laws of nature because of an invariable experience in their favor, then exceptions have been observed, and finally these propositions have ceased to be regarded as laws of nature. But the first reported exception was, to anyone who had not personally observed it, in precisely the same position as a story of a miracle, if Hume be right.[24]

Secondly, Hume ignores other important sources of evidence for miracle. Two deserve mention. First, there is the whole range of indirect evidence. For example, in the case of the resurrection of Jesus there are such considerations as reports about the empty tomb, the radical change and boldness of the disciples despite the crucifixion, the conversion of Paul, the spread of the Christian faith, the theological developments in early Christianity directly related to the resurrection, and so on. Such evidence bears considerable weight, yet Hume pays no attention to it.

In addition, there are important theological considerations, which have to be weighed very sensitively. The point this time is that Hume totally ignores the fact that a miracle by definition is an act of God brought about to achieve certain intentions and purposes. This introduces a whole new dimension, which is either glossed over or treated in a flat-footed manner. Mackie, for example, contends that "the usual purpose of stories about miracles is to establish the authority of the particular figures who perform them or are associated with them. . . ."[25] This is a misleading half-truth, which overlooks the varied reasons why God may perform a miracle. If we must speak in general terms, miracles in the Christian tradition need to be seen as part of the vast redemptive purposes of God. The relevance of this to belief in miracle is well expressed by Austin Farrer.

> What Christians find in Christ through faith inclines them at certain points to accept with regard to him testimony about matters of fact which would be inconclusive if offered with regard to any other man. The Christian who refused to take that step would in my opinion be pedantic and irrational, like a man who required the same guarantee for trusting a friend which he would re-

[24] C. D. Broad, "Hume's Theory of the Credibility of Miracles," *Proceedings of the Aristotelian Society XVII* (1916-17), pp. 77-94.

[25] Mackie, *Miracle of Theism*, p. 13.

quire for trusting a stranger. Thus it is possible through faith and evidence together, and through neither alone, to believe that Christ corporeally rose from the dead, not merely that his death on the cross had a silver lining significant for our salvation.[26]

Farrer speaks here of faith in contrast to evidence. Perhaps it were better to speak of different kinds of evidence, some internal and some external. The evidence he hints at is that furnished by religious experience. But this is part of a wider set of phenomena which includes putative divine action in creation, in history, in the lives of the prophets and apostles, and in providence as well as in one's own personal experience. In other words, besides considering such external evidence as that furnished by direct testimony and indirect consequence, we need to take into account considerations which are internal to the religious tradition in which the miracle story is to be found. This is a complex matter, but it is not to be ignored.[27]

THE APOLOGETIC SIGNIFICANCE OF MIRACLE

In conclusion, something should be said about the apologetic value of miracle. It is common to draw a distinction at this point between two sorts of situations. Thus we can imagine a debate about the reality and significance of a miracle between theists of different religious persuasions. Equally we can imagine a debate between a theist and an atheist or agnostic. It is in this latter context that we locate the question of the primary apologetic value of a miracle.

Prima facie it would seem that miracles can have no apologetic value. This follows from the fact that the believer will appeal to theistic considerations in order to confirm other evidence to a miracle. In other words, far from miracles' constituting evidence for God, evidence for God constitutes evidence of a general sort for miracles. But this need not necessarily be the whole story. We can envisage a situation where a miracle could be weak evidence for theism.

Consider a case where someone witnesses, say, a major healing. If there is direct personal experience, if there is good supporting testimony, if there is a religious context such as that supplied by prayer or laying on of hands, if there is no plausible alternative explanation, then the event designated as a miracle will serve to give some evidence for the existence of God. The underlying logic is that of the argument from design. The event concerned exhibits a degree of design which is explained by the activity of God. It can therefore take its place in a cumulative-case argument for religious belief. The evidence will be cautious and modest, so those who want more decisive arguments will be disappointed. Others, like the Syrophoenician woman in the Gospels, may be well satisfied with the crumbs which fall from a miracle's table.[28]

[26] Austin Farrer, "An English Appreciation," in *Kerygma and Myth,* ed. Hans Werner Bartsch (New York: Harper and Row, 1961), p. 220.
[27] I sketch more fully what is at stake in *Divine Revelation,* pp. 132–37.
[28] Mark 7:28.

Chapter Fourteen
Revelation

The idea of revelation has come to have a peripheral position in modern philosophy of religion. Those working in the tradition of linguistic analysis have ignored it, which is surely strange, for revelation is an interesting and significant concept in religion. Those who have written about it tend to borrow analyses of the idea from a favored theological tradition. Thus John Hick relies on a concept of revelation developed by a school of modern biblical scholars.[1] To find an original philosophical account of revelation one has to reach back to idealists like William Temple.[2] Let us begin our discussion by asking why revelation tends to have a marginal status in philosophy of religion.

PHILOSOPHICAL AVERSION TO REVELATION

It is very understandable why philosophers should be reluctant to discuss the topic of revelation. Aside from the general abuse of revelation when it is used as a warrant for bizarre, dangerous, or self-serving courses of action, there are obvious reasons

---

[1]John Hick, *Philosophy of Religion* (Englewood Cliffs, N.J.: Prentice-Hall, 1973), pp. 59–67.

[2]William Temple, *Nature, Man and God* (London: Macmillan, 1935), chap. 12. One obvious exception to this would be the work of Austin Farrer. See his *The Glass of Vision* (London: Dacre Press, 1948); *Faith and Speculation* (London: Adam and Charles Black, 1967), chap. 6.

why philosophers shy away from it. Austin Farrer draws attention to two of them. First, philosophy claims to work with what is reasonable, while revelation suggests something secured by authority. The idea of revealed truth seems a priori objectionable:

> For philosophy is reasonable examination, and must resist the claim of any doctrine to exempt itself from criticism. And revealed truth is commonly said to be accepted on the mere authority of its revealer; not on any empirical evidence for it, nor on any logical self-evidence contained in it.[3]

Secondly, in discussing revelation it is impossible to avoid falling into writing theology pure and simple.

> Revelation is what God manifestly does, and is shown to be possible by His doing it. All we can do with it is to unfold it, to explain by any means we have what is said to have been received by those who claim to have received it; and this is just Christian, or some other, theology.[4]

Philosophers, therefore, understandably keep their distance for many do not want to get involved in the details of religious doctrine. Theologians from their side are happy to encourage this, not necessarily because they want to monopolize the territory but because they know that any fruitful account of revelation in the Christian tradition must ultimately reckon with the chief source of revelation, the biblical traditions. Philosophers tend to be removed from this area due to the vast, specialist industry related to biblical studies. Their natural inclination is to assimilate revelation to religious experience or to ignore it entirely. So the concept is repugnant because of either its intrinsic associations or its remote and specialist context.

This is a pity. The topic of revelation is rich enough to stand up to philosophical scrutiny, and philosophers have their own distinctive contribution to make to the discussion. It is worth remembering that initial reaction is often a poor guide to adequate reflection on any issue. Indeed, that revelation is inimical to reason is not something that can be assumed at the outset. It must be argued in its own right. Moreover, there is nothing wrong with philosophers straying into theology proper. That would be so if the two disciplines were insulated from each other, a thesis which is thoroughly questionable. Besides, leaving revelation in the hands of systematic theologians and biblical scholars has not been a conspicuous success. What we need here surely is sensitive interaction. Perhaps cross-fertilization of ideas in this area is long overdue. Theologians, philosophers, and biblical scholars might benefit from eavesdropping on each other's conversations.

On the philosophical side three overlapping issues deserve extended attention. First, we need to do some sorting out of the concept. More particularly, we need to know how the term is used and what some of its essential features are as applied to

---

[3] Austin Farrer, "Revelation," in *Faith and Logic,* ed. Basil Mitchell (London: George Allen and Unwin, 1957), p. 84.

[4] Ibid., p. 99.

God. Secondly, we need to focus on the relation between revelation and reason. Is revelation an inferior relation to reason in religion, something we have to rely on but which we only turn to as a last resort? Furthermore, can we speak of criteria for divine revelation? In other words, how do we judge whether a revelation has actually taken place? These questions intrude on a third area, namely, How important is a doctrine of revelation? Can we give up the concept without there being any major loss in theology? Clearly we cannot hope to settle these matters. We can, however, indicate something of the fascinating vitality and complexity of the issue.

It needs to be kept in mind throughout the discussion that we shall be working with rival accounts of divine revelation within the Christian tradition. Hence I shall draw on concepts and considerations which will seem foreign to many philosophers of religion. Moreover, in order to sharpen up the issues I shall take sides on the theological issues at stake. My aim is to awaken the reader to the relevance of philosophical discussion to the debate about revelation within Christianity. At the end I shall indicate that there are other philosophical problems which any doctrine of divine revelation must ultimately face.

REVELATION AND MEANING

Revelation is not a concept which can be given a neat or exclusive definition. Ordinary language allows lots of latitude in usage, and theologians have propounded a host of possibilities. In the end, if one so desires, there is nothing to stop one from stipulating an entirely new account of the concept to serve one's theological purposes. Escaping to the Bible will not help, for it has no developed concept of revelation. The term, as Van Harvey points out, is the product of later theological reflection.[5] Yet the impact of that reflection has been so pervasive that dictionary definitions virtually mediate the classical Christian doctrine of special revelation. Generally revelation is defined as the disclosure or communication of knowledge by a divine or supernatural agency.[6] On this definition revelation involves the giving of revealed truth; it is the imparting of information which could not otherwise be known. Hence it has been common to talk of propositional revelation and to associate it with some kind of direct divine speaking. Both of these, in turn, have been commonly affixed to a widely held conception of the inspiration of the Bible. Thus divine revelation, divine speaking, and divine inspiration have often been used interchangeably.

This definition has been subject to considerable strain in recent theology. The pressure emanates from several sources. For one thing, it seems strange to treat revelation and inspiration, for example, as if they were one and the same divine activity. Both philosophers and theologians have perpetuated confusion at this point. Sec-

---

[5]Van A. Harvey, *A Handbook of Theological Terms* (New York: Macmillan, 1964), p. 207.
[6]See the *Oxford English Dictionary* (Oxford: Clarendon Press, 1933), vol. VIII, pp. 594–95.

ondly, the account of inspiration associated with the classical definition of revelation conflicts with both the spirit and the findings of the historical study of the Bible. Thus hostility to one has led inevitably to hostility to the other. Lastly, and most important, other uses of the term *revelation* have seemed to express more adequately what theologians want to maintain. Let me explain more fully what I mean, for it introduces us to an entirely new stream of thought on the concept.

Suppose we have an eye for fashion and we attend a party where we come across a strikingly beautiful new dress worn by a charming young lady. In such circumstances it might be natural to think of the new outfit as something of a revelation. We can imagine going away and telling friends that we had just had a revelation of what fashions would be like over the next decade. Of course we might not convince them of this but they would understand what we mean. Revelation here means "a striking disclosure of something previously unknown or unrealised."[7] As applied to the divine, revelation in this case would refer to any event, insight, person, or process which is believed to disclose the character or purposes of God. It would not necessarily refer to a revealed truth.

If one works with this more moderate conception of revelation, then clearly one takes on board much less theological luggage than is the case with the classical notion of revelation. With the latter there is a definite commitment to divine intervention in history. God is said to communicate information, for example, about his character and purposes through his word to prophets and apostles and through divine incarnation in Jesus Christ. In the more moderate usage one holds that God's nature is revealed in certain events, persons, and so forth, but one is not committed to the view that God actively intervenes to bring about or create these events, processes, and such. One may still talk of God's performing certain specific acts such as divine speaking or divine incarnation, but this is intended wholly metaphorically or mythologically. In this case God works in, with, and through everything that happens, but some things that happen, i.e., some events or insights or persons more readily display or disclose the ultimate purposes of God than do others.

Ordinary language analysis of the concept of revelation can fully endorse both stronger and more moderate conceptions of revelation. This is borne out by the fact that even those committed to the stronger conception will sometimes make use of the more moderate account to describe their experience. Imagine the new convert who goes home to share her faith with her sceptical father who has no time for religion. After being pestered, as he sees it, for weeks on end by a religious freak, he may turn and tell her angrily that he has had enough. She is disappointed and yields. Reflecting on her father's deep hostility, she may come to believe that God has spoken to her through this experience of rejection. She may speak of God's telling her to be less dogmatic and heavy-handed in her evangelism. Such an experience might more naturally be described as a case of human insight than of divine speaking, for it arose out of reflection, prayer, meditation on the Gospels, and the like, but the language of particular divine action is entirely appropriate. Many religious believers would resort to it without hesitation. As far as ordinary usage goes, it is

[7] *Oxford English Dictionary*, p. 595.

perfectly acceptable. Hence those who appeal to the more moderate conception of revelation are entirely within their linguistic rights.

THE SIGNIFICANCE OF SPECIAL REVELATION

The question of usage is only the first word, however, on this issue. We also want to find out if a theology which works exclusively with the more moderate conception of revelation is overall adequate. Clearly a decision at this level will always be a complex affair. The philosopher cannot expect to legislate one way or the other in a simple manner. Yet there are crucial philosophical factors which require attention, and the philosopher has every right to have his or her say in the debate. As we pursue these, the following points seem to me to be important.

First, it is surely obvious that a strong conception of revelation more adequately describes the content of divine revelation in the Christian tradition than the more moderate one sketched above. According to the classical tradition, God is conceived as a transcendent person. Persons characteristically reveal themselves through what they say and do. For example, I reveal myself to my friends through the words I speak, the letters I write, the presents I give, the favors I perform. I reveal myself, therefore, through particular actions in space and time. Likewise with God. He reveals himself in many and varied ways: through creating and sustaining the world, through the exodus from Egypt, through his Word to the prophets, through the incarnation in Jesus Christ, through the witness of the Spirit to the human heart. The moderate account of revelation has enormous difficulty accommodating these specific divine acts. It either seeks to develop an unattainable general theory of divine action, which fails to do full justice to these claims, or it treats them all as metaphors for something else which remains exceedingly vague and Pickwickian.[8] In either case, it is admitted that the whole Christian tradition has to be radically reinterpreted.

The philosopher can point out not only that the stronger conception more readily coheres with the personal character of God but, secondly, that it makes sense of relevant considerations generally accepted by both parties. We can see this quite clearly when we remember that revelation is a polymorphous activity. Consider another polymorphous activity, teaching. Teaching is an activity which involves a host of subordinate acts and activities. Thus one teaches by writing on the blackboard, giving talks and lectures, setting homework, questioning students, supervising experiments, setting examinations, and so on. One teaches by performing certain subactions. It is precisely the same with revelation. One reveals oneself by speaking, writing, performing this or that action, and the like. The same applies to God, as we have seen. Divine revelation is a polymorphous activity which encompasses a wide variety of events and experiences in creation, history and the lives of individuals.

---

[8] As it stands their claim is sheer assertion. I plan to make good this claim in a future publication.

The more moderate account of revelation, however, tends to limit divine revelation to human insight, treating it as a kind of poetic inspiration where there is a sense of givenness about what is said to be discovered. As a consequence it has to explain away the experience of prophets like Jeremiah or apostles like Paul who speak of a direct divine address. It also has to explain away the evidence for those signs, like the resurrection, and those other considerations in the life of Jesus which led the early church to speak of divine incarnation. The same applies to cases of personal revelation in the life of the believer, whether this be the inner testimony of God's Spirit or a matter of direct divine communication. The events and experiences behind these claims have a certain independent weight about them. A strong doctrine of revelation which stresses its polymorphous nature makes better sense of these factors overall and has to engage in much less explaining away to make sense of them than does a more moderate account.

Thirdly, it is indeed true that the strong conception of revelation advocated here does have unwelcome associations. It has tended to limit revelation to revealed propositions, and it has been fixed to conceptions of divine inspiration which have generated hostility to the historical study of scripture. Against this, however, it can be said that the stronger doctrine of revelation can easily be reoriented in its emphasis to handle revelation in creation and in events in history with relative ease. A polymorphous conception of revelation not only allows that revelation is a matter of both general acts of God in creation and special acts of God in history and the lives of prophets and apostles, it shows how that is so. It suggests that the concept of revelation can very naturally range over divine activity in both creation and history. Just as human agents can reveal themselves through what they create and what they do in history, as well as through what they say, so too can God. Revelation need not in itself be restricted to any one class of divine actions such as God's acts of speaking to particular individuals. Furthermore, the kind of repair work required to furnish a more adequate account of inspiration is not impossible to develop. Once we learn to distinguish clearly between divine revelation, divine speaking, and divine inspiration, then the clues for a viable and valuable doctrine of inspiration lie before us.[9] Hence the standard difficulties associated with a strong conception of divine revelation on the conceptual level dissolve quite readily.

It will be asked, however, whether we need a strong conception of revelation and whether we have any criteria for marking off special acts of divine revelation. This takes us to the relation between revelation and reason, which we will now pursue in some detail.

REVELATION AND REASON

At first sight it might seem that the issues here are too complex to detain us. The situation, however, is not that depressing, for it is not difficult to see why the stronger conception of revelation has much in its favor. Revelation is not a last

[9] See William J. Abraham, *The Divine Inspiration of Holy Scripture* (Oxford: Oxford University Press, 1981), chap. 4.

resort that believers turn to because they are afraid to use their reason. On the contrary, revelation is well-nigh essential if we are really to know the purposes of God for creation. That is a rather bold claim, but I think it merits very serious consideration.

As we have seen, a doctrine of revelation develops in part because God is understood to be a personal agent, analogous to human agents. In the case of a human agent it is patently obvious that we must have access to the specific actions of that agent if we are to know anything of substance about him or her. Suppose you have a friend and you want me to know what she is like. The standard way to do this is to tell me the story of what she has done and said. Without that story I remain in the dark; at best I can guess what your friend is like, but even then I may have nothing to go on so that my guessing is reduced to fantasizing. Within that story certain acts may have crucial significance. Perhaps your friend has done something truly heroic; if that is the case, such an act will be specially revelatory. Whatever the case, what your friend says has a privileged status because it is by speaking that we normally declare our intentions and purposes. Sometimes we can infer a person's intentions simply by seeing what he or she does, but this inference depends very much on the context and is usually supplementary to what is revealed through what is said or written by the agent.

This has a direct bearing on the question before us. If God is a personal agent analogous in nature to human agents then we would expect to be dependent on the equivalent to human speaking in the human situation. Just as human agents generally reveal their intentions by speaking, it is likely that divine agents will also need to speak to reveal their intentions and purposes. Relying on pure reason unrelated to exposure to some act of divine speaking would seem to be a precarious exercise. It would be like always having to work out the intentions and purposes of human agents merely from what they did and never from what they said. Let us expand this point and see where it leads.

My first argument has been that dependence on revelation is what we should expect if coming to know God is analogous to coming to know a human agent. The two are strikingly analogous, therefore this argument is entirely sound. It gains in plausibility when we remember that both sides in the debate generally agree that God does not have a body. There is nothing equivalent therefore to human body language when it comes to discerning the purposes of God. In the human situation one can often try and guess what human agents are up to. One can identify their bodies and read their bodily movements in order to try and discern what they are about. This does not seem to be available in the case of God. This suggests we are even more dependent on special acts of God to reveal to us both what he is doing in creation, in history, and in our own lives and why he does what he does in these areas. In particular, we are even more dependent on the prophet and apostle than we might at first imagine.[10]

---

[10] See William J. Abraham, *Divine Revelation and the Limits of Historical Criticism* (Oxford: Oxford University Press, 1982), pp. 14–24.

This is further supported when we considered the effects of sin and rebellion in our lives. Christians generally agree sin is pervasive in the world. If that is so, it is bound to make the reading of God's purposes all that more difficult and precarious. We certainly know rebellious and perverted attitudes distort our reading of what human agents do and intend. How much more so in the case of God if there is considerable distrust between human beings and God.

We can reach a similar conclusion about the cruciality of special revelation when we approach the issue from another direction. Let us ask, How are theists to provide warrants for substantial claims about God? If they do not rely on special revelation, to what shall they turn? They could simply be fideists and make their claims about God a matter of basic belief. This will not help, however, for if the existence of God is an unlikely candidate for basic beliefs, it is less likely that more specific claims about God's purposes and intentions can ever be located in this very privileged position. Another alternative would be to turn to natural theology. We attempt to infer God's purposes from creation as a whole or from certain parts of it. But this is a very precarious position as the history of natural theology makes only too obvious. Surely the general dissatisfaction with natural theology counts decisively against this way out of the dilemma. Much the same applies to any appeal to religious experience. Taken on its own, it cannot yield the kind of assurance the responsible theist seeks in order to make sense of commitment. It certainly cannot be dismissed as useless, yet to rely on it exclusively is to ignore the caution we saw was essential when we looked at it in detail.[11] The only alternative is to appeal to some other source, say, some sort of intuition or divinely implanted knowledge, or to appeal to a combination of the factors indicated here. The former option is either unreliable or ill-founded in experience; the latter sounds plausible only so long as we think of a hypothetical possibility and refrain from going through the hard work of presenting the detailed evidence to be culled from each source. All in all, the prospects of delivering the goods are bleak. In such circumstances special revelation takes on entirely new significance as a means of access to God's intentions and purposes. Perhaps Aquinas said as much when he remarked, "None of the philosophers before the coming of Christ could, by bending all effort to the task, know as much about God and things necessary for eternal life as after the coming of Christ a little old woman knows through her faith."[12]

This can easily be overlooked because theists committed to a moderate conception of revelation can live indefinitely off the theological capital of the past. Certainly a strong conception of divine revelation is mediated through the Bible and the classical liturgy of the church and theologians have little or no control over these. Thus Christian communities are to a great extent shielded from the long-term effects of moderate views of revelation on faith and practice because the long hand of the orthodox past supplies the data and warrants for substantial claims about God's character and purposes.

[11] See above p. 49.

[12] Mary T. Clark, *An Aquinas Reader* (London: Hodder and Stoughton, 1972), p. 404.

It can also be overlooked because it is easy to become impatient with philosophical argument. Thus it is tempting to dismiss the arguments I have deployed as the concern of theoreticians who do not have to work with the putative sources of special revelation. It is all very well, it will be said, for the philosopher to argue that Christian theology needs revelation, but what is needed may not be available. In such circumstances the Christian theologian has every right to live with the facts as they are and get on with the task of reconstruction.[13]

This is a fair protest but only if two important conditions are met. First, it must actually be shown that there are no genuine cases of such revelation available. That has certainly not been done, and it is unlikely to be done. Secondly, those theologians who embark on the task of reconstructing Christian theology without relying on the strong account of divine revelation must squarely face and address the issue of the warrants for their proposals about God. They have a responsibility to defend their new epistemological proposals. At this point in the debate the onus is clearly on their side, for the case against relying on natural theology, religious experience, intuition, and the like, has been developed at length and is something of a consensus. As it stands, the philosophical side cannot be set aside as the abstract concern of theoreticians.[14] Perhaps this is one point where there is great need for sensitive and patient dialogue among philosophers, theologians, and biblical scholars.

CRITERIA FOR DIVINE REVELATION

An important topic which emerges out of this discussion is the criteria for divine revelation. One of the reasons people are reluctant to advance claims about actual special revelation is that they are at a loss as to how to decide when they can be substantiated. To find any serious discussion of this we have to go back to philosophers like John Locke (1632-1704) or J. B. Mozley (1813-78). Both deployed the argument that miracles were the fundamental criterion for special revelation. Very few now take this argument very seriously.[15]

Locke, however, makes a general point which has been quoted repeatedly, and we do well to take a fresh look at it.

> God when he makes the prophet does not unmake the man. He leaves all his faculties in the natural state, to enable him to judge of his inspirations, whether they be of divine original or no. When he illuminates the mind with supernatural light, he does not extinguish that which is natural. If he would have us assent to the truth of any proposition, he either evidences that truth by the usual methods of natural reason, or else makes it known to be a truth which

---

[13] This point is well made in an indirect way by Maurice Wiles in *The Remaking of Christian Doctrine* (London: SCM, 1974), p. 48.

[14] Adherents of the more moderate conception of divine revelation have gladly accepted their responsibility. See, for example, Gordon D. Kaufman, *The Theological Imagination* (Philadelphia: Westminster Press, 1981), pp. 263-79.

[15] I outline and evaluate this argument in *Divine Revelation*, chap. 2.

he would have us assent to by his authority, and convinces us that it is from him, by some marks which reason cannot be mistaken in. Reason must be our last judge and guide in everything. I do not mean that we must consult reason, and examine whether a proposition revealed from God can be made out by natural principles, and if it cannot, that then we may reject it: but consult it we must, and by it examine whether it be a revelation from God or no: and if reason finds it to be revealed from God, reason then declares for it as much as for any other truth, and makes it one of her dictates. Every conceit that thoroughly warms our fancies must pass for an inspiration, if there be nothing but the strength of our persuasions, whereby to judge of our persuasions: if reason must not examine their truth by something extrinsical to the persuasions themselves, inspirations and delusions, truth and falsehood, will have the same measure, and will not be possible to be distinguished.[16]

One cannot but have sympathy with some of the sentiments expressed by Locke. We know that prophets remain human despite their holy vocation; we know that the unwary can be led astray by imposters, therefore we want some reason for accepting a claim to revelation as being genuine; we know also that if what is known by revelation can be worked out by natural principles, then the appeal to revelation is superfluous. Yet we can surely hear the strident voice of hard rationalism raised within this passage. The quest for absolute certainty, the search for external marks of authenticity, the commitment to the omnicompetence of pure reason, the agonizing fear of falling into error, all these are the characteristic insignia of hard rationalism. The inadequacy of hard rationalism in this area is surely not difficult to establish. As we seek to demolish it, let us try to replace it with an account of the criteria of revelation, which is altogether more appropriate.

We should note, first, that no such conditions have been suggested by those who came to believe that revelation has actually occurred. Distinguishing between true and false prophecy has always been a precarious business where religious believers acted partly in faith rather than completely by sight.[17] It is equally so in the identification of Jesus of Nazareth as the incarnate embodiment of the divine and therefore as uniquely revelatory. Austin Farrer's comment on this is much to the point.

In most fields of enquiry it is possible to set up models of argument and canons of proof. The usefulness of such aids varies greatly from one field to another. In the matter of revelation it must surely reach a vanishing point. If there is no *a priori* model for the form of God's self-disclosure, how can there be *a priori* canons for the marks of its authenticity? There is no major premise which lays it down that every child virginally born, or every good man making divine claims, or every crucified man raised from the dead, is a Person of the Godhead. There existed in the minds of Christ's contemporaries certain premises about the supreme human instrument of divine intervention. The Gospels devote a surprising amount of space to the demolition of them.[18]

[16] John Locke, *Essay Concerning Human Understanding*, bk. IV, chap. 19, sec. 14.

[17] The point is well made by James A. Sanders in a review of the literature. See "Hermeneutics in True and False Prophecy," in *Canon and Authority*, ed. George W. Coats and Burke O. Long (Philadelphia: Fortress Press, 1977), pp. 21–41.

[18] Farrer, "Revelation," p. 101.

Locke's demands, therefore, do not grow out of sensitive interaction with serious candidates for special revelation. Rather he wants to lay down the law in advance. Using our reason, we are supposed to develop external marks of divine revelation and then using these as a yardstick go off and discover what does or does not fit. This is certainly not how it has worked in practice, so we should pause for thought before we accept it.

But maybe Locke is right, and the practice within the tradition is just wrong? To side uncritically with actual practice is just to beg the question against Locke and open the floodgates to any and every claimant to revelation. Presumably rival traditions will have rival criteria of revelation, and each tradition can conveniently appeal to its own criteria to validate its own position. So we are caught in a classic dilemma: either we yield to Locke's demands for external criteria and end up with nothing to show for our trouble or we yield to the demands of tradition and beg the question about its validity.

The emergence of these options is the voice of hard rationalism being raised again. Typically we are told that there can be two and only two alternatives in the quest for criteria of divine revelation. But is this the case? Surely it is not so at all. The pattern of reasoning one should deploy is entirely different from that proposed in either option but no less genuine for that. Let us follow through on this briefly.

It is surely the case that in speaking of revelation outside theology in everyday life we do not have hard and fast rules as to how to operate. Suppose we have a neighbor who, given what we know of him, is a rather dull soul. What we have seen and heard leaves us bored. Then one day we stumble across a learned journal in the library and discover to our amazement that our neighbor is an expert on certain species of butterly. When we next meet him we mention butterflies and before we leave he catches fire as he holds us spellbound enthusing about their habits and beauty. We would speak very naturally of such a chain of events as being a revelation. "What a revelation of his true character," we tell our friends and neighbors.

The hard rationalist has no way to make sense of such everyday experiences. The soft rationalist does, for he or she can see that we can indeed have criteria, but they are loose and mostly retrospective. We have to work with preliminary considerations of a rather vague sort, with considerations furnished by the experience itself, and with confirming evidence picked up afterwards. Exactly the same kind of logic, suitably adapted to fit the context, applies in the case of divine revelation. To fill out this point let me work with a concrete example, namely, the place of Paul in the Christian tradition.

A PARADIGM CASE

Paul is a good case to discuss because he represents a significant figure in the historical development of the Christian tradition, who lays claim to speak on behalf of God and expects to be taken seriously on this basis. Clearly he was accepted in the early church as a major source of divine revelation. What sort of evidence led to such a conclusion? The answer is complex, but we can still discern some salient factors in it.

There is, to begin, his dramatic conversion and call on the Damascus road along with subsequent religious experience. Fundamental to all this is Paul's claim that he has been appointed not on the basis of his genius nor on the basis of human decision but on the basis of divine election, made known to him personally by the risen Christ. This was taken seriously not because it was made much of on the part of Paul but because it was linked to a radical reversal of life-style, to penetrating and sacrificial service to Jew and Gentile, and to a sense of humility and even reserve when he spoke of its details. Such a claim could not easily be assimilated to those "conceits which warm our fancies" or to clear cases of mental insanity. In other words, the principle of initial credulity stood firm for many who watched Paul preach and work.

James S. Stewart captures this point about Paul in this way:

> It is significant . . . to find that on occasions when his apostolic authority was called in question and attacked, he reminded his critics that in the Damascus experience there lay a full vindication of his claim. No one could bear apostolic rank—so the mind of the Church decreed—who had not personally seen the risen Jesus. . . . And Paul always insisted that he possessed this essential qualification. "Am I not an apostle? Am I not free? Have I not seen Jesus our Lord?" In the face of all this to speak of Paul's vision as "illusion," "projection," "hallucination," and so on, simply betrays a lack of spiritual perception and a defective understanding of the ways of God. What shattered the flaming career of persecution, wrenched the stubborn Pharisee right round in his track, killed the blasphemer, and gave birth to the saint was nothing illusory; it was the most real thing in life, as real as the fact of God, as real as the risen life of Christ. It was, in the apostle's own words, an "arrest." It was a "revelation." It was a new divine "Let there be light!" And the glorious words in which Paul's great disciple of a later day, St. Augustine, described his own redeeming experience of God in Christ might have come straight from the apostle himself.
>
> "With Thy calling and shouting Thou didst break my deafness; with Thy flashing and shining Thou didst scatter my blindness. At the scent of Thee I drew in breath, and I pant for Thee. I have tasted, and I hunger and thirst. Thou hast touched me, and I am on fire for Thy peace."[19]

A second factor that clearly had weight was the content of what Paul revealed. Negatively it was not something trivial; nor was it something which could be worked out from natural principles or from shared, general religious experience. Positively it sought to illuminate and explain those controversial events associated with the life, death, and resurrection of Jesus. Equally it sought to root itself in deep continuity with the traditions of revelation gathered together in the Old Testament. Thus Paul argued at length that his message fulfilled rather than destroyed those fundamental purposes of God already made known in the past through general and special

---

[19] James S. Stewart, *A Man in Christ* (London: Hodder and Stoughton, 1934), pp. 126–27. Reprinted by permission of Hodder and Stoughton Limited.

revelation. Moreover, what Paul said made sense of the charismatic and personal experience which had been discerned as the work of God's Spirit. Indeed Paul himself claimed to perform signs and wonders which confirmed his message, although he himself was reluctant to make much of this.

A further factor is the sheer impressiveness of Paul's theological proposals when judged over time in the Christian community. They fitted into a wider symphony of revelation both in Jesus and in other apostles and outwitted and outshone other efforts to make sense of a wide range of controversial but fundamental religious events, experiences, insights, and other phenomena. Part of what is at issue here is very subtle. Paul's theology and ethics simply stretched what was previously to be known of God; so much so that Paul could be seen as one who abrogated rather than fulfilled earlier accounts of God's will. Yet what is seen to have happened with Paul is often what happens when we are confronted with revelation in any sphere. Old ways of thinking and living have to yield to the sheer weight of what has been newly revealed.

Nowhere in this process are there the kind of fool-proof criteria that the hard rationalist desires. As it stands, there are no external proofs to settle it once for all that someone has received a revelation from God. Attempts to codify the discussion into hard and fast criteria for divine revelation do not look very fruitful or promising.[20] Yet this does not at all mean that deciding to accept a particular revelation is a purely arbitrary matter. One can give reasons even though they must remain loose and suggestive. The best we can say in advance is that any putative revelation should have something relevant and significant to transmit to the world as it is. The one who claims to receive revelation should give a relatively convincing avowal and account of having had a significant encounter with God. The revelation itself should make sense of those events and experiences to which it refers and should not be contradicted by established facts related to the same experiences and events. The purported revelation should actually mediate substantial information about the actions, intentions, and purposes of God regarding the matter of which it speaks. It should illuminate wider aspects of human life and experience as a whole. Moreover it should fit in naturally with what can be known of God from other sources, whether these be other cases of special revelation or more general revelation in creation. It is by means of these kinds of considerations that the problem of criteria for divine revelation is to be approached.

OTHER ISSUES

Our discussion to this point has concentrated on the doctrine of revelation within Christianity. I have therefore assumed the existence of experiences, events, proposals, and claims that are peculiar to Christianity. My intention has been very modest: I want to point out that there are important philosophical considerations

---

[20] Farrer, "Revelation," pp. 101–2.

about the general concept of revelation, about our knowledge of an agent's intentions and purposes, and about the nature of reason and argument, which are relevant to a fully viable doctrine of divine revelation. What doctrine a theologian ultimately espouses cannot be settled by these factors alone but it is crucial that they be considered and given their due weight.

There is a further set of questions which are very important in debates about the nature of revelation. Chief among these questions is the issue of the coherence of the concept of divine agency. Traditionally God is construed as an incorporeal agent. But does this concept make logical sense? If it does not, does it help to construe God as corporeal, treating the world as his body? More specifically, we can ask, How are particular divine actions to be identified in the world? And what exactly does it mean to predicate particular actions of God? What, for example, does it mean to say that "God spoke to x"? Does a doctrine of analogy help here? Clearly such issues call for patient philosophical scrutiny although we shall not pursue them here.

Chapter Fifteen
Religion And History

The systematic development of historical study is one of the great achievements of the modern world. Interest in the past has always been with us. Indeed there were ancient scholars who showed remarkable historical insight and ability. However, it is only in the last two centuries that history as a critical, intellectual discipline has flourished. We take the study of history for granted, given our educational conventions, but our forefathers knew little of the delight and agony it can evoke among religious believers. Even yet we are unsure whether to look upon it as a bane or a blessing.

THE IMPORTANCE OF HISTORY

Clearly history matters to religious believers and especially to Christians and Jews. All religious believers are interested in history, if for no greater reason than that they are interested in the rise and development of their own religious doctrines, heroes, and institutions. But Jews and Christians have a special interest in history because they believe that God has acted decisively in the past, and therefore the record of that past acts in a significant way to mediate the revelation of the divine will. One of the reasons for the rise of a canon of literature and the passionate defense of that canon stems from this fact.

E. L. Mascall highlighted the significance of history for the Christian faith in this way. "It has often been emphasised that Christianity is historical in a sense in which no other religion is, for it stands or falls by certain events which are alleged to have taken place during a particular period of forty-eight hours in Palestine nearly two thousand years ago."[1] Others have echoed this comment, making it a warrant for the pivotal role assigned to historical study within theology as an intellectual discipline.

Mascall focuses on what we might call the epistemic relation between faith and history. The reference to standing or falling suggests that somehow historical study validates or invalidates the Christian faith. Given our discussion on the rationality of religious belief in earlier chapters, clearly this is a gross oversimplification as it stands. Moreover, it highlights only one of the ways in which history relates to faith. Nevertheless, it is useful to begin at this level, for this has been a matter of considerable interest. On the one side, there are those who have looked to history as a kind of intellectual or apologetic savior after religious experience failed to replace classical natural theology as a defense of theological doctrine. When wedded to a doctrine of revelation which construed revelation exclusively as acts of God in history, this tradition had enormous attraction for modern theologians. On the other side, there have always been those who have held that to make faith depend on the results of historical investigation is a form of theological madness. Not only does it make faith dependent on the work of learned professors, it also drastically misreads the true nature of religious commitment. Perhaps when positions polarize like this we have a clear signal for the philosopher of religion to set to work.

In this chapter I plan to explore the territory already staked out by the last option mentioned. I shall work indirectly and, perhaps appropriately, historically. I want to expound and evaluate the thought of Gotthold Ephraim Lessing (1729-81) on this issue. What I intend to show is that, although the details of his position are unacceptable, he does begin to highlight some of the central topics generated by the interaction between faith and history. Let us begin with some introductory comments on Lessing.

LESSING'S CONTRIBUTION TO THE DEBATE

Lessing was not an original philosopher, and he refused to be called a theologian, yet he is an interesting and indeed extraordinary figure. He was in turn a theological student, dramatist, librarian, editor, historian, polemicist, and Freemason. His influence on later theologians was profound, particularly on Kierkegaard and through him on the theologies of Karl Barth and Rudolf Bultmann. This is one reason why his views are important. There are two others. First, for good or ill, Lessing's way of posing the relation between faith and history has been taken as the

---

[1] Quoted in Maurice Wiles, "In What Sense Is Christianity a 'Historical' Religion?" *Theology,* LXXXI (1978), p. 5.

standard for subsequent discussion. David A. Pailin has stated this very clearly: "The fundamental question of the relation between faith and history was classically posed by Lessing in the eighteenth century. In its most challenging form it has been studiously avoided by most theologians ever since."[2] Secondly, it is generally agreed that Lessing's views had a profound impact on the rise of biblical criticism and that they continue therefore to be of contemporary relevance.[3]

Lessing develops his more formal views in a little book published in 1777 called *On the Proof of the Spirit and of Power.*[4] This was the follow-up to the appearance of some five fragments of Reimarus, an early biblical critic, which Lessing had edited for publication. These fragments amounted to a spirited attack on the possibility of special revelation and on the historical claims of the Bible, particularly the accounts of the crossing of the Red Sea and the resurrection of Jesus. This attack, as we might expect, evoked a general mobilization of the orthodox of the day, first against Reimarus and then against Lessing. Lessing had his own weapons ready, it would seem, for he threw himself into the fray with dexterity and coolness, as we shall see. In time the discussion degenerated into a pamphlet war, which eventually led to Lessing's writings on religion being subject to censorship. Not to be outdone, Lessing then turned to what he referred to as his former pulpit, the theatre, to propagate his views.

On the Proof of the Spirit and of Power comes from Lessing's earlier, non-polemical period. The title sounds strange, but the terms in it were well known in the eighteenth century. They came originally from Origen's gloss on what Paul wrote in 1 Cor. 2:4. There Paul had said: ". . . my speech and my message were not in plausible words of wisdom, but in demonstration of the Spirit and of power. . . ." Origen took this to mean that there was a proof peculiar to the truth of the gospel. More particularly, Jesus was proved to be the Son of God by two facts: first, by the fact that he directly fulfills Old Testament prophecies—the proof of the Spirit—and secondly, by the fact that he performed miracles—the proof of power. These two proofs constituted the standard arguments for special revelation in the time of Lessing, and it was these that the orthodox theologians had presented as a reply to the thought of Reimarus as edited and published by Lessing. Lessing set out to discredit this response. In the process he raised some very important questions about the relation between history and faith.

In outlining Lessing's arguments we shall treat the two traditional arguments cited above as one. We can do this because Lessing says exactly the same about the one as he does about the other. Moreover, in logic the two are essentially the same, for on the proposed account prophecy is a matter of having access to information about future events by means which transcend the normal course of nature. This is

[2] See David A. Pailin, "Lessing's Ditch Revisited—The Problem of Faith and History," in *Theology and Change,* ed. R. H. Preston (London: SCM, 1975), pp. 78–103.

[3] See Henry E. Allison, *Lessing and the Enlightenment* (Ann Arbor: University of Michigan Press, 1966).

[4] G. E. Lessing, "On the Proof of the Spirit and of Power," in *Lessing's Theological Writings,* trans. Henry Chadwick (London: Adam and Charles Black, 1956).

clearly akin to, if not identical with, a miracle. There are three basic phases in Lessing's proposals.

LESSING'S CENTRAL PROPOSALS

Lessing begins his arguments against the traditional apologetic for special revelation with a distinction which he thinks is beyond controversy. "Miracles, which I see with my own eyes, and which I have the opportunity to verify for myself, are one thing; miracles, of which I know only from history that others say they have seen and verified are another."[5] Against miracles in themselves Lessing has no objection. If he had actually seen them performed in the time of Christ or if he were to see them before his own eyes, he is quite emphatic that they would have a strong effect on him. The effect here is not just a matter of psychological impact, it is a matter of rational impact. Thus not only would he have been led to pay attention to Christ "I would have gained so much confidence that I would willingly have submitted my intellect to his."[6] ". . . if even now miracles were done by believing Christians which I had to recognise as true miracles: what could prevent me from accepting this proof of Power as the Apostle calls it."[7] Lessing's problem is that the supply of miracles has run out. All he has is the reports of miracles, and reports of miracles do not possess the rational force which holds in the case of the original miracles. The problem is that reports of fulfilled prophecies are not fulfilled prophecies; that reports of miracles are not miracles. "These, the prophecies fulfilled before my eyes, are immediate in their effect. But those, the reports of fulfilled prophecies and miracles, have to work through a medium which takes away all their force."[8] Or as Lessing expresses it more briefly: "The problem is that this proof of the spirit and of power no longer has any spirit or power, but has sunk to the level of human testimonies."[9] Lessing's first move then is to draw a distinction between miracles and reports of miracles and to insist thereafter that the logical force attributable to the former cannot be predicated of the latter.

Lessing's second move grows out of a rejoinder to this first move. We accept your distinction, the critic might reply, and we agree that the reports we have of these prophecies and miracles are as reliable as historical truths ever can be, but we can still rely on these reports as part of our apologetic. They may not have the force of miracles actually experienced, but they have the force of reports of miracles. It is at this point that Lessing plays what he thinks is his trump card.

Lessing rejects this rejoinder because it ignores a logical distinction between the nature of the propositions in the premises and the nature of the propositions in the conclusion. The historical truths of the premises and the theological, metaphysi-

---

[5] Ibid., p. 51.
[6] Ibid., p. 52.
[7] Ibid.
[8] Ibid.
[9] Ibid.

cal, and moral truths of the conclusion are separated by a broad, ugly ditch, which, he says, ". . . I cannot get across, however often and however earnestly I have tried to make the leap."[10] There are three separate contrasts at issue here.

> Historical propositions are reliable, theological propositions are infinitely more reliable.
>
> Historical propositions are accidental truths, theological propositions are necessary truths of reason.
>
> Historical propositions are open to doubt, theological propositions are not open to doubt.

Be it noted that Lessing is not objecting to historical investigation. Indeed, in practice he was something of an historian himself, for he attempted to explain how the early church grew so quickly, and he was one of the first in the history of biblical criticism to set John apart from the other three synoptic Gospels. What he objected to was the attempt to argue for the truth of theological claims by appeal to historical fact.

> That the Christ, against whose resurrection I can raise no important historical objection, therefore declared himself to be the Son of God; that his disciples therefore believed him to be such; this I gladly believe from my heart. For these truths, as truths of one and the same class, follow quite naturally on one another.
>
> But to jump with that historical truth to a quite different class of truths, and to demand of me that I should from all my metaphysical and moral ideas accordingly; to expect me to alter all my fundamental ideas of the nature of the Godhead because I cannot set any credible testimony against the resurrection of Christ: if that is not a $\mu\epsilon\tau\dot{\alpha}\ \beta\alpha\sigma\iota\varsigma\ \epsilon\iota\varsigma\ \overset{\prime}{\alpha}\lambda\lambda o\ \gamma\dot{\epsilon}\nu o\varsigma$ then I do not know what Aristotle meant by this phrase.[11]

Not even an attempt to rest the appeal on a strong doctrine of inspiration will do. "If you press me still further and say: 'Oh Yes! This is more than historically certain. For it is asserted by inspired historians who cannot make a mistake.' But unfortunately, that also is only historically certain, that these historians were inspired."[12] Lessing strategy, then, is to point to the broad, ugly ditch which separates historical and theological propositions and then set a guard to drown you should you dare venture to cross.

That he cannot himself get across poses no problem for him, for as Lessing sees it, he is already safely grounded on the right side of the ditch. This brings us to the third phrase of his proposals. He does not appeal to any historical propositions for his theological beliefs because by their nature these beliefs do not need this kind of support. What binds Lessing to the teachings of Christ is nothing but the teachings themselves. In other words, Lessing has found more appropriate arguments for

[10] Ibid., p. 55.

[11] Ibid., p. 54.

[12] Ibid., p. 55.

his religious position. As Henry Chadwick points out, like all truths of reason, they are tidy, mathematically certain, and known a priori.[13]

In the early days of the church theological claims did need to be supported by miracles. "Eighteen hundred years ago they were so new, so alien, so foreign to the entire mass of truths recognised in their age, but nothing less than miracles and fulfilled prophecies were required if the multitude were to attend to them at all."[14] What miracles did was put common sense on the right track to truth. The truth, however, does not depend on the miracles for theological propositions have their own inner truth, and so they stand in no need of external confirmation. Some remarks by Lessing in his comments as editor on Reimarus bring this out clearly and vividly. Lessing is, as the following shows, not at all embarrassed by the attack of Reimarus on miracles.

> ... how much could be said in reply to all these objections and difficulties! And even if no answer was forthcoming, what then? The learned theologian might in the last resort be embarrassed but certainly not the Christian. To the former it might at most cause confusion to see the supports with which he would have made it safe and sound. But how do this man's hypotheses, explanations, and proofs affect the Christian? For him it is simply a fact—the Christianity which he feels to be true and in which he feels blessed. When the paralytic feels the beneficial shocks of the electrical sparks, does it worry him whether Nollet or Franklin or neither of them is right. In short, the letter is not the spirit, and the Bible is not religion. Consequently objections to the letter and to the Bible are not also objections to the spirit and to religion.[15]

In summary we can note that Lessing's third argument is a positive one. Theological claims do not depend on historical propositions, for they are like necessary truths of reason, and therefore they are true in themselves.

EVALUATION OF LESSING'S POSITION

What are we to make of Lessing's arguments? It is tempting to focus on Lessing's remarks about miracles and see his thought as simply a variation of the modern dissatisfaction with them in the realm of apologetics. On this reading Lessing is really offering supplementary additions to Hume's arguments. This interpretation would be a mistake. What makes Lessing important is his determination to see how faith and history stand in relation to each other. Lessing in this seeks to give each its due so does not concentrate on one at the expense of the other. Both faith and history are to be taken seriously. This is of capital importance, for much modern writing on faith and history has not matched Lessing in this respect.[16] Moreover, Lessing is im-

---

[13] Ibid., p. 30.

[14] Ibid., p. 55.

[15] Ibid., p. 17.

[16] Even the best have failed. Van A. Harvey, for example, in *The Historian and the Believer* (Toronto: Macmillan, 1969), leaves theology to the last chapter by which time his account of history has already predetermined how theology will be construed.

portant because his position is an extreme one, and thus it forces us to face up to the radical significance history may have for faith. However, we do need to attend to Lessing's material on miracle as we take stock of his overall position.

We can agree with Lessing that we ought to distinguish between miracles and reports of miracles. We clearly do prefer to see things with our own eyes rather than depend upon reports of what others see. There may well be exceptions to this, of course. For example, consider a debate in Parliament or Congress. We might well prefer to have the report of a seasoned political commentator, who will set the debate in context and interpret its veiled allusions, rather than our own naive reading as given by personal experience. This is almost certainly the case with complex scientific experiments. The layperson will gain far more from suitably informed reports than from personal experience. But let us treat these cases as exceptions.

Let us agree also with Lessing that miracles will not deductively prove any theological proposal. Thus we reject the orthodox apologetic of the eighteenth century against which he fought. However, two comments are immediately in order, and the second is fatal for Lessing's second argument. First, Lessing never considers whether miracles might not be of a more limited or modest value in arguing for a theological claim. This is a viable position to maintain.[17] Secondly, Lessing may have to concede this possibility because he has already agreed that miracles can rightly have not just a psychological but a rational effect on our beliefs. In other words, Lessing at the outset accepts that claims about present miracles can have epistemic relevance to theology. The only issue for him at this stage is that he only has reports of miracles before him. But claims about present miracles before our own eyes are contingent claims. They are not truths of reason but fall on the accidental side of his broad, ugly ditch. Hence in his first argument Lessing has contradicted what he argues in the second. He has allowed contingent truths about present events to support theological claims about Jesus Christ.

Having shown that Lessing contradicts himself, I do not think that we should make too much of this. The likelihood is that Lessing's initial concession about contemporary miracles was a deliberate move on his part. It is well known that Lessing was prepared to wear the outward garb of orthodoxy in order to make space for a more radical upheaval of the whole orthodox system at a later juncture. That is understandable, for the age in which he lived made life difficult for those who did not toe the orthodox line. From our radically different situation we need to exercise our historical imagination in evaluating Lessing. Lessing may well have been aware of the internal contradiction in his own position. What really mattered to him was the distinction between faith and history as developed in his second and third arguments. Let us now turn to these.

Central to them is Lessing's claim that the truth or falsity of one is irrelevant to the truth or falsity of the other. Between them there is a broad, ugly ditch which cannot be crossed. As Henry E. Allison points out, we need to acknowledge the radical character of Lessing's position.

[17]See chap. 12.

. . . for the first time in the eighteenth century the question of the facticity of the Christian revelation was held to be irrelevant for the truth of the Christian religion. This religion contains an intrinsic truth, immediately grasped by the believer, and this truth retains its validity whether or not the various accounts of the resurrection agree, and in fact, whether or not Jesus of Nazareth actually arose from the tomb after three days.[18]

This is a fascinating and attractive position to take up. If accepted it immediately dissolves a problem that has plagued theology since the rise of biblical criticism. According to this solution, historical study can have no logical bearing on theology; hence we need not worry about the results of historical criticism. Bultmann aptly sums up the resulting relief as applied to information about Jesus.

I calmly let the fire burn, for I see that what is consumed is only the fanciful portraits of life-of-Jesus theology, and that means nothing other than "Christ after the flesh." But the "Christ after the flesh" is no concern of ours. How things looked in the heart of Jesus I do not know and do not want to know.[19]

What are we to make of this important proposal? Can Lessing in particular sustain his position? I do not think he can. The first problem in his position is that it involves a radical misinterpretation of theological claims. He treats theological claims as if they are truths of reason, but that is exactly what they are not. Theological claims are not like mathematical claims; their denials are entirely coherent. Hence if we speak of a ditch between various kinds of statements, theology is on the same side of the ditch as history. In other words, given the options Lessing has offered us, theological claims are less reliable than truths of reason, they are accidental rather than necessary, and they are clearly open to theoretical doubt. Lessing's account of the relation between faith and history is therefore doomed to failure. It is hopelessly deficient in its interpretation of one factor in the relation.

This deficiency is confirmed when we recall that some theological claims although they cannot be proved by historical investigation can clearly be falsified by historical inquiry. It is perfectly conceivable that Jesus never existed or that his life and death could never bear the interpretation which Christians minimally give them. History therefore cannot be set aside as epistemically irrelevant. Historical fire can consume theology. Indeed it has forced Christian theologians to reinterpret the significance of wide tracts of the biblical material. This has caused considerable agony, and even yet there is no consensus as to how best to appropriate much in the biblical traditions. This lack of consensus is no accident. It stems from the character of the Christian religion and the clear relevance of historical study to its content.

Lessing failed to see this because of general tendency in his age to construe Christianity as a combination of inner feeling and moral commitment. The latter

[18] Allison, *Lessing and the Enlightenment,* p. 96.
[19] Rudolf Bultmann, *Faith and Understanding,* trans. L. P. Smith (London: SCM, 1969), p. 132.

especially appealed to him. For Lessing the heart of Christianity was its command to love one another. This alone was its heart and soul.[20] Obviously Christianity thus construed cannot be falsified by historical investigation, for it is now interpreted in moral terms, and moral claims have a different logical space from that occupied by historical study. The problem with this, however, is that it fails to do justice to what Christianity really is. In its essence the Christian religion construes certain past events as constitutive of its very nature. Besides, the moralism suggested by Lessing does scant justice to the primacy of grace in the classical doctrines of the Christian life.[21]

ISSUES PROVOKED BY LESSING'S WORK

Although Lessing's main proposals are far from satisfactory, his work does provoke some of the central questions posed by the rise of historical investigation as it interacts with faith. I want now to indicate what these questions are and make some comments on them. My aim is not to resolve these issues. I shall indicate the direction of my own thought, sometimes very briefly, sometimes at greater length, but my primary concern is to map what the issues are. I hope it will be clear that there are some vital questions which philosophers of religion should pursue with some diligence.

The first issue that Lessing's work provokes is the question of the distinction between history and theology. Lessing was very sure that history and theology should be distinguished quite sharply. The distinction he proposes is inaccurate. Theology and history, as we have seen, fall on the same side of his broad, ugly ditch. If this distinction fails, how should we distinguish between faith and history? Should we in fact distinguish between faith and history at all?

Intuitively we feel we should. Theology and history surely differ from one another; their division within our educational curricula bears witness to this. What then distinguishes them? I suggest at least three factors are relevant here. First, they differ in subject matter. History deals fundamentally with the activity of human beings. Theology deals basically with questions about God and what he has done. Secondly, they differ in the range of arguments deployed. Theology makes appeal to the kind of considerations historians may offer, but it also appeals to wider philosophical considerations as represented by natural theology, religious experience, and moral insight. Finally, they differ in their relation to historic communities, especially the church. Theology is done as part of the life of the church; history serves no particular institution as a matter of deliberate vocation. Certainly history contributes to the welfare of governments and society, but this is more of a by-product than it is deliberate policy.

A second issue prompted by Lessing's work is this: How are faith and history

[20] See G. E. Lessing, "The Testament of John," *Lessing's Theological Writings*, p. 59.
[21] We saw this in chap. 11.

rationally related to one another? Although they are distinct from one another, this does not mean that history and faith are separated by thick walls which prevent interpenetration. On the contrary, there can be deep interaction which is clearly epistemic in nature. First, as we have seen, historical investigation can falsify claims about divine action or make them look strained and implausible. Secondly, historical investigation can go some way to confirming theological claims about divine action. This is a controversial point but it is one that a soft rationalist would argue. At the very least historical considerations will be one element in giving reasons for a claim about divine action in the past. Appeal, that is, will be made to reports of what certain people have seen, heard, or otherwise witnessed.

The interaction is not, moreover, just one way. Theological conviction may affect historical decisions about what has happened. This may occur in a general way when the historian makes assumptions about human nature or the historical process as a whole.[22] It may also happen in a more specific way when a historian's commitment to the possibility of divine intervention may influence how he or she evaluates the value of testimony.[23]

A third question posed by Lessing's work arises out of my criticism that Lessing fails to do justice to what Christianity actually is. I claimed that Lessing was working with a reduced and inadequate account of faith. The rise of historical study makes possible a fascinating counterattack on this, which has important ramifications of a philosophical character.

What history shows, it might be said, is that contrary to what is assumed Christianity has no fixed essence. Over time and space it has changed and developed. Things once deemed essential have been scrapped or reabsorbed in new ways. Hence it is possible to abandon the very close connection with history envisaged in the argument canvassed earlier without abandoning the Christian faith. This point has been well made by Maurice Wiles. Speaking of those events normally held to be essential to Christianity, he writes:

> When the objector says that without this historical dependence Christianity would simply cease to be Christianity, how does he know? Let us grant that in one form or another it has been a feature of Christianity throughout its history. That does not of itself prove his point. Other things have characterised Christianity for the greater part of its history without our being led thereby to regard them as indispensable or unalterable—the absolute reliability of the sacred text, God's special creation of man, a negative attitude to other religions, even the refusal of ordination to woman. One needs to be able to say more than that it has always been a feature of Christianity; one needs to be able to say that it belongs to the essence of Christianity. How is such a claim to be made? Can it be supported by argument or is it something one either sees to be so—or fails to see, as the case may be?[24]

---

[22] For more on this see William J. Abraham, *Divine Revelation and the Limits of Historical Criticism* (Oxford: Oxford University Press, 1982), chap. 7.

[23] I discuss this in *Divine Revelation,* pp. 133-37.

[24] Wiles, "In What Sense Is Christianity a 'Historical' Religion?" p. 9.

Wiles is correct to press this point, for it highlights one way in which historical study generates a very complex question about the criteria for the identity of the Christian tradition. Historical investigation does make it impossible to speak in a simplistic fashion about the essence of Christianity. It thus forces us to come to terms with the contested character of most religious traditions. Christianity is not a rigid, static system of belief. It has changed and will change. Hence there is no easy way to discredit those attempts which seek to develop a version of Christian theology which does not depend critically on appeal to past events.

Yet I would stand by my verdict on Lessing and would apply it also to Wiles's program to develop a version of the Christian faith which does not require any essential reference to past events in history.[25] What matters here is not the merits of either side in this dispute but the kind of evidence that is relevant.

I suggest that the following set of considerations captures the crucial material relevant to deciding whether a proposed interpretation is a genuine version of the Christian faith rather than a rejection of it. Let me express them in terms of a set of questions. Do the objections to the element to be rejected succeed? Is there a substantive case to show that the proposed alternative has genuine continuity with agreed elements in the existing Christian tradition? Is the intrinsic nature of the change acceptable to our considered judgment? Does the proposed change involve the loss of crucial warrants for vital parts of the Christian claim as a whole? Does the proposed change have drastic consequences for other significant areas of Christian doctrine, such as the trinity, grace, and so forth? Are there any historical precedents which can act as case studies for potential development given the proposed change? As we pursue these questions, we will be able to discern the criteria of identity for legitimate continuity in the Christian tradition. It is historical investigation which has forced us to face this issue in modern times.

A fourth issue lies close by. Historical study also confronts us with another question, which is even more acute. Thus some have suggested that our knowledge of the past shows that there is a vast gap between past and present. So much so that it is going to be quite impossible for modern believers to appropriate even those elements which were central to the canonical writers.[26] Therefore considerable attention must be given to the hermeneutical task of translating what the text meant into what it presently means for faith and practice. This is a vast topic, but it is obvious that it demands painstaking philosophical scrutiny. Lessing was perhaps unaware of this issue, yet there is surely a hint of it when he pointed out that what was once significant to people as an argument in theology could cease to be compelling to later generations. Maybe he hit on that gap, which has now for many become a yawning chasm.

In mentioning a fifth and final issue, let us note that the foregoing discussion makes it very clear that accounts of the relation between faith and history need to

[25] I discuss Wiles's position in *Divine Revelation,* chap. 4.

[26] This matter has been pressed very forthrightly by Dennis Nineham, *The Use and Abuse of the Bible* (London: Macmillan, 1976).

attend to particular versions of the Christian faith. History may raise one set of issues for a liberal version of Christianity and another set for a conservative version. Concerning the latter, one of the most interesting questions to be raised in the last century of study is whether commitment to divine intervention is compatible with the rational structure of historical investigation. This issue was posed acutely by Ernst Troeltsch in the nineteenth century and has been raised even more clearly by Van Harvey in our own.[27] Expressed rather bluntly the question is this: Does belief in direct divine action in the world grind sound historical judgment to a halt? My own considered judgment is that it does not.[28]

However we resolve this question, it is obvious that the relation between faith and history is one which calls for extended philosophical investigation. No doubt the philosopher will have to cross boundaries which provoke disquiet in some quarters. No doubt also, crossing those boundaries will call for sensitive openness to skills and conclusions which lie outside normal philosophical competence. Sensible philosophers will try not to step on too many theological and historical toes. Yet whatever the risks, the effort must be made, for the issues involved are far too important to be left exclusively in the hands of theologians and historians. Let philosophers walk in where angels have feared to tread.

[27] A full exposition of Troeltsch and Harvey can be found in *Divine Revelation*, chaps. 5 and 6.

[28] This is the burden of the argument developed in *Divine Revelation*, chaps. 5 to 7.

Chapter Sixteen
Religion And Science

To a great extent the discussion of the relation between religion and science has become stale and boring. Even when it is raised in a dramatic fashion, as has happened recently with the debate between "creationism" and evolution, few outside the circles directly involved take it very seriously. Although there is still opposition to Darwin the general feeling is that the issue has been thrashed to death and it is best left buried for good. Every schoolchild knows that in the warfare between science and religion, science has won and religion remains defeated. Weariness propels us to move on to another issue.

Philosophers, however, will want to proceed more cautiously. There are good reasons for this posture. To begin, bold generalizations about the relation between religion and science are bound to be misleading. Both elements in the relation are extremely complicated enterprises; any account of the relation between them must reflect this fact. Moreover, emotive talk about warfare between science and religion does more justice to sensational debate which for a time catches the public eye than it does to sober historical reality. Some religious believers have indeed resisted some well established scientific theories, but this is not the whole story. It is too easily forgotten that mysterious as the origins of science still are, science grew on soil which was well watered by belief in the rationality and order of nature. That belief in turn was nurtured by the classical Judaic-Christian heritage. In this chapter we shall stand back and identify some of the more important questions raised for religion by the development of science. Fundamentally, religion and science interact at two distinct though not unrelated levels.

RELIGION AND THE RESULTS OF SCIENCE

Clearly one way in which science has an impact on religion is that it can call into question the truth of particular religious doctrines. It is at this level that most people first come across questions about the relation between faith and science. Undoubtedly the most famous example in this regard is the conflict generated by Darwin's theory of evolution. Let us pause and take note of the way in which the theory of evolution challenged religious belief. It did so in two separate areas.

First, it challenged the appeal to design as it was enshrined in classical natural theology. That appeal attempted to prove the existence of God by invoking divine action to explain why specific developments took place in nature. Thus divine action explained the complex working and purpose, say, of the human eye. Somehow it seemed as if the eye could not just arrive out of nowhere. Evolution, however, allowed one to explain the development of organs like the eye without referring directly to divine action. According to evolution, all forms of life are related by descent. Various mechanisms arise as a matter of natural selection without any divine intervention. Hence adequate naturalistic explanations are available for what formerly required supernaturalistic causes. In the process, the classical argument from design collapsed because theological explanations became redundant.

Secondly, and more important, the theory of evolution challenged the classical Christian account of the origins of human beings. The heart of that account maintained that God literally and miraculously created Adam and Eve out of the dust of the earth. These first parents of the race proceeded to rebel against God, falling into grievous sin. The effect of their sin has been transmitted to all human beings since then, so much so that in traditional Christian thought baptism of infants is essential if the stains of original sin and guilt are to be washed away and the punishment of God avoided. In other words, belief in a literal Adam and Eve had ramifications which not only touched one's conception of what it was to be a human being but had very specific relevance to religious rite and liturgy.

In addition, evolution called in question much traditional thinking about the meaning and origins of the Bible. It made impossible a literal reading of the early chapters of Genesis. This in turn elicited the complex question of how one interpreted ancient texts. More particularly, it posed the issue of how one distinguished historical from nonhistorical material in the biblical traditions. As to the origins of the Bible, evolution indirectly threatened traditional theories of inspiration. The classical Christian tradition has again and again construed divine inspiration in terms of divine dictation and divine speaking.[1] The corollary of this is what scripture says,

---

[1] See William J. Abraham, *The Divine Inspiration of Holy Scripture* (Oxford: Oxford University Press, 1981), chap. 1.

God says. But if God says it, it must be true; hence all of scripture is inerrant. When such a theory is linked to a literal reading of Genesis, the conflict with evolution is inevitable. It is only too obvious, therefore, that the theory of evolution has had profound doctrinal consequences for traditional accounts of the meaning and origin of scripture. Those who think these issues have been resolved satisfactorily can do so only if they ignore the debates about hermeneutics and authority which continue to enliven modern theology.

When we consider the impact of evolution in these terms, what should surprise is less the crisis that it engendered and more the speed with which the vast majority of theologians have quite naturally come to terms with it. The most popular trend has been to adopt the position of theistic evolution. On this view what is essential to the health of theism is that God is the creator and sustainer of all that is. How God actually creates is a matter for scientific research and discovery. God may well have created *homo sapiens* through the process of natural selection. If he did not, then this can only be known not by appeal to special revelation but by the development of more adequate scientific accounts of human origins. Biblical exegesis does not resolve the issue because the Bible does not address this matter directly and because it speaks from within the cultural context of its own times. Hence belief in divine creation and belief in evolution are entirely compatible.

THE SEARCH FOR COMPATIBILITY

The underlying principle at work here is the simple one that theology should seek to build on established accounts of the world as furnished by natural science. This does not imply that theology will not have its own unique sources for its reflection. Thus it will still draw on special revelation, on religious experience, and on past religious reflection. Yet it will also make judicious appeal to reasoned conclusions as furnished by science and will seek to interpret and reinterpret its own unique sources in the light of scientific truth. Out of this matrix the theologian proceeds to develop a religious understanding of the world and human nature. To achieve success at this point is one of the great challenges of modern systematic theology. In other words, the theologian has the unenviable task of bringing together the relevant considerations from scripture, tradition, experience, and reason and uniting them to develop a clear, coherent, and healthy doctrine of creation.

This is easier said than done. One reason for the difficulty stems from the contested character of scientific claims. At this point relying on evolution as a paradigm case of the relation between science and particular religious doctrines can be misleading. Where evolution is concerned, there is a relatively stable consensus among scientists. To be sure, there are those within both science and theology who have challenged the traditional theory of evolution. However, this does not radically alter the situation. On the one hand, those who challenge it within science normally want to call for drastic modification rather than total rejection. On the other hand, those who challenge evolution from within theology have failed to convince the scientific community as a whole that it is wrong and have failed to offer an agreed account of those parts of the biblical traditions which are a crucial factor in their proposed alternative. Hence evolution still remains a cornerstone of modern biology. So in this instance the theologian has relatively solid ground to start from.

Other cases may be more difficult. This was the situation some time ago when there were competing theories of the origins of the cosmos. Thus some scientists argued for a steady-state theory where creation was construed as continuous, while others supported the big bang theory where the universe was construed as beginning at a single moment of time. In this case theologians simply had to try to accommodate either possibility, as neither is incompatible with divine creation. More recent research tends to confirm the big bang theory; hence the option is more clear-cut now than it was earlier. In present circumstances the possibility of affirming the traditional doctrine of creation *ex nihilo* would seem to be much enhanced. In fact, as Robert Jastrow graphically suggests, astronomers have reached the summit of the mountain of truth only to find the theologians already there.[2]

Some scientists may sense this as an embarrassment, but there is no reason why this should be so. Any scientific proposal will be acceptable in the end not because it neatly coheres with a particular religious tradition but because it has its own data and warrants. Equally, any theological proposal will have to be defended in its own right. Coherence with a particular scientific theory will not in itself show it to be true. At best it will only be a necessary and not a sufficient basis for its truth. Hence those scientists who studiously avoid theories which in principle seem to lend indirect support to a religious position have totally failed to appreciate the complex logic of religious belief. Scientific theories do not prove or verify in any strict sense particular religious doctrines. With sufficient intellectual dexterity they can be located in nontheistic visions of the universe.

Extremely interesting issues arise where religious doctrine comes into conflict with highly disputed theories in science. Consider in this regard, the account of human nature furnished by a behaviorist like B. F. Skinner. Skinner's view of human beings reduces them to much less than what is affirmed by scripture, religious experience, and classical religious reflection. It is difficult to see how the two accounts can be at all reconciled. What should religious believers do in such a case? Should Skinner be ignored because he offers a minority report within modern psychology? Should they wait for further light on the matter and just live with the tensions? Should they treat Skinner's proposals simply as a methodological device for psychological research, thus denying them any explanatory status and thereby making them theologically harmless? Or should they rely on theological considerations to reject Skinner's account of human nature? All four of these seem to me to be viable options.

What this example shows is that we should avoid blanket generalizations about the relation between the results of science and particular religious doctrines. Theologians tend to have a bad conscience about the past, which understandably leads them to want to avoid serious conflict in the future. Some unbelievers, keen to con-

---

[2] Robert Jastrow, *God and the Astronomers* (New York: W. W. Norton, 1978), p. 116.

strue science as the only avenue to truth, are apt to use scientific theory to discredit religious belief. Each case must be worked through on its merits, and no one can assuredly predict the outcome. Everyone is vulnerable. Liberal theologians can too readily accept as final what turns out to be provisional if not false. Thus, for example, some nineteenth-century theologians happily accepted current scientific theory on racial origins, which in turn undergirded the moral and social claim that for black people servitude was the fulfillment of their proper destiny.[3] Conservative theologians, on the other side, can be too resistant to change, as history very readily proves. What is required is sensitive judgment. There is a time for bold reinterpretation of religious doctrine, and there is a time for dogged resistance to change. There is even a time for patient agnosticism where confession of ignorance as to what to do is the best policy. Only good judgment can enable us to discern which option to take. We can be helped at this point by exploring the kinds of explanations which are on offer in both science and religion. To that we now turn.

RELIGION AND THE LOGIC OF SCIENCE

The results of science and particular religious doctrines have come into conflict in the past only because they offer incompatible accounts of the same phenomena. Thus the theory of evolution posed a problem for faith because it made traditional claims about divine action in creation implausible or redundant. The way out of this involved a recasting of the doctrine of divine creation which was compatible with evolution. This issue leads very naturally therefore to the more general question of how scientific explanations are to be related to theological explanations. More particularly, we want to know if there can be any value from a scientific point of view in resorting to a theological explanation which speaks of direct divine intervention in the world.

It is often thought that the answer to this question must be an emphatic no. Philosophers, until recently, have paid little or no attention to it mainly because they have failed to realize that theological discourse can be, and sometimes is, explanatory. Theologians, for their part, have thought that it involves an implicit appeal to what they call the god of the gaps and that it involves a repudiation of the scientific world view. Rudolf Bultmann expressed the general distaste in a passage which is now justly famous.

> It is impossible to use electric light and the wireless and to avail ourselves of modern medical and surgical discoveries, and at the same time to believe in the New Testament world of spirits and miracles. We may think we can manage it in our own lives, but to expect others to do so is to make the Christian faith unintelligible and unacceptable to the modern world.[4]

[3] For specific cases see Ralph E. Luckner, "Liberal Theology and Social Conservativism: A Southern Tradition, 1840–1920," *Church History,* 1981, pp. 193–204.

[4] Rudolf Bultmann, "New Testament and Mythology," in *Kerygma and Myth,* ed. Hans Werner Bartsch, trans. Reginald H. Fuller (New York: Harper and Row, 1961), p. 5.

As it stands, this is a splendid piece of philosophical dogmatism. Bultmann offers us no reasoned argument for his conclusion. To decide whether he is right or not we need to explore the logic of scientific explanation in some detail. For the sake of clarity we shall concentrate on the standard account of scientific explanation to be found in the hard sciences such as physics and chemistry. Moreover, we shall not enter into those disputes surrounding the role of paradigm shifts or internal revolution within science. We shall work, that is, with the kind of explanation on offer within normal science.

Scientific explanations are a remarkably simple achievement. Thus science explains an event E by showing that E can be predicted to a greater or lesser degree of certainty by relating E to a set of laws and preceding conditions which together entail or make inductively probable the occurrence of E.[5] Thus the movement of a billiard ball can be explained by showing that it is inevitable given the various positions of the agents in operation on the table and the forces governing their motion.

What then of theological explanations? How do they compare with scientific explanations? Theological explanations differ in that they involve an appeal to divine agency; hence they differ radically in content. They differ also in the kind of explanation on offer; hence they differ in logic. Typically theological explanations explain an event E by showing that E is brought about by God for certain intentions and purposes. What we have in this case is a personal explanation which makes intelligible what has happened by relating it to the activity of God and relating that activity in turn to divine intentions and purposes.

The obvious analogy for this is those explanations where we explain events in terms of the activity and intentions of human agents. Thus we explain Smith's bleeding ear by pointing out that it was caused by Jones's biting him in the rugby scrum and we explain Jones's biting Smith by saying that he did it to settle an old score where Smith had kicked him ten minutes earlier. This is not a scientific explanation, for there are no laws and no predictions of the specific sort utilized in science. It is a personal explanation which is unique and irreducible.

THE SEARCH FOR HARMONY

Bearing this in mind, we can see immediately that there is a natural harmony in using both scientific explanations and theological explanations for the same event. Consider the case where Susan gets ill and goes to the doctor. He prescribes certain medicine, and she recovers. Later she thanks God for her recovery. Prima facie this seems odd. On the one hand, her recovery can be given a scientific explanation. On the other, she attributes it in some sense to God. How can this be? The answer lies in the fact that as a theist Susan believes that the laws governing the medicine which cured her are the result of divine creation, both past and ongoing. Hence there is

---

[5] See, for example, Carl G. Hempel, "Explanation in Science and History," *The Philosophy of Science*, ed. P. H. Nidditch (Oxford: Oxford University Press, 1968), pp. 54–79.

harmony between the different explanations invoked in the contexts of surgery and worship. We might say that the explanations work at two different levels.

The issue becomes even more interesting when we change the story dramatically. Suppose Susan collapses and dies. A postmortem examination shows the cause of death to be a heart attack. All involved in the case agree. Three days later, however, to everyone's amazement Susan comes back to life. As they are about to bury her, she calls out to be released. They open the coffin, and she steps out. All agree that it is Susan; all normal criteria of identity show it to be so. As most stand astonished, her grandmother sings the doxology. Later she explains how her prayers for a resurrection have been answered; God, she says, has raised Susan from the dead.

This story is entirely fictional and is designed to focus sharply the relation between scientific explanation and the theological explanation when the latter involves direct intervention in the world. What are we to make of this situation? How are we to explain what has happened?

As it stands we have no scientific explanation to hand. The medical profession is completely baffled. There are no known laws to cover the case before us. Could they come up with some? From a logical point of view they could, but it is unlikely that they would be very successful. There are two reasons for this. First, the event concerned is rare. Hence their ability to reflect on a class of events of a like nature cannot be exercised in any stringent sense. Secondly, and much more important, the laws they attempt to think up turn out to be so complicated and awkward that they have to sacrifice a crucial condition for any good law of science, namely, simplicity. Moreover, what they propose plays havoc with a host of laws which they have found invaluable in explaining a host of other phenomena.

Suppose now we invite them seriously to consider that God really did intervene. We mount a soft-rationalist case for direct divine intervention. What intellectual effect will this have on their work as scientists? If they are convinced, it not only explains what has happened but also relieves them of the need to alter their beliefs about the normal course of nature and the laws which govern it. They can retain their present explanatory beliefs intact and turn their attention to those events which are much more likely to be susceptible of lawlike explanation. The event is a rare and unique occurrence brought about by God to fulfill certain intentions and purposes. In this instance the search for scientific explanation is unnecessary and redundant.[6]

REBUTTING OBJECTIONS

The argument I have just deployed asserts that there can be manifest harmony between science and belief in divine intervention. This is a bold claim, which will inevitably be looked on with suspicion. I want now to defuse some of that suspicion

[6] I have made use of the argument set out here to defend the resurrection of Jesus in *Divine Revelation and the Limits of Historical Criticism* (Oxford: Oxford University Press, 1982), chap. 8.

by considering some objections. The primary objection will come from theologians who fear that my position suggests that God is a kind of push-button deity, who shows up only when all else fails. Let us call this the occasionalist objection. Scientists, for their part, may worry that resort to divine intervention opens the door to all sorts of nonsense. Once we appeal to divine action, then there seems to be no control on what happens. Let us call this the floodgate objection.

The answer to the floodgate objection is quite simple. It rests on the assumption that belief in divine intervention in the world is logically of the same status as belief in UFOs, witches, ghosts, poltergeists, irrational psychic powers, visitors from outer space, and any other kind of nonsensical agents we care to mention. Such an assumption seems to me to be patently false. At the very least, it must be set out and argued rather than dogmatically stated. It may, of course, be part of the common sense of our culture that belief in divine intervention is a legacy of past superstition, but this is a poor guide to sound intellectual judgment. As I have argued in some detail already, religious belief is not entirely without its own controls, and there is no good reason why one who believes in divine intervention should thereby be committed to allowing nonsense to rule where it will.

It might also be the case that the floodgate objection rests on the assumption that science and science alone can explain what happens in the world. Hence theological explanations are unacceptable a priori. This has had widespread support in our modern culture insofar as science has successfully addressed a host of questions previously left unanswered. The problems in this proposal, however, are manifold. I mention two here. First, this is a philosophical or metaphysical thesis, which has long been associated with logical positivism. As such, it is not something that science itself has shown to be true. At best it is a statement of faith; at worst it is unsubstantiated prejudice. Secondly, if personal explanations do differ from scientific explanations, then it is simply false to say that science and science alone can explain what happens. Clearly we do rely on personal explanations both in everyday life and in history to explain events. Appeal to divine action simply extends the range of explanatory agents we use in accounting for what happens. As yet no one has proved that there is an insurmountable philosophical barrier to exercising this option.

But is there a theological barrier? This leads us very neatly to the occasionalist objection to my position. Hidden beneath this objection are a number of concerns, which need to be identified and answered separately. It is not easy to do justice to all the issues involved, but let us approach them as sensitively as possible.

Part of the theologian's worry is that talk of divine intervention seems to imply that God is absent from the world when he is not intervening. This is simply false. If God exists, whatever else he may do, he continually sustains the universe. Perhaps the problem arises here from a failure of the imagination. We forget that God, being omnipotent, can perform a host of actions at once. Because we focus on one particular act of intervention we forget what else he may be doing. In other words, divine intervention in no way implies or entails an absentee deity.

A further worry is that if God intervenes, then his intervention must somehow be capricious and unpredictable. Now certainly it will not be predictable, for God remains free in all that he does. It will not, however, be capricious. If God intervenes, we can be sure that he will do so for some legitimate intention or purpose. It will, to be sure, often be very difficult to discern why God intervenes or, for that matter, why he does not intervene. His ways are not always our ways or our thoughts his thoughts. But that his action should be capricious seems on the face of it false.

Yet another worry is that some feel that the view of God suggested here implies a kind of God of magic who waves his wand or presses the appropriate button and behold his will is done. The problem this time is that such descriptions of God's activity rely on crude and inappropriate analogies. Were God to intervene directly, there would of course be a basic action on his part. He would bring about some state of affairs without first bringing about some other state of affairs. This would be no more magical than a human agent's raising an arm or performing any other basic action. Besides, when God intervenes, the relation between God and the world remains an ultimate mystery far removed from what we know takes place in the case of magic.

Perhaps there is still a lingering fear that the theologian steps in with a theological explanation only when all else fails. Thus the propriety of divine action depends on the inability of science to furnish an answer. Therefore God becomes a last-resort explanation, and he is in constant danger of being squeezed out of the gaps of scientific failure. Were it not better, it might be argued, to keep on looking for a scientific explanation for all events and retain God's activity at the level of generally creating and sustaining all that is?

This objection has considerable force, but it is not ultimately successful. To begin, it is an act of faith of messianic proportions to believe that scientists will make the kind of revisions needed to cope with the example given. Moreover, the theological explanation may not at all be brought forward as a last resort to save the day. On the contrary, it may appear by far the most natural and plausible way to deal with all the relevant phenomena. Failure to find an adequate scientific explanation will be part of the data which will have to be weighed. Theoretically it will always be possible to be proved wrong in that a scientific explanation might, logically speaking, be found. But this is not something to fear; it is part of the risk of offering an explanation in the first place. If nothing is ventured, nothing is gained. We can well live with the risks of being proved wrong.

Back of all these concerns there may still be the lingering suspicion that the radical transcendence of God is being denied. God seems to be reduced to one agent among other agents in the working of the universe. The only difference seems to be that God is more ingenious and powerful in what he does. To this I reply that I do not see that I at all deny the transcendence of God. On the contrary, construing God as an agent seems essential to any serious account of the theistic traditions of the world. Anything less would be both religiously and intellectually deficient. Moreover, divine intervention of the kind postulated above seems by far the most economical and clear way of understanding those acts of God which are central to the Christian tradition. Any account of divine transcendence must assume and work from this. Hence I do not think that I have at all put divine transcendence at risk in what I have argued.

CONCLUDING COMMENTS

Our attention in this chapter has been directed to the relation between religion and science. I have argued that religious believers have no need to fear either the results or the logic of science. A mature religious tradition will appropriate all that is best in science, duly weighing the kind of information made available and its fallible status. Indeed it is a religious duty to pursue science as a means of reading the book of nature and as fulfillment of the mandate to act as responsible stewards of the natural world. A healthy religious tradition need fear nothing of the truth which science reveals.

Equally, science need not fear religion as a hindrance to the pursuit of scientific explanations for events in the world. Science and religion are compatible at a deep conceptual level. This is even the case when appeal may be made to direct divine intervention on the side of theology. The latter may be a positive gain, for it can relieve science of a burden that may be much too great to bear.

We can perhaps sense this more fully if we bear the following factors in mind. First, theological language can be, and often is, explanatory in function. The concept of divine agency has real power to explain both lawlike, regular activity in nature and particular events within space and time. It is not just pious emotion aimed to soothe people's nerves or to shield them from the truth. Secondly, belief in divine intervention is not an option to be taken at whim when all else fails. It is a serious and even rational attempt to understand and explain what has happened in the world. Aware of the complexity and even pitfalls it involves, those committed to it need to support such belief by appeal to the appropriate data and warrants. Lastly, we should not exaggerate past failure. That some have looked too exclusively or too hastily to direct divine action as a means of coping with failure in science is sober historical reality. Yet no one has shown that science explains everything. Let us follow the evidence where it leads and use whatever concepts and explanations will ultimately work. The soft rationalist will tread such a path with joy, seizing it as an opportunity to exercise all the wisdom we can muster.

Chapter Seventeen
Life After Death

There are few topics more bewildering in the philosophy of religion than that of life after death. One good reason for this lies close at hand. Death is not a pleasant topic; for most people it is very naturally a forbidding and emotional matter. After all, death can have a devastating effect upon us, as happens when someone very close to us dies. Moreover, when we stop to think of our own death, there is often a sense of fear and mystery which can leave us confused and uncertain.

PHILOSOPHY AND LIFE AFTER DEATH

Philosophical perplexity runs much deeper than this and manifests itself on two distinct levels. To begin, we are at a loss to know how to evaluate putative evidence for or against claims about immortality. We can set about finding out what happens when we fall asleep, but how do we set about finding out what happens when we die? In the abstract it is not easy to know where to turn to answer this. Concrete proposals can leave us baffled because those who claim to have positive evidence do not always present themselves dressed out in generally accepted credentials. Some, such as mediums and their interpreters, are initially associated with the weird and the abnormal, if not the occult and the absurd. Even ordinary people who may themselves have experiences which suggest an afterlife are tempted to take them as a sign of madness rather than evidence for immortality.

As we probe deeper into putative evidence, we find ourselves unsettled at another level. We find ourselves baffled, that is, by a set of conceptional issues which are demanding in the extreme. We are informed, for example, that a certain person who is dead has sent a message to a friend through a medium. But how can a person exist as a spirit without a body? What in fact are persons? Are they complicated, physical bodies which happen to feel and think? Or are they simple, immaterial substances or souls? And is the soul a series of mental events, running parallel to physical events in the brain? Or are persons a combination of body and soul?

In addition, we want to know how we are to identify persons. Is it by means of identifying bodies? Or is it by memory and personality traits? Or is it by a combination of all three?

Moreover, we find it difficult even to conceive of an afterlife. Indeed, can we conceive of it at all? If we can, is it a kind of shadowy existence, such as we find in Homer or early Hebrew thought? Or is it an immortality of the soul, such as we find in Plato? Or a resurrection of the body, as we find in Paul? Or a series of reincarnations, ending in some kind of nonindividual immortality, as suggested by Hinduism? Or is it a complex combination of these arranged in temporal order, as ingeniously worked out of late by John Hick?[1] Or is discourse about immortality when construed along any such lines being radically misinterpreted? Perhaps talk about eternal life or life after death has nothing to do with life beyond the grave and more to do with the kind of life a person is living, as has been suggested by D. Z. Phillips.[2]

Clearly great patience is needed if we are to make any progress, for it is important that we set the issue in its appropriate context. If we are to treat life after death as an issue in philosophy of religion rather than, say, philosophy of mind, it is imperative that we try to work with a serious religious option which has been embraced by a living religious community rather than work with imaginative suggestions or personal speculation.

This, of course, has its own problems. What religious options shall we consider? Should we look at those of the West? Or the East? Or both? Preliminary work such as is our concern here must narrow the field. It is not just a matter of saving space. If we are to deal seriously with relevant evidence, then too much time cannot be given to the complex, hermeneutical issues involved in presenting the main religious options available. What is at stake here is a serious treatment of the topic itself. Unless we have a reasonably rich account of one serious option, then it is unlikely that any account will receive the attention it merits. This is so for two reasons. First, a tour of various accounts tends to induce an air of unreality into the discussion. Things are surely bad enough in this domain without making them worse as a matter of inadvertent policy. Secondly, claims about life after death when treated in religion do not exist in a vacuum. They are part of a wider metaphysical proposal which should not be set aside as irrelevant. For these reasons I shall concentrate in what follows on a Christian vision of life after death.

[1] John Hick, *Death and Eternal Life* (Glasgow: William Collins, 1976), chap. 22.
[2] D. Z. Phillips, *Death and Immortality* (London: Macmillan, 1970).

It should be noted that this approach does not entail either any disrespect for, or lack of interest in, alternative accounts, whether these be religious or nonreligious, communal or personal. Nor does it mean that I think it is easy even to articulate or defend what any particular Christian account is, purely on the level of description. My concern is simply to introduce the topic by working with a view of life after death which will allow some of the central issues which arise to be covered in some detail.

THE CLASSICAL CHRISTIAN CONCEPTION OF IMMORTALITY

Immortality in the classical Christian tradition is a contested doctrine. Generally it has been construed as a synthesis of biblical and Greek thought.[3] This assumption needs to be treated with some caution, however, for it can suggest that Greek categories are somehow being imposed on the biblical material. There are at times clear differences between, say, Paul and Plato, but even if one concentrates on the New Testament and tries to make sense of all that is said there, it is extremely difficult to avoid categories which are not analogous with Greek ideas. In particular, despite much emphasis on bodily resurrection as essential ultimately to life after death, some concept of the soul is needed to capture Christian convictions about the nature of the intermediate state between death and resurrection.[4] With this in mind, how might we lay out a version of the classical tradition? Perhaps the following will suffice.[5]

Life on earth is clearly an embodied existence; people live and move and have their being in bodies. At death the body dies but the soul lives on. The soul separates from the body and those who die in the Lord are immediately with God and in the presence of Christ. There they participate in a form of conscious existence. In such a state they remain until the general resurrection of the dead. At that point their souls will be given a new body; that body will be different in some respects from the bodies we know, so much so that it is often called a spiritual body. There will be continuity with the old, earthly body though there will not necessarily be any strict material or numerical identity with it. This resurrected body will be placed in an environment appropriate to it after a general judgment. This, in turn will be a prelude to the consummation of God's plans wherein the people of God are given the fullness of eternal life.

The reader will note that I have omitted several elements which are to be

[3] See, for example, Van A. Harvey, *A Handbook of Theological Terms* (New York: Macmillan, 1964), p. 128.

[4] Even Oscar Cullman, who has made much of the contrast between Greek and biblical thought on immortality, has to posit some kind of intermediate state where people "sleep" but are near to Christ. The "inner man" lives on even without a body. See Cullman's "Immortality of the Soul or Resurrection of the Dead? The Witness of the New Testament?" in *Immortality*, ed. Terence Penelhum (Belmont, Calif.: Wadsworth, 1973), pp. 81–83.

[5] For a fuller account by a philosopher see Ninian Smart, "Death in the Judaeo-Christian Tradition," in *Man's Concern with Death*, Arnold Toynbee et al. (London: Hodder and Stoughton, 1968), pp. 116–21.

found in Christian accounts of life after death. Thus there is no mention of such matters as the return of Christ, purgatory, hell, limbo, the beatific vision, conditional annihilation, and so on. This is entirely appropriate, for the aim is to lay out the bare essentials of the classical Christian conception of immortality. Central to that is some kind of intermediate state without a body and an ultimate state in a resurrected body. Beyond that we need not venture any further into systematic theology.

Despite the brevity, this way of construing talk about immortality has been vigorously attacked by D. Z. Phillips. Phillips contends that it involves a radical misconception of the meaning of questions about death and immortality. Philosophical reflection, he argues, should begin with what belief in immortality means in the life of religious devotion. In that case we shall see, for example, that talk about whether a man has a soul has nothing to do with any kind of empirical question.

> It is not like asking whether he has a larynx or not. Neither is asking whether a man would sell his soul like asking whether he would sell his body, say for medical research. One can investigate whether a man has a larynx or not quite independently of any knowledge of the kind of life he is living. The investigation is into the existence or state of a physical object. But an investigation as to whether a man has a soul or not, or into the state his soul is in, has nothing to do with the location or examination of an object. Questions about the state of a man's soul are questions about the kind of life he is living. If the soul were some quite distinct entity within a man, it would follow that whatever a man did would not affect it. But this is not how we speak of soul. The relation between the soul and how a man lives is not a contingent one. It is when a man sinks to depths of bestiality that someone might say that he had lost his soul. It is a man's relation to what is morally praiseworthy and fine that would determine whether this judgement was applicable or not.[6]

Phillips is correct to insist that the logic of language about souls is more complex than most philosophers have recognized. Clearly some uses do fit his analysis. But it is simply false to claim that the uses to which he attends exhaust the full range of usage. Phillips seems to be focusing on those which fit his own philosophical commitments. Any use which would suggest any ontological commitments about a life beyond the grave are ignored or dismissed as superstitious. Talk about souls does at times have ontological implications within religion. To prove that would be pedantic for anyone acquainted with the history of religious thought.

It is ironical that Phillips should miss this, for he insists, with most ordinary language philosophers, that the ideal for philosophers is to attend to the actual usage of religious language if we are to understand the meaning of religious discourse. Phillips's practice falls short of his precept. Indeed it is clear that Phillips has imported into the discussion at the outset the standard philosophical objections to life after death. Such objections, as he sees it, render traditional discourse otiose and incoherent. Hence it is natural to cast around and find more attractive uses which will cohere with this conclusion. Even then, however, Phillips's own analysis re-

---

[6] Phillips, *Death and Immortality*, p. 44.

mains thoroughly obscure. I know of no religious community which actually operates with Phillips's account of life after death. We could, of course, reinterpret discourse about life after death in the direction he commends. But this is a private matter which does not affect the present discussion.

What are the main arguments for the kind of life after death I have just set forth? In all, four different kinds of argument have been given: metaphysical, moral, empirical, and theological. In presenting and evaluating these arguments I shall concentrate on the last two, especially on empirical arguments. I am presuming, at this point, that discourse about life after death is coherent. This has, of course, been vigorously contested in some quarters. For reasons which will become clear as we proceed, I prefer to deal with this issue when we come to examine some arguments against the traditional conception of immortality.

THE METAPHYSICAL AND MORAL ARGUMENTS

The metaphysical argument for life after death focuses on what it is to be a soul. The heart of this argument is that the soul is naturally immortal. In various forms it has been embraced by Plato, Aquinas, Butler, and Maritain. In its most popular form it attempts to prove that the idea of indestructability is logically implied by the idea of a soul. On this view only composite things can be destroyed. Destruction, in fact, involves the breaking down of a thing into its composite parts; so my body perishes by being broken into pieces or by being separated into parts. The soul, however, is not a composite thing; it does not have parts; it is an immaterial substance. Hence it cannot be destroyed. Maritain expresses this point forcefully as follows:

> A spiritual soul cannot be corrupted, since it possesses no matter; it cannot be disintegrated, since it has no substantial parts; it cannot lose its individual unity, since it is self-subsisting, nor its internal energy, since it contains within itself all the sources of its energies. The human soul cannot die. Once it exists, it cannot disappear; it will necessarily exist for ever, endure without end.[7]

There are several difficulties in this argument. To succeed it would have to be shown that the soul is a simple substance; this has not been done. Prima facie it is implausible even to move in this direction for, insofar as the soul is identified with consciousness and mental life, the latter appear to be subject to division and perhaps even dissolution. The more obvious objection to it is that there may well be a mode of destruction appropriate to a soul. Perhaps souls just peter out gradually like a flame flickering until it dies. Hence it is wrong to argue that destruction necessarily involves the dissolution into parts. For these reasons the argument from the nature of the soul in itself carries very little conviction. The very concept of the soul is so strange, obscure, and contested that claims about its necessary immortality appear rhetorical and strained.

[7] Jacques Maritain, *The Range of Reason* (London: Godfrey Bles, 1953), p. 60.

Much the same can be said about arguments from morality. Indeed it is difficult to find a good argument even intended as a serious reason for life after death. The thrust of the argument stems from Kant and maintains that without immortality, morality becomes senseless. Morality, for example, requires that happiness and virtue kiss in happy union. Clearly that does not happen in this life; but it ought to happen; therefore there is a life after death where it will happen.

The flaws in this argument hardly need stating. Morality can make perfectly good sense even if death is the end of human existence. Indeed believing that life ends with the death of the body can conceivably enhance morality. After all, if life is short, should we not be more kind and considerate to each other? Moreover, even though we may think that virtue *ought* to be crowned with happiness, this is no guarantee that it will. Perhaps it is wishful thinking to believe that everything will work out the way we think it ought to work out. Hence the moral argument fails completely.

THE EMPIRICAL EVIDENCE

How do empirical arguments fare? Can they provide a more solid basis for belief in a life after death? In modern times distinguished philosophers have been much interested in this question and have been favorably impressed. The main body of evidence considered to date by philosophers has been furnished by parapsychology. However, important new material is now surfacing which deserves to be considered with diligence. Let us take the evidence from parapsychology first. The most relevant considerations involve either appearances of dead people to someone still alive or communications from dead people through a medium to people now alive. Let us take these in turn.

The former is well illustrated by the well-known translator of the New Testament, J. B. Phillips. After pointing out that he is incredulous by nature and as unsuperstitious as they come, he mentions the following experience.

> Many of us who believe in what is technically known as the Communion of Saints, must have experienced the sense of nearness, for a fairly short time, of those whom we love soon after they have died. This has certainly happened to me several times. But the late C. S. Lewis, whom I did not know very well, and had only seen in the flesh once, but with whom I had corresponded a fair amount, gave me an unusual experience. A few days after his death, while I was watching television, he "appeared" sitting in a chair within a few feet of me, and spoke a few words which were particularly relevant to the difficult circumstances through which I was passing. He was ruddier in complexion than ever, grinning all over his face, and as the old-fashioned saying has it, positively glowing with health. The interesting thing to me was that I had not been thinking about him at all. I was neither alarmed nor surprised nor, to satisfy the Bishop of Woolwich, did I look up to see the hole in the ceiling that he might have made on arrival. He was just there—"large as life and twice as natural"! A week later, this time when I was in bed reading before going to sleep, he appeared again, even more rosily radiant than before, and repeated

to me the same message, which was very important to me at the time. I was a little puzzled by this, and I mentioned it to a certain saintly Bishop who was then living in retirement here in Dorset. His reply was, "My dear J . . . , this sort of thing is happening all the time."[8]

What is impressive here is the integrity of the witness and the apparent purpose in Lewis's appearance and communication.

Matters become much more complicated when we turn to the case of communication through mediums. Nothing can substitute for reading some of the particular reports for oneself. The most interesting cases are those where the information transmitted seems only to be available to the person who has died and those where there are clear indications of continuing intention and planning after death. The former is well illustrated in the following example.

> Professor E. R. Dodds, at the time Regius Professor of Greek at Oxford, who, incidentally, does not believe in survival, asked Mr. Drayton Thomas, a Methodist minister, to take a proxy sitting with Mrs. Leonard. (In a proxy sitting, the sitter represents someone else and knows no details about the life of the deceased person with whom it is hoped to make contact.) The sitting was not even at second-hand, on behalf of Professor Dodds himself, but at third-hand, for a friend of his, a Mrs. Lewis. She wanted to try to get proofs of identity from her dead father, Mr. Macaulay, who in life had been a water engineer. All Mr. Thomas was told was his name, home town and date of death, presumably the essential minimum if the medium was to locate any one person among the countless millions of the dead. This minimum seemed to be enough for Freda, Mrs. Leonard's Control, since she set about identifying Mr. Macaulay right away. First she described his tools and drawing office, very well for a person who was not an engineer. Then she mentioned his great interest in saving water, particularly bath water. She gave his pet name, Puggy, for his daughter. She referred to his damaged hand, and so on. And she added one tiny item which seemed uniquely applicable to the Macaulay family. This was to give the names of some persons, who were now, she said, with Mr. Macaulay (these persons were in fact dead), and who had shared a specially happy period during his life on earth. One name puzzled her. "It might be Reece, R.E.E.C.E.," she said "but it sounds like Riss, R.I.S.S." She also added as further proof of identity that Mr. Macaulay had proposed to his first wife on a bridge.
>
> All this meant nothing to Mr. Thomas and he sent the records to Professor Dodds, who sent them on to Mrs. Lewis. She confirmed that all the items given were correct, including names, and added that her father's passion for saving bath water had been a family joke, also that during the happy period referred to, her schoolboy brother had hero-worshipped another boy called Rees and had said so often that his name was spelt R.E.E.S., not R.E.E.C.E., that to tease him his young sisters had taken to singing, "Not Reece but Riss." And Mr. Macaulay did propose to his first wife on a bridge.[9]

[8] J. B. Phillips, *Ring of Truth* (London: Hodder and Stoughton, 1967), p. 117. Reprinted by permission of Hodder and Stoughton Limited.

[9] Rosalind Heywood, "Death and Psychical Research," in *Man's Concern with Death*, Arnold Toynbee, ed. (London: Hodder and Stoughton, 1968), pp. 234–5. Reprinted by permission of Hodder and Stoughton Limited.

Cases of continued intention and planning after death are best seen in reports of cross-correspondence. One famous example involves putative communications from three distinguished Cambridge scholars who died in 1900. Shortly after they died, several women began to get messages which claimed to originate from them. The messages were mere fragments when taken alone, but when put together by an outside person, they formed a coherent message. There were other impressive factors; the receivers were scattered throughout the world; the messages referred to abstruse classical subjects which few but scholars would know; the messages ultimately formed parts of elaborate jigsaw puzzles which seemed to be deliberately designed; and so on.[10]

Another strand of empirical evidence for life after death has been furnished of late by investigation into what is known as the near-death experience. Owing to advanced medical care, many people who have come close to death, if not died, have been brought back to conscious life. Some of these people have been talking, and what they report is of considerable interest. A general pattern has emerged in the reports studied so far. Thus some or all of the following have been recorded: separation of the mind from the body; sensations of drifting and passing through solid objects; knowledge of events in the physical universe; moving through a dark tunnel; coming into a warm, bright light; meeting others and recognizing them; experiencing great bliss and peace; and returning to inhabit one's body.[11] In most cases the experiences have been pleasant.

Once again nothing can substitute for first-hand exposure to detailed reports of the experiences involved. What is impressive is the number of people involved, the considerable degree of agreement, the difficulty of providing standard pharmacological, physiological, neurological, psychological, or sociological explanations for them and the strong sense that they differ radically from dreams or hallucination.

What are we to make of all this empirical data? For the present let us take the evidence one piece at a time. In none of these cases do we have a conclusive argument for life after death. Each sample of evidence can theoretically be explained without resorting to the hypothesis that certain individuals survive death. The "appearance" of C. S. Lewis to J. B. Phillips could clearly be a case of projection from Phillips's imagination. The cases of alleged communications through mediums could be examples of very special extrasensory perception. The near-death experience could simply be an expansion of our knowledge of mental events closely associated with death. Hence any talk of dramatic proof for life after death is exaggerated nonsense.

It would be premature and insensitive, however, to leave the discussion at this level. We need to ask if some of the evidence taken on its own or all of it taken together can give good reason rather than a conclusive argument for immortality. When we raise the issue in this way, then things are much more complex. I would sum up the weight of the evidence in this fashion.

[10] For full details see Heywood, "Death and Psychical Research," pp. 236–38.

[11] Case studies of these factors can be readily found in Kenneth Ring, *Life at Death* (New York: Coward, McCann and Geoghegan, 1980), chaps. 3 and 4.

First, nobody has given an entirely satisfactory explanation of all the phenomena to be explained. Clearly there is data here which needs explaining and some of the evidence is impressive. Especially so when we look at the whole data taken together. Even the near-death experience taken on its own is impressive. In the absence of compelling alternatives, the hypothesis of survival will surely be an attractive solution which will have its defenders. However, in the last analysis we just do not know for certain what is happening. We need continued investigation which will seek to examine the evidence with fearless objectivity. For now the question is an open one.

Secondly, it should be recognized that there may well be conflict between such evidence as there is and the claims of the Christian tradition. H. H. Price has hinted at this conflict. He points out that other-world-describing communications do raise theological problems.

> Some of them are very repugnant to religious people (and not without reason). I am afraid there are the beginnings of a kind of conflict between psychical research and religion here; and this distresses me, because I happen to have a foot in both camps.[12]

Thirdly, and most important, suppose we take the empirical evidence in a wholly positive spirit, giving the benefit of the doubt and agreeing that a good case can be made for survival. Where does that leave us? The answer is unavoidable: it leaves us far short of what the Christian faith claims. On the one hand, it is always possible with atheists like C. J. Ducasse,[13] to treat life after death as a surprising natural fact which has nothing to do with the plans or activity of God. On the other hand, the picture presented gives no hint of the kind of long-range, eternal existence, involving a bodily resurrection, which we encounter in the Christian tradition. Hence there is no substantial, direct empirical evidence for the classical Christian conception of immortality.

THEOLOGICAL CONSIDERATIONS

If claims about immortality cannot be secured by metaphysical, moral, or empirical arguments, then the only alternative would appear to be a straight appeal to theological considerations. But what kind of appeal is possible here? In the nature of the case, the fundamental basis for the Christian hope of immortality must be some doctrine of divine revelation. The reason is not difficult to find.

Let us explore this by noting the common suggestion that the Christian hope of immortality rests fundamentally on the resurrection of Christ. This, however,

---

[12] H. H. Price, "The Problem of Life After Death," in *Immortality*, p. 117. This has long been recognized. See A. E. Taylor, *The Christian Hope of Immortality* (London: Geoffrey Bles, 1938), pp. 67–68.

[13] C. J. Ducasse, *The Belief in a Life After Death* (Springfield, Ill.: Charles C. Thomas, 1961), pp. 14–15, 203.

cannot be so. The argument here has nothing to do with the contested status of the resurrection either as a miracle or as a historical event. It derives in part from the fact that the Christian claim is that Christ was unique. What happened to Christ cannot be extended without warrant to others. In addition, the resurrection of one person in the past cannot be extrapolated to cover all persons in the future. Further warrants are essential to make this move. The obvious warrant in this regard is some kind of teaching or some kind of promise given or endorsed by special divine revelation. Traditionally, Christian theology has located such a warrant in the teaching of Christ and of apostles like Paul. In other words, appeal has been made to the canon of scripture, backed by the claim that it embodies revelation from God.

This is an entirely sensible approach to the issue. The Christian conception of immortality involves reference to the deliberate intentions and activity of God. Eternal life, it is said, is a gift which begins on earth but is consummated by further divine action hereafter. It is surely difficult to know what God will do in the future unless he somehow reveals it. This is because God alone knows what he has in store for the future, for as the crucial agent involved, he has privileged access to his own intentions and plans. What human agents can know depends on how much he reveals to them and even that is not something over which they can have any control. Perhaps God reveals enough to give them hopes of heaven but not enough of heaven to distract them from the projects and tasks which should absorb them here on earth.

In the past theologians have sought to supplement the appeal to special revelation by appeal either to the general character of God or to religious experience. Thus it might be said that a benevolent God would not create human beings in his own image only to see them rot in black holes where they will be eaten by worms. Equally the believer's relation with God is one which has the kind of quality about it which suggests continued existence beyond death. Indeed, it is no accident that Christians speak of eternal life beginning here and now; the covenant relationship with God they claim to enjoy already bears the marks of eternity, so to speak.

These considerations can have a place, but it is a limited and impressionistic place. Inferences from the general omnipotence and benevolence of God are bound to be precarious and speculative. The options are just too numerous for anyone to be very certain. Indeed there is an air of presumption about claiming what God should do with human beings after death. Equally, it is far from clear what we can claim on the basis of religious experience. Either the experience comes couched in terms which are too vague for us to make any inferences or they come couched in terms rich enough for this purpose but which already appeal to special revelation. Hence I think that those who appeal exclusively to the general character of God or religious experience or both taken together have radically inadequate warrants. At best such considerations are impressionistic and supplementary to divine revelation.

It should come as no surprise, therefore, that I find John Hick's recent proposals highly speculative and even fanciful.[14] It is logically possible that we live

---

[14] Hick, *Death and Eternal Life*, chap. 22.

here on earth, proceed after death through a series of lives, spent in other worlds in spaces other than that in which we now live, and then, transcending our personal individuality, live forever in mutual coinherence and unity. Unfortunately, however, the theological and philosophical insurance policies offered by Hick do not have enough of the right kind of material in the small print to underwrite such a project. Having rejected special revelation, Hick must rely on general assumptions about human nature, on philosophical reflection about ultimate reality, on religious experience, and on diverse empirical considerations. What I have argued is that the yield from all of these sources is much more modest than Hick allows.

Interestingly, this has been recognized of late by a theologian who has much in common with Hick. Maurice Wiles, who with Hick rejects any appeal to special revelation, not only questions the traditional doctrine of resurrection but also resolutely refuses to develop any kind of specific alternative.[15] He still holds to belief in immortality, but he cautiously confesses ignorance on how this is to be envisaged. Wiles surely is entirely consistent as he moves in this direction. Without special revelation, great caution if not outright agnosticism rather than cosmopolitan speculation is the natural consequence.

AN IMPORTANT OBJECTION CONSIDERED

I promised earlier to look briefly at the case against belief in immortality. Let me now make good that promise by looking at the most obvious objection to what I have set out heretofore. This focuses on the fact that I have assumed all along that the idea of personal survival is coherent. After all, it might be said, we should establish that the idea of an afterlife is logically possible before we examine the evidence for or against it. When we proceed in this manner, we shall soon discover serious logical obstacles to any claim about life after death. More particularly, we shall find it impossible to preserve the thread of personal identity through the drastic changes necessary to take one through an intermediate state to ultimate resurrection.

This is a fair criticism, but the point about procedure should be challenged. I have reversed the discussion for two reasons. First, the present climate of opinion makes it difficult for the issue of immortality to be pursued with sustained seriousness. Western intellectual circles tend to assume that belief in an afterlife is a mark of superstition; the weight of cultural authority counts against it. In my view this is of no more value than the old argument often heard and printed that the almost universal belief in an afterlife makes it tenable. By beginning with putative evidence, we start to cut into this cultural prejudice against immortality.

A second reason for beginning there is of greater philosophical relevance. One of the great problems we have in this area is lack of imagination. We find it very

[15] Maurice Wiles, *The Remaking of Christian Doctrine* (London: SCM, 1974), pp. 125–46.

difficult to conceive of what immortality could be like and thus need considerable philosophical dexterity, as H. H. Price has shown,[16] to begin thinking clearly in this field. Looking at putative evidence can help us here, for it exposes us to expanded horizons. In particular, reports of empirical investigation such as we find in stories of near-death experience are invaluable in this regard.

This, of course, does not answer the philosophical objection proposed, so let us look at that more closely. The claim as it stands is a very strong one: it alleges that the idea of survival is incoherent. "Person words," as Antony Flew puts it, mean what they mean.

> Words like "you," "I," "person," "somebody," "Flew," "woman,"—though very different in their several particular functions—are all used to refer in one way or another to objects . . . which you can point at, touch, hear, see and talk to. Person words refer to people. And how can such objects as people survive physical dissolution?[17]
>
> In their present use person words have logical liaisons of the very greatest importance: personal identity is the necessary condition of both accountability and expectation; which is only to say that it is unjust to reward or punish someone unless . . . he is the same person who did the deed; and also that it is absurd to expect experiences for Flew in 1984 unless . . . there is going to be a person in existence in 1984 who will be the same person as I. The difficulty is to change the use of person words so radically that it becomes significant to talk of people surviving dissolution: without changing it to such an extent that these vital logical liaisons are lost.[18]

When we apply this to talk about a disembodied intermediate state and an embodied final state, the results are obvious. A disembodied intermediate state is quite literally nonsensical. If bodies are essential to persons, there just cannot be the state envisaged. With final resurrection the conclusion is more difficult to arrive at but no less dismal. The sceptic can always argue that the resurrected individual may be only an imitation replica rather than the same individual who existed prior to the final resurrection. What are we to say to this?

Before we reply, we should note two things. First, we cannot take refuge, as many have sought to do, in the doctrine of a final resurrection. To do so ignores the claim about some kind of intermediate state clearly attested in the canonical literature and the classical Christian tradition. In addition, it ignores the claim that God himself is a person and is not an embodied agent. Secondly, I think there is an element of equivocation in the objection under review. It is not always clear whether the objection is a difficulty, rhetorically presented as a proof of incoherence, or a real, knock-down proof of outright incoherence. Even Flew confesses that we do seem to be able to understand the hopes of warriors expecting to go to a paradise or the fears of the slum mother warned about the penalties of mortal sin.[19] In other

---

[16] H. H. Price, "Survival and the Idea of 'Another World'," in *Immortality*, pp. 21–46.

[17] Antony Flew, "Death," in *New Essays in Philosophical Theology*, ed. Antony Flew and Alasdair MacIntyre (London: SCM, 1955), p. 269.

[18] Ibid., pp. 270–71.

[19] Ibid., p. 267.

words, prima facie we can make sense of survival. This leads in naturally to the main point I want to make.

'In the last analysis everything turns on whether we can believe that our language about persons can take the strain that the drastic changes envisaged entail. To make out the strongest case Flew would have to prove that it cannot do so. Neither he nor any other philosopher has ever achieved this distinction. Nor do I believe that anyone has come close or is likely to. Here is the reason why.

Arguments about personal identity and the nature of persons generally begin with a rough and ready account of the relevant criteria we employ in our present existence. At this level bodily reference is invariably essential. They proceed by envisaging new situations involving drastic changes and then asking whether we can still speak of persons or the same person. Thus from Locke onwards, philosophers have imagined situations where people seem to exchange bodies or where two spheres of consciousness are to be found related to the one brain.[20] We are then invited to think through whether we would say that we have in such situations the same person or a different person. Concerning this, two points should be made.

First, very often we simply do not know for certain what to say. There is a large measure of subjectivity in anything we may say, and sometimes we may just have to decide by stipulation or rely on our intuitions. Thomas Nagel strikes the right note at the end of a recent paper which discusses a problem case.

> The concept of a person might possibly survive an application to cases which require us to speak of two or more persons in one body, but it seems strongly committed to some form of whole number countability. Since even this seems open to doubt, it is possible that the ordinary, simple idea of a single person will come to seem quaint some day, when the complexities of the human control system become clearer and we become less certain that there is anything very important that we are one of. But it is also possible that we shall be able to abandon the idea no matter what we discover.[21]

Nagel captures very succinctly our difficulties in deciding conclusively the contours of the concept of a person. Our language about persons is rooted in our common experience of embodied agents but it is not fully determined by that experience. It is difficult to know in advance of new experiences how far the concept can be stretched to cover new situations. Therefore it is extremely difficult to prove or disprove the coherence or incoherence of the concept as applied to putative claims about immortality. This is an unsettling conclusion but one that has to be faced.

Secondly, it seems clear to me that the concept of a person can cope with the kind of changes that are envisaged in the classical account of immortality. Thus we can surely make sense of the story of disembodied existence recently laid out by H. H. Price, where he construed survival in terms of a mental world in which recog-

---

[20] For a famous case of this see Derek Parfitt, "Personal Identity in *The Philosophy of Mind*, ed. Jonathan Glover (Oxford: Oxford University Press, 1976), pp. 144–46.

[21] Thomas Nagel, "Brain Bisection and the Unity of Consciousness," in *Philosophy of Mind*, p. 125.

nition is made possible by telepathy.[22] Equally, we can understand the story of bodily resurrection developed by John Hick.[23] I do not therefore find the standard argument against immortality at all convincing. In the nature of the case readers must work this through for themselves.

[22] Price, "Survival and the Idea of 'Another World'."
[23] John Hick, "Theology and Verification," in *Immortality*, pp. 86-91.

Chapter Eighteen
World Religions

One of the most important issues facing theologians today is how they meet the challenge posed by the new awareness of the existence of diverse religious traditions around the world. The issue is not entirely new, for theologians have often addressed it, and one significant religious tradition, the Hindu tradition, has for centuries claimed to resolve it, making this resolution a part of its positive apologetic. What is new is that we are now at the point where the issue is explicitly addressed by the major theologians of our day. Indeed within the Christian tradition, it has been taken up by both the second Vatican Council and the World Council of Churches. My judgment is that it will be on the theological agenda for some time to come. Hopefully, philosophers will make their own distinctive contribution to the debate.

One crucially important issue to be faced is this: How do we address the fact that world religions make conflicting truth claims? Thus the world religions differ on matters of fundamental significance. They differ on whether God's will is made known in the Koran or the Bhagavad Gita or the Bible; they differ on whether God became incarnate in Jesus Christ; they differ on whether the divine reality is personal or nonpersonal; they differ on whether human beings become reincarnate on earth, and so on. How should we react when confronted with these alternatives?

THE EXCLUSIVIST TRADITION

One way to resolve the obvious tension between these claims is to adopt an exclusi-
ist position. This position can take a number of different forms, for there can be
more moderate or extreme versions within this family of positions. The heart of the
tradition is the claim that the fundamentals of religious truth are mediated uniquely
and most fully in one religious tradition.

Expressed in terms of the Christian tradition, one way to develop this would
be to say that the Christian religion is the only true religion; all others are false,
perhaps even demonic. In fact, other religions are a temptation to be avoided; the
only appropriate attitude is to work for complete conversion to Christianity. Nothing of the non-Christian tradition held prior to conversion can be brought over into
the new life of faith. Moreover, failure to hear of Christ and failure to convert to
Christianity have eternal consequences. All who do not hear and do not positively
respond go to hell for ever.

It is difficult to be sure how many have adopted this edition of the exclusivist
tradition. It is certainly not easy to find a serious presentation of this position within modern theology. How far it has been held in the past must await the labors of
historians of Christian doctrine. If it were the only possible version of the tradition,
it is unlikely that it would be taken very seriously. There are, however, much more
promising ways of stating it, and I shall review two of these before I set out some of
the objections which have been made against the tradition as a whole.

One way of expressing it has been developed by Karl Barth and his followers.
According to Barth, only in Jesus Christ is there true revelation. This revelation
stands in judgment over all religion, including the Christian religion. Religion apart
from true revelation is really unbelief; it is an attempt to know God without there
being available the necessary conditions for knowing God.

> Because it is a grasping, religion is the contradiction of revelation, the concen-
> trated expression of human unbelief, i.e. an attitude and an activity which is
> directly opposed to faith. It is a feeble but defiant, an arrogant but hopeless,
> attempt to create something which man could do, but now cannot do, or can
> now do only because and if God himself creates it for him: the knowledge of
> the truth, the knowledge of God. We cannot therefore interpret the attempt
> as a harmonious co-operating of man with the revelation of God, as though
> religion were a kind of outstretched hand which is fitted by God in his reve-
> lation.[1]

Moreover, religion is an attempt to justify oneself by human works rather
than a recognition that salvation is by grace alone.

> Where we want what is wanted in religion, i.e. justification and sanctification
> as our own work, we do not find ourselves . . . on the direct way to God, who
> can then bring us to our goal at some higher stage on the way. On the contra-

[1] Karl Barth, "The Revelation of God as the Abolition of Religion," in *Christianity and
Other Religions,* eds. John Hick and Brian Hebblethwaite (Glasgow: Collins, 1980), p. 38.

ry, we lock the door against God, we alienate ourselves from him, we come into direct opposition to him. God in his revelation will not allow man to try to come to terms with life, to justify and sanctify himself. God in his revelation, God in Jesus Christ, is the one who takes on himself the sin of the world, who wills that all our care should be cast upon him, because he careth for us. . . . [2]

Religion in and of itself, therefore, is opposed to revelation. Revelation, however, can adopt a religion and mark it off as true religion. "There is a true religion: just as there are justified sinners. If we abide strictly by that analogy . . . we need have no hesitation in saying that the Christian religion is the true religion."[3] Such a claim is itself made from the standpoint of revelation. It is not something argued on the basis of the phenomena of the Christian religion compared to other religions; it is expressed in faith and from faith. Given this, the appropriate attitude to non-Christian religions is one of great forbearance and one of witness. There will be no attempt to resist and conquer other religions, appealing to this or that immanent truth. There will be neither praise nor reproach. Rather in weakness, witness will be borne to the righteousness and salvation of God made available in Christ.

A very different exclusivist position to that of Barth has been suggested by Karl Rahner. Rahner does not mask the exclusivist nature of his claims. ". . . Christianity understands itself as the absolute religion, intended for all men, which cannot recognise any other religion beside itself as of equal right."[4] This Rahner takes to be basic and self-evident. It does not mean, however, that non-Christian faiths are to be seen merely as elements of natural knowledge of God mixed up with human depravity. They may be and often are erroneous, but they also contain "supernatural elements arising out of the grace which is given to men as a gratuitous gift on account of Christ."[5] The decisive reason that they contain these elements is not an empirical study of religion but theological considerations stemming from the universality of God's love and the nature of salvation. God desires the salvation of all people; that salvation is mediated through Christ, the essential agent of supernatural grace; if God seriously intends helpless human beings to be saved, then they must be offered supernatural grace; but it is impossible to think that God's offer should generally be ineffective; hence, in a great many cases, grace gains the victory by the free acceptance of it.

> . . . if one believes seriously in the universal salvific purpose of God towards all men in Christ, it need not and cannot really be doubted that gratuitous influences of properly Christian supernatural grace are conceivable in the life of all men . . . and that these influences can presume to be accepted in spite of the sinful state of men and in spite of their apparent estrangement from God.[6]

[2] Ibid., p. 42.
[3] Ibid., p. 44.
[4] Karl Rahner, "Christianity and the Non-Christian Religions," in *Christianity and Other Religions*, p. 56.
[5] Ibid., p. 61.
[6] Ibid., p. 66.

To move from this to the positive significance of non-Christian religious traditions is a comparatively easy step to take. Salvation, as Rahner sees it, is inescapably social in character. Hence those who respond to God's grace will express that response in a social religious order. Indeed it is through such a concrete religious order that God reaches the individual. Therefore the religious traditions of the world must bear traces of God's grace. This is not to say that every religion is acceptable nor that acceptable religions are acceptable in all their elements. But it does mean that individuals have a duty to express their relationship with God within the religious and social realities offered to them in their particular historical situations.

Rahner refers to those who positively respond to grace outside the Christian religion as anonymous Christians. What happens then when such a person hears the Gospel? Rahner answers as follows:

> . . . the proclamation of the Gospel does not simply turn someone absolutely abandoned by God and Christ into a Christian, but turns an anonymous Christian into someone who now also knows about his Christian belief in the depths of his grace-endowed being by objective reflection and in the profession of faith which is given a social form in the Church.[7]

Thus the explicit preaching of Christianity is not at all superfluous. It makes available the incarnational and social structure of grace and, because it is a clearer, purer, and more reflective expression of grace, it makes the actual chance of salvation much greater. The church on this view is not the exclusive community of salvation but rather "the historically tangible vanguard and the historically and socially constituted explicit expression of what the Christian hopes is present as a hidden reality even outside the visible Church."[8] In other words, the church is the communion of those who can explicitly confess what they and anonymous Christians hope to be. Such a view clearly involves a presumption in favor of the Christian religion; that presumption cannot, however, be given up. Correctly interpreted it can be a source of profound humility and firmness.

SOME OBJECTIONS TO EXCLUSIVISM EXAMINED

How might the exclusivist tradition be attacked from a philosophical point of view? By far the most important objections to it have been made by John Hick. Let us expound these in some detail. There are three in all.

First, and perhaps most important of all, the exclusivist tradition is at odds with its own commitment to the universal love of God. Indeed the tradition involves not just a paradox but a contradiction.

[7] Ibid., p. 76.
[8] Ibid., p. 77.

We say as Christians that God is the God of universal love, that he is the creator and Father of all mankind, that he wills the ultimate good and salvation of all men. But we also say, traditionally, that the only way to salvation is the christian way. And yet we know, when we stop to think about it, that the large majority of the human race who have lived and died up to the present moment have lived either before Christ or outside the borders of Christendom. Can we then accept the conclusion that the God of love who seeks to save all mankind has nevertheless ordained that men must be saved in such a way that only a small minority in fact receive this salvation? It is the weight of this moral contradiction that has driven christian thinkers in modern times to explore other ways of understanding the human religious situation.[9]

Secondly, standard attempts to resolve this contradiction within the exclusivist tradition can at best be seen as interim measures. They do not go far enough, for they tend to assume theism as essential to true religion, and this cannot accommodate nontheistic faiths; or they resort to purely ad hoc supplementary theories, which are introduced arbitrarily to save the tradition from defeat; or they really abandon the heart of the exclusivist position without facing that fact squarely.

Hick's favorite way of stating this objection is by comparing it to the switch from a Ptolemaic to a Copernican theory of the universe.

For a time those who believed that the earth was at the centre of the universe could hold out by investing supplementary theories. In the end, however, these theories became so artificial and burdensome that people adopted the view that the sun was at the centre of the universe. Likewise with the relation between Christianity and other religions. . . . much the same . . . applies to what I shall call the Ptolemaic theology whose fixed point is the principle that outside the church, or outside Christianity, there is no salvation. When we find men of other faiths we add an epicycle of theory to the effect that although they are consciously adherents of a different faith, nevertheless they may unconsciously or implicitly be Christians. In theory one can carry on such manoeuvres indefinitely. But anyone who is not firmly committed to the original dogma is likely to find the resulting picture artificial, implausible and unconvincing, and to be ready for a Copernican revolution in his theology of religion.[10]

Such a revolution is, in fact, mandatory given the new knowledge and evidence made known to us by the study of other faiths.

Thirdly, the exclusivist position completely ignores the culturally relative, if not culturally determined, nature of religious belief. So long as we stay within our own restricted circles, then it seems natural enough to adopt a Ptolemaic theology where our own religion is at the center of the universe. Awareness of other religions, however, brings home the fact that others adopt the same posture, and thus

[9] John Hick, *God and the Universe of Faiths* (London: Macmillan, 1977), pp. 122–23. By permission of Macmillan, London and Basingstoke.

[10] Ibid., p. 125.

we can see that Ptolemaic theologies are built on the accidents of cultural geography. Hick makes his own confession of this as follows:

> I myself used to hold a Ptolemaic Christian theology; but if I had been born into a devout Hindu family in India and had studied philosophy at, let us say, the University of Madras, I should probably have held a Ptolemaic Hindu theology instead. And if I had been born to Muslim parents, say in Egypt or Pakistan, I should probably have held a Ptolemaic Muslim theology. And so on. This is an evident fact; and an intellectual position which ignores it or fails to make sense of it can hardly be adequate.[11]

For these reasons Hick suggests that the time is now ripe for a switch to a new philosophy of world religions. Before we turn to that, let us take stock of his objections to the exclusivist tradition. As we begin, it is worth reflecting on Hick's use of the Copernican analogy. As Hick is generally well aware, analogies can be as dangerous as they are illuminating. It is not entirely clear, however, that Hick has not been misled by his own analogy. Prima facie, the analogy with Copernicus and his situation is thoroughly misleading. Initially it suggests that issues in religion can be resolved just as neatly as they can be in the switch from a Ptolemaic to a Copernican view of the universe. In the latter case the issue does look relatively straightforward. The evidence accumulated, and it counted clearly against the Ptolemaic theory. Moreover, there was a compelling, single alternative which accommodated the evidence more economically. Also there was general agreement on the criteria relevant to deciding the issue. Hence simplicity, for example, was crucial. In the light of these three factors, the defenses mounted in favor of the Ptolemaic theory did indeed look strained and burdensome.

The situation in relation, however, is exactly the reverse of this. First, the evidence is much more controversial. All agree that the study of world religions shows that there is very serious conflict among the truth claims of religions. What then shall we make of this? Does the fact of conflict count for or against an exclusivist position? Or is it perhaps neutral? Certainly the existence of conflict does not obviously count against exclusivism per se. On the contrary, conflict is what one would expect given any exclusivist position. If one religion is true to a greater degree than all others, then religions will differ on significant issues. Clearly they do. So does that not weakly confirm the exclusivist tradition broadly conceived? Secondly, there is no agreement on the criteria for deciding between religious-truth claims in the way there seems to have been for deciding between the Ptolemaic and Copernican theories. Obviously simplicity mattered. But how far does this matter, say, in history or religion? I suggest it is a criterion of limited value.[12] Hence the complexity of a theory is much less of a disadvantage than the Copernican analogy

[11] Ibid., p. 132.
[12] See p. 122.

and Hick's use of it would suggest. Thirdly, it is simply not the case that there is a single alternative which every scholar in the field is queuing up to accept. Hick's own philosophy of world religions is but one possibility within a family of inclusivist positions.[13]

These observations are very important, for they highlight the insensitive way in which Hick lays out the issue. The question, for example, whether Rahner's position involves arbitrary, ad hoc inventions is far from easy to decide. Surely the crucial question is not whether the notion of an anonymous Christian is an epicycle to a worn-out theory but whether it follows from the theological premises from which he begins and whether those premises themselves are secure. We need not decide that here, for it would take us deep into Rahner's whole theology. Hick, however, seems to think that this crucial but complex task can be conveniently bypassed by a piece of verbal description. It cannot; hence his second objection fails to carry very much force.

His first objection carries even less, for it carries none at all as it stands. Of course, applied to crude versions of the exclusivist tradition the charge of contradiction may well work. Even then we must be cautious, for moral contradictions are more difficult to establish than logical contradictions and especially so with reference to the divine. However, let us ignore such a quibble. The point to make is that the charge of contradiction does not apply to the versions of exclusivism developed by either Barth or Rahner. Whatever problems they face, internal contradiction is not one of them, for their positions are internally consistent. Certainly Hick has not shown that they contain any formal contradictions.

Hick's third objection is more difficult to answer, not least because it is hard to know what to say when asked what one would believe if one had been born elsewhere. Hick insists that knowledge of cultural origins settles the issue. Surely this is exaggerated. People convert from one religious tradition to another, and they reject the religious heritage into which they were born, so birth is not a certain guide to commitment. In any case, it is important to distinguish between questions about the sociology or psychology of belief and questions about the rationality of belief. Thus a person may have become a Ptolemaic Christian, to use Hick's language, or a Ptolemaic Hindu or whatever, because of his or her cultural setting, but this does not show in itself that it is right or wrong to be a Ptolemaic Christian or a Ptolemaic Hindu or whatever. To be sure, not all of these positions can be correct, for they contradict each other. However, Hick's evident sociological fact, even if we grant it, does not in itself show them all to be wrong. One could still well be correct and rational; only independent considerations about the nature of ultimate reality and how it is known can settle that question. We can see this as we explore Hick's own account of the relation between the world religions.

---

[13] An alternative inclusivist position is presented by Wilfred Cantwell Smith in *Towards A World Theology* (Philadelphia: Westminster Press, 1981).

JOHN HICK'S INCLUSIVIST ALTERNATIVE

That account seeks to establish that all the major world religions can be held together in one all-embracing, inclusive theory of ultimate reality. Hick's central suggestion is that rather than non-Christian religions being seen as revolving around Christianity, all religions should be seen as revolving around God. Each in its own way represents an authentic revelation of the divine world and a fully authentic means of salvation. The latter is morally required if God is a God of universal love. The former is historically likely because of the fragmented character of the ancient world. If God is to reveal himself to different cultures separated from each other, creative moments of revelation are bound to be pluriform in nature; they will be adapted to the varied streams of human history.

This means that the great religious traditions of the world are not rivals. It is true that most of the various traditions have been missionary traditions. But those missionary movements were most successful when they worked downwards into primitive religion rather than sideways into another world faith. Therefore the missionary character of religion should not be exaggerated. In any case a whole series of considerations will radically change our initial perceptions. A greater grasp of the infinite character of ultimate reality, a proper account of the mysterious duality of ultimate reality, an accurate portrayal of what is truly significant within religion, a proper analysis of the concept of truth in religion, a proper epistemology for deciding religious truth claims, all these will allow one to see that what appear to be rival systems of belief and action are really complementary accounts of the one ultimate reality.

Before we unpack these considerations, it is important to see that Hick recognizes the obstacles to his position. Hick is fully aware of the serious conflicts to be found in the truth claims of the world religions. Thus he quite rightly has no time for those naive inclusivists who think that they can synthesize the diverse claims of the world religions and so develop a superreligion which shall do justice to them all while transcending them all. Equally Hick is aware that the existence of conflicting claims can give a toehold for scepticism about all religions. Perhaps all religions, says the sceptic, are false rather than all being true, or one being true, or whatever. So he accepts that the sceptical case has to be answered. The differences between the religions of the world are real. Nevertheless it is his view that these differences do not disconfirm the claim that all are equally valid accounts of the ultimate divine reality. To make this point he uses the well-known story of the blind men and the elephant.

> An elephant was brought to a group of blind men who had never encountered such an animal before. One felt a leg and reported that an elephant is a great living pillar. Another felt the trunk and reported that an elephant is a great snake. Another felt a tusk and reported that an elephant is like a sharp ploughshare. And so on. And then they are quarrelled together, each claiming that his own account was the truth and therefore all the others false. In fact of

course they were all true, but each referring only to one aspect of the total reality and all expressed in very imperfect analogies.[14]

As I have indicated, Hick supports this conclusion by a number of separate arguments, which we now need to unpack. The first argument focuses on the infinite nature of the ultimate divine reality.

> God, to use our christian term, is infinite. He is not a thing, a part of the universe, existing alongside other things; nor is he a being falling under a certain kind. And therefore he cannot be defined or encompassed by human thought. We cannot draw boundaries round his nature and say that he is this and no more. If we could fully define God, describing his inner being and his outer limits, this would not be God. The God whom our minds can penetrate and whom our thoughts can circumnavigate is merely a finite and partial image of God.
>   From this it follows that the different encounters with the transcendent within the different religious traditions may all be encounters with the one infinite reality, though with partially different and overlapping aspects of that reality.[15]

Hick's second argument can be expressed in various ways. Its central thrust is that the infinite reality needs to be seen in dualistic categories. Using categories made famous by Kant, Hick suggests that as a thing-in-itself, as noumena, the ultimate reality can be known in and through encounters with it as phenomena, that is, as it appears to us. Hence each religious tradition grasps a phenomenal part of the noumenal divine reality behind all of them. Adopting categories of Hindu thought, Hick expresses the same point this way:

> Theologically, the Hindu distinction between Nirguna Brahman and Saguna Brahman is important and should be adopted into western religious thought. Detaching the distinction, then, from its Hindu context we may say that Nirguna God is the eternal self-existent divine reality, beyond the scope of all human categories, including personality; and Saguna God is God in relation to his creation and with the attributes which express this relationship, such as personality, omnipotence, goodness, love and omniscience. Thus the one ultimate reality is both Nirguna and non-personal, and Saguna and personal, in a duality which is in principle acceptable to human understanding.[16]

By means of this move Hick hopes to solve the problem of how theistic and non-theistic religions can both be seen to refer to the same ultimate reality.

Hick's third, fourth, and fifth arguments belong together. The third suggests that doctrinal matters are not really the stuff of religion. It is in prayer and worship that belief in God comes alive and does its work. So when we examine the prayers

---

[14] As retold in Hick, *God and the Universe of Faiths*, p. 140.
[15] Ibid., p. 139.
[16] Ibid., p. 144.

and hymns of the various religions we see that religions overlap. Hence the differences are more peripheral than central. The fourth argument goes further to suggest that truth in relation is expressed not in theological theory but in myth. Myths are not true or false in the way scientific theory is true or false. Religious myths, like that of the fall or the incarnation, are attempts to express and evoke these experiences which are central in religion. They are "true" in virtue of their power to evoke appropriate attitudes to the real character of what is encountered in religious experience.[17] Hence the various myths of the world's religions are not conflicting, competing theories which are mutually exclusive; they are more like different art forms, each appropriate for its native culture. Moreover, the various myths of the major religious traditions are valid, for they arise out of genuine encounters with ultimate reality. This takes us to the core of Hick's fifth argument. The fifth argument maintains that religious experience is the ground for claiming that a particular conception of the divine is valid and not illusory. Hick sums up the epistemology behind this as follows: " . . . every conception of the divine which has come out of a great revelatory experience and has been tested through a long tradition of worship, and has sustained human faith over time and in millions of lives, is likely to represent a genuine encounter with divine reality."[18] On this criterion Hick's claim that the world religions have complementary rather than contradictory conceptions of the divine appears vindicated. Taken as a whole the arguments for his position look very impressive.

EVALUATION OF HICK'S POSITION

The task now is to examine Hick's position with some care. I want to show that Hick's arguments are vulnerable to very damaging criticism. Let us work back from the fifth to the first, taking each in turn.

The problem with the fifth argument is that religious experience plus numerical strength is a poor basis for judging whether a particular religious tradition really gives us access to the truth about ultimate reality. For Hick it is all that is needed; surely it is more accurate to claim that religious experience and its consequences give only necessary, but not sufficient, warrants for a claim to truth.[19]

Even then, this point only applies if we adopt the standard account of truth in religion which construes religious language as informative rather than evocative. For Hick, however, truth in religion has more to do with the response that is evoked in religious experience than it has to do with what is said about the object of religious experience. This is the core claim in his fourth argument. Thus he suggests that the incarnation of God in Jesus Christ is true not because it expresses the true

---

[17]Ibid., p. 175. For fuller exposition of this see William J. Abraham, *Divine Revelation and the Limits of Historical Criticism* (Oxford: Oxford University Press, 1982), chap. 4.

[18]Hick, *God and the Universe of Faiths*, p. 141.

[19] I have suggested this above, chap. 4.

ontological claim that God was incarnate in Jesus but because it evokes an appropriate attitude to God as encountered through Jesus. As an interpretation of the incarnation, this account fails to do justice to its historical content.[20] Moreover, as Peter Byrne has pointed out, Hick's general theory of truth fails to reckon with the logical relations between language, belief, and experience in religion. A concern for truth, accuracy, and reliability in thought about the object of faith cannot be displaced as quickly as Hick suggests. Byrne explains why this way:

> This is because the sorts of responses to that object Hick is alluding to are intentional in character. To say that worship, prayer, etc., are intentional activities is to say that they involve making a reference to something in thought or speech. But thought or speech only succeeds in referring to an object if it contains some true or accurate thoughts about the nature of that object. So if people's thoughts about an object are sufficiently mistaken, they will just not be able to connect their thoughts with the object at all. It follows that whether two men worship the same thing or not depends not so much on a similarity in how they respond *to* that thing, but rather in there being a sufficient similarity in what they say *about* that thing.[21]

This point applies equally well to Hick's third argument in which he seeks to play down the place of belief in religion. To claim, for example, that all religious believers are worshipping the same object requires some agreement in belief about that object of worship. Otherwise there is a basic failure in reference, and thus to speak of worshipping the *same* object cannot arise. Moreover, it is simply false to claim that in all religions doctrinal considerations are a peripheral concern. The situation differs from one religion to another. Thus Hick is not facing up to the conflict that exists among religions on the ranking of doctrine in their schemes of values. Accurate description at this level is enormously complex and controversial, but it is too easy by far to set doctrine aside as of secondary significance.

This takes us to Hick's second argument in which he suggests that we need to construe the ultimate divine reality in dualistic categories. The difficulties this time are twofold. First, this suggestion has all the marks of an ad hoc distinction brought in to cope with the radical differences between theistic and nontheistic religions. To be sure, it has some support in some Christian mystics, but this is slender support which depends on a very favorable account of religious experience. It has much more support within Hinduism, as Hick points out, but in its own context within that religion it is a central element in a thoroughly inclusivist account of the relation between world religions. Secondly, Hick has enormous difficulty articulating the dualism he proposes. If we accept the Kantian version of his dualism, then we are offered a notoriously obscure and contentious distinction. It is a case of *obscurum per obscurius,* explaining what is obscure by what is more obscure. On the other

---

[20] I have defended this claim over against Hick in *Divine Revelation,* pp. 72–76.

[21] Peter Byrne, "John Hick's Philosophy of World Religions," *Scottish Journal of Theology* XXXV (1982), 293–94. For more on this see Peter Geach, "On Worshipping the Right God," in *God and the Soul* (London: Routledge, 1969), pp. 100–16.

hand, the Hindu version is prima facie self-contradictory. The one ultimate reality is at once both nonpersonal and personal. If we were told that this was paradoxical then well and good. But this is precisely what Hick does not say and cannot say. Hick simply claims that this duality is in principle acceptable to human understanding. He must claim this because otherwise his dualism is unnecessary. After all, it was introduced to cope with the contradictions between the claims of the world religions; clearly it does little good to get rid of these by appealing to a paradox elsewhere.

What then of Hick's first argument? There Hick stressed the infinite character of God and the inevitably finite nature of our thought about ultimate reality. From these he inferred that the different religious traditions may well be genuine encounters with different aspects of ultimate reality. There are several comments to be made about this.

First, the conclusion is very weak. Given the collapse of his other arguments, what Hick needs is the conclusion that the different religions really are genuine encounters with different aspects of divine reality. Without this conclusion the argument is of little value. Secondly, if we are even to allow Hick's weak conclusion to stand, we must still show that the various descriptions of the divine which Hick actually allows should be consistent with one another. However inexhaustible the qualities of ultimate reality are, or however partial the qualities human beings attribute to it may be, this condition still applies so long as we claim to describe the same thing. But this is precisely what we do not find in religion. Hence appeal to the infinite character of God does not come to grips with the problem it is meant to resolve. Thirdly, it is worth noting how close Hick comes to total scepticism about the divine.[22] He does so when he suggests that *infinite* as applied to God should be taken to mean that God is not a being falling under a certain kind and therefore cannot be defined or encompassed by human thought. If this is really the case then all thought about God is logically impossible. Equally belief in God is impossible, for one cannot believe in God without thought. However, we need not press this sceptical conclusion. The case against Hick's first argument is strong enough without it.

CONCLUSIONS

Our evaluation of Hick's arguments has shown that they will not work. Yet without them his claim that all the major religions give complemtary rather than rival descriptions of the same ultimate reality cannot cope with the long recognized conflict between the truth claims of the various religions.

Does this evaluation also show that some kind of exclusivist position is to be preferred? The answer here must be a firm no. The reasons for this go much deeper

---

[22] This is cogently argued by Byrne in "John Hick's Philosophy of World Religions," pp. 297–98.

than the common observation that the demolition of one position does not establish the superiority of a rival position.

First, there are alternative accounts which deploy other arguments to defend an inclusivist position. Moreover, Hick may still come up with much better arguments than he has offered to date. In the nature of the case, these alternative accounts have not been examined here. Secondly, it is surely obvious that exclusivist or inclusivist positions are not the only options available to us. Both presuppose that either one religion is true or some or all religions are true. However, it has also been argued, as it was by Karl Marx, that all are false. Were that case to succeed then clearly both inclusivist and exclusivist positions would be wrong.

Lastly, our discussion indirectly shows that any account of the relation between world religions cannot be separated from an account of what ultimately exists. Clearly any proposal, whether inclusivist or exclusivist, whether sceptical or nonsceptical, must be consistent within itself, and it must not deny evident facts about the nature of the religions under consideration. But these are only necessary conditions of a satisfactory proposal. To be fully satisfactory a proposal will also need to show that its content best describes how things ultimately are. This stems from the fact that religions either presuppose or self-consciously offer a creed as an essential part of their nature. Any appropriation or rejection of these creeds cannot be done without coming to a decision as to whether they are true or not; that cannot in turn be done in most cases without at some stage deciding what ultimately is. Therefore, philosophers who seek to develop a serious account of the relation among the world religions are faced with daunting alternatives. They must either articulate and defend some particular religious creed and thus, in Christian terms, venture boldly into systematic theology; or they must articulate and defend some atheological vision of reality. If they do one or the other, then the necessary costs and risks should be fully acknowledged, reckoned, and paid for; if they do not, then they must content themselves with rather limited conclusions. In this chapter I am content to conclude that the conflict between religious-truth claims constitutes a serious barrier to any inclusivist proposal about the relation between world religions.

Chapter Nineteen
Christianity And Marxism

When we consider thinkers who stand outside the Christian tradition, there are few in modern times who can lay more claim to attention than Karl Marx. There are at least three reasons why this is so. First, Marx offers a profound and searching critique of all religious belief that ranks him with the likes of such intellectual giants as Sigmund Freud and Emile Durkheim. Secondly, about one-third of the world's population live in societies whose official aims and outlooks are highly colored, if not considerably conditioned, by Marxist thinking. To attend to the views of Marx is to attend to the views of a very large minority of the world's inhabitants. Thirdly, the thinking of Marx has sufficient truth or sufficient contemporary attraction to be the inspiration for a significant school of present-day theology. Marx, then, in my view cannot be ignored by the contemporary philosopher of religion.

We can say this despite Marx's avowed opposition to Christianity both in theory and in practice. This opposition was a relatively late development in his own life, although we must be cautious in what we claim about Marx's own religious commitments in his early life. He was born in 1818 into a Jewish family, but his parents became nominal Christians in 1824 more for social and economic convenience than for religious reasons. The young Marx did show an interest in Christianity. While at school he wrote an essay on John's Gospel, which was highly commended. Moreover, some have claimed that he went through a passionate Christian phase when he was nineteen. However, he early abandoned the Protestantism in which he was nominally raised to become a convinced materialist and atheist for the rest of his life. As a thinker he had a checkered career: as a student (he received a doctorate from Jena in 1842), as a journalist, as a revolutionary strategist, as a scholar, and as a political activist. The last years of his life were lived in obscurity. He died in 1883, when to the great masses of people he was not even a name.

In this chapter I plan to do three things. First, I shall offer an account of his general philosophy. Secondly, I shall summarize his views on religion. Thirdly, I shall offer a balanced assessment of his views, concentrating in the main on his critique of Christianity. By concentrating on these three areas I hope to provide a reasonable comprehensive and sane introduction to an area which can easily become the arena for animated, if not acrimonious, debate.

MARX'S GENERAL PHILOSOPHY

To understand the views of Karl Marx one must have some grasp of the philosophy of Hegel. This can be a daunting prospect. According to Bertrand Russell, Hegel is "the hardest to understand of all the great philosophers."[1] And yet we must not be discouraged, for the general thrust of Hegel's philosophy is well within our reach, and those who desire to pursue his position are blessed by renewed attempts of late to come to terms with his ideas and concepts.

We can begin by reviewing the leading idea for Hegel, namely, the idea of historical development. According to Hegel, history goes through various stages. Each stage is linked to what comes before and goes after it by certain laws. These laws are mental or spiritual; in fact they are nothing less than the expression of what Hegel called on varying occasions the Absolute, the Absolute Spirit, the World-Self, or simply the Idea. The development of history, on this analysis, is the progressive self-realization of the Absolute-Spirit. As D. W. D. Shaw summarizes it:

> For Hegel, ultimate reality was rational, mind, Absolute Mind; and what is going on in our world, our universe is a movement or process whereby Absolute Spirit, infinity, eternal, realises itself by becoming that which it is not— finity, temporal.[2]

Hegel's Absolute is akin in its conception to the classical conception of God. The relationship between the two is as follows: the Christian God is a symbol for the Absolute Spirit. The two are not identical. The former (the Christian God) is an untutored, unsophisticated symbol useful for the man or woman in the street, but inadequate for those who can grasp the real truth about ultimate reality and hence appreciate the philosophical truth of Absolute Spirit. On this analysis there is a real

[1] Bertrand Russell, *A History of Western Philosophy* (London: George Allen and Unwin, 1965), p. 201.
[2] D. W. D. Shaw, *The Dissuaders* (London: SCM, 1978), p. 30.

difference between the God of the ordinary Christian and the Absolute Spirit of the academic, philosophical theologian. It is the latter that is at work in the process of history. Through history this Absolute Spirit is at work, progressively involved in its own self-realization.

This philosophy, or this theology, has obvious implications for political and social life. Hegel's philosophical disciples split into two camps at this point. On the one side there were those who followed Hegel himself: the Right Hegelians. They drew conservative implications from his doctrine of development: history is all right as it is; after all, it is here and now expressive of the Absolute Spirit. On the other side were the Left or Young Hegelians. They took an opposite position: the present is just one stage in a total, ongoing development within history, so the present must be changed. The task at hand is to assist the development of the next stage; hence the Young Hegelians were radical in their political views.

Marx spent his student days immersed in the general philosophy of Hegel. This was virtually inevitable, for Hegel was uncrowned king of the philosophical world of his day. But within this tradition Marx sided with the radical Young Hegelians. More important, he gave Hegel's philosophy a twist or turn which completely transformed its content and yet retained a large measure of continuity. So in Marx's philosophy we have a delicate balance of continuity and discontinuity in his relationship with Hegel.

A key element of continuity is his espousal of the view that history goes through various stages. Here he agreed in principle with Hegel. For Marx, as for Hegel, history is a dynamic arena where something of great significance is taking place. And from Hegel, Marx borrowed some of the concepts with which to understand that. Thus he borrowed the concept of a dialectic as a way of grasping something that is not static but on the move and the concept of alienation as a way of expressing the estrangement between people and their environment and work. But the key element is the belief that history goes through certain stages which are governed by specifiable laws.

The discontinuity is to be seen in two areas, which are closely related. First, Marx abandons the sophisticated, elusive, and speculative theism that pervades Hegel's philosophy. Here Marx drew on the work of a fellow Young Hegelian, Ludwig Feuerbach, who argued that the idea of Absolute Spirit was unnecessary. Reality was what was available to the senses; there was no need to posit the Absolute Spirit to explain the concrete acts of human agents in history. "Man is what he eats": "Er ist was er isst." Abstract, formal, and speculative ideas must be shunned. Theology, when properly understood, is not about God, it is about human beings. Thus the ontological commitments of Hegel can be first transcended and then scrapped. Marx accepted this radical critique of Hegel, as formulated with great fervor by Feuerbach. This is the first major break with Hegel.

The second break is even more momentous. Keeping the idea that history goes through stages, Marx proposed that the laws governing these stages were not mental or spiritual but economic. History was not determined by reason or mind, it was determined by economic factors. More particularly it was determined by the key element in any economic system, namely the means of production. Whoever controlled these, controlled history.

For Marx this thesis was not a matter of philosophical speculation, it was a matter of scientific truth. All around he could see the evidence that established his position in a clear-cut manner. For example, it was obvious more or less to the naked eye, so Marx held, that production was a key factor in the origin and development of society. People must eat, drink, and have shelter before they can do anything else. Science, religion, and politics, for example, cannot be pursued if one does not possess the basic necessities that are a prerequisite of any kind of life. Control the means of production that in turn control these necessities and you control life. To control the means of production is to control the crucial political and social relations that are developed in any society. To grasp this is, for Marx, to grasp the foundation stone of society. Friedrich Engels expressed this succinctly in his funeral oration for Marx at Highgate Cemetery.

> He discovered the simple fact, hitherto concealed by an overgrowth of ideology, that mankind must first of all eat and drink, have shelter and clothing, before it can pursue politics, science, religion, art etc.; and that therefore the production of the immediate material means of subsistence and consequently the degree of economic development attained by a given people or during a given epoch, form the foundation upon which the State institutions, the legal conceptions, the art and even the religious ideas of the people concerned have been evolved, and in the light of which these things must therefore be explained, instead of vice-versa as had hitherto been the case.[3]

Secondly, Marx saw confirmation of his views in the actual development of history. History could in fact be divided into four main stages. There was, to begin, the Asiatic. The Asiatic period was one of primitive communism, with a simple undeveloped form of social organization; religion took the form of Asiatic religion: this is a vague entity covering religions of the Far East and Hinduism. Then there was an ancient phase: this was a period of greater productive power, marked by the rise of masters who owned the means of production, including the workers. Again Marx was vague about religion: religion was of the "ancient" type, namely, Graeco-Roman religion. This was followed by the feudal stage of the Middle Ages. Productive power increased; slaves became serfs, because of the greater initiative required from them. Roman Catholicism went hand in glove with this feudal period of production. This in turn was followed by the modern phase: capitalism. In this the rise of manufacturing industry pushed aside the nobility, elevated the bourgeoisie, or the middle class, and gave the worker freedom to be exploited. At this time Protestantism came into its own as the appropriate religious development.

For Marx, then, history and life combined to prove the claim that society in all its forms was determined by economic forces. Economic factors were the foundation of society; on top of this foundation developed a complex superstructure of

---

[3]Quoted in Edward Rogers, *A Christian Commentary on Communism* (London: Epworth, 1959), p. 83.

life determined by this economic foundation. And this view was scientific truth about life rather than refined philosophical speculation.

If this theory is true then, for Marx, two things should follow. First, we can predict the future. We know where we are in history, we know the laws that govern history, hence we know where history is going. We can map it roughly as follows.

Capitalism will destroy itself. In due course there will be a vast conflict in which the bourgeois will war with the proletarait in a major class struggle. The latter will inevitably increase in strength and number and win, forming for a time a phase known as the dictatorship of the proletariat. This paves the way for the abolition of all classes in a classless society. Marx saw this as utopia, although he has in fact very little to say of this in detail. One celebrated passage deserves a mention at this point.

> In communist society, where nobody has one exclusive sphere of activity but each can become accomplished in any branch he wishes, society regulates the general production and this makes it possible for me to do one thing today and another tomorrow, to hunt in the morning, fish in the afternoon, rear cattle in the evening, criticise after dinner, just as I have a mind without even becoming hunter, fisherman, shepherd or critic.[4]

It is at this point that we can apply the slogan: "From each according to his ability, to each according to his need." The first thing that follows from Marx's views, then, is that we can predict the future.

The second is this: we know what to prescribe for action. Given what we know in theory we know what to do in practice: we must change the world in a radical fashion. The philosophers have only interpreted the world in different ways; the point is to change it. This change must be radical; limited, piecemeal reforms are out; campaigns for higher wages and shorter working hours are cosmetic in character. What is needed is complete revolution; politics are essentially impotent; revolution is the only answer to the ills that bedevil society.

This in broad terms is Marx's philosophy: history goes through stages; these stages are determined by economic factors; usher in the future by means of violent revolution.

MARX'S ACCOUNT OF RELIGION

From the above analysis of society it is not difficult to imagine the account of religion that emerges. The danger, if there is one, is that we will oversimplify and thus minimize the radical consequences that follow. Marx was in fact quite sophisticated in his analysis of religion and did not apply his overall theory of life to religion without attempting to take account of the religious realities of his own day. Thus Marx was well acquainted with the New Testament scholarship such as it was in the

[4] Quoted in Ibid., p. 96.

Germany of the 1840s. Marx accepted the view of such scholars as David Strauss and Bruno Bauer, who held that there was no valid, historical foundation for the Christian faith. The Gospels, on this view, were the product of the myth-making consciousness of the early church.

We can summarize Marx's central conviction about religion by noting that, for Marx, religion is a part of the wider culture which is determined by the economic foundations of society. Religion is an element in the general consciousness of society; this consciousness is determined by economic life. The point is well made in the *Communist Manifesto:*

> The charges against communism made from a religious, a philosophical, and, generally, from an ideological standpoint are not deserving of serious examination. Does it require deep intuition to comprehend that man's ideas, views, and conceptions, in one word, man's consciousness, changes with every change in the conditions of his material existence, in his social relation and in his social life? What else does the history of ideas prove, than that intellectual production changes its character in proportion as material production changes? The ruling ideas of each age have ever been the ideas of its ruling classes. When people speak of ideas that revolutionise society, they do but express the fact that within the old society the elements of a new one have been created, and that the dissolution of the old ideas keep even pace with the dissolution of the old conditions in existence. When the ancient world was in its last throes, the ancient religions were overcome by Christianity. When Christian ideas succumbed in the eighteenth century to rationalist ideas, a feudal society fought its death battle with the then revolutionary bourgeoisie. The ideas of religious liberty and freedom of conscience merely gave expressions to the sway of free competition within the domain of knowledge.[5]

In this analysis religion is an epiphenomena. It has its origin in the economic contradiction in society. As a system of belief it is an illusion; it is false. And yet false though it is, it still has a significant function to play in society. Indeed it has at least two functions.

In a positive sense religion can provide consolation. It enables people to cope with suffering. It holds out a hope for the future. As this hope is ill founded, religion however is more likely to be dangerous. By focusing on heaven it takes people's eyes off earth. It is in this context that Marx speaks of religion as the opium of the people: it is a drug that puts people to sleep in the midst of cruel and unjust circumstances. So its role as a consoling agent is both positive and negative, but mostly negative.

The other function that religion performs is entirely negative. It has an exploitive role; it supports and sanctifies the status quo. It gives backing to the interests, privileges, and property of the dominant class. Thus Christians were opposed to the Poor Law in the time of Marx, because it destroyed the harmony that God had supposedly established in nature and in the world. In due course, however, religion will fade away. When communism arrives in all its glory, religion will cease

[5] *The Communist Manifesto* (Chicago: Henry Regency, 1954), pp. 51-52.

to be; it will wither away. One does not need to persecute to destroy it, for there will come a time when talk of theism and atheism will be meaningless. On this view the future of religion is simple: it simply has no future.

A BALANCED ASSESSMENT

Any comprehensive evaluation of the views of Marx on religion must begin from the fact that his philosophy has won the allegiance of millions. Marxism is a very live option to many, especially for those oppressed by hunger and political exploitation. It has within it a prophetic vision that is fearless and passionate. Moreover, as Edward Rogers points out, Marxism is rich in explanatory power.

> It offers a coherent and comprehensive explanation of the manifold of experience, providing a frame of reference for every event of history, every claim of religion, and every conflict of politics.[6]

For this faith many are ready to die. This is because built into this comprehensive account of life and history is an intense moral fervor. There is in Marx a deep concern for the poor and the oppressed: this is part of the attraction of the theory, an attraction which is at heart moral. There is a passionate commitment to the betterment of mankind, for the chains of exploitation are to be burst, and the burdens of the weak and afflicted are to be lifted. Marx offers an ingenious blend of theory with idealism, thought through by a highly educated genius who was cosmopolitan and yet steeped in the statistical horrors of industrial life in the nineteenth century as captured in the volumes of the British Museum. In its own right this philosophy is an incredible achievement.

Nor can one deny the impetus that Marx has given to a whole galaxy of subjects in the academic field. Marx has deeply enriched the modern understanding of history, economics, sociology, social philosophy, and the history of ideas. He has brought to light the role of economic factors in these areas in a way that was undreamt of and unrealized before his time. For all this we should be grateful. Despite this it is difficult to be enthusiastic about the actual content and outcome of Marx's philosophy and his critique of religion. The major issues are these.

First, Marx is far too confident and dogmatic about the truth of his overall theory. It comes to us dressed out in the garb of empirical science. In essence it is nothing of the kind. It is a vast speculative theory about the world as a whole, rather than an argued small-scale theory about something in the world, which is what it would be if it were science. Marx is in fact in the business of metaphysics. There is nothing wrong in this so long as we do not dress it up as a piece of empirical science. That it is metaphysics is borne out by at least three facts: by its broad or general character; by its reliance on Hegel, a speculative metaphysician par excellence; and by the absence of any experiment to test out its claims. The danger here

---

[6] Rogers, *Christian Commentary on Communism*, p. 110.

is that we shall be deceived on a vast scale. The prestige of science will be drawn on to give backing to a theory that can rightly have great initial appeal to our moral intuitions.

Secondly, Marx has the problems of all determinists. To begin, one wants to know why his own philosophy is not an illusion, caused by certain economic forces at work in his life. Somehow he must claim a privileged position for his own belief, and yet that privileged position is never established. It is assumed or ignored as a problem. Another problem generated by Marx's determinism is that it is not clear how he can issue a call for revolutionary action in society. The dilemma is simple: if we make a difference then economic forces are not the only determinants in the total situation; if we cannot make a difference, then the call to act is empty and pointless. It requires much greater sophistication to respond to this than Marx at any time displayed. As it stands Marx will have to sacrifice either his economic determinism or his call to action.

Thirdly, Marx's account of past history is crude and unsatisfactory. Those historians most competent to judge cannot be satisfied with his account of the past with its simplistic divisions and one-way causal relations between economic and noneconomic factors. Even if we concentrate on one stage, the capitalist stage, he is inaccurate, for it is quite impossible to divide society neatly into two classes, the bourgeoisie and the proletariat.

Fourthly, Marx's predictions about the future are equally unsatisfactory. They have failed to come true. In those countries where revolution would be most expected it has not happened, i.e., in the capitalist West. On the contrary Britain, France, Germany, and America have seen the emergence of a new class of managers and skilled technical advisers. Here we have ownership without control and control without ownership. On the other hand, revolution has come in countries with little or no capitalist development: in Russia in 1917, in Yugoslavia in 1945, and in China in 1949.

Fifthly, with all the gains that revolution has undoubtedly brought to certain countries, it is difficult to be enthusiastic about the actual application of Marx's philosophy in concrete societies. Religious believers can have sympathy with Marx at this point for they know from their own past how much can be wrought in the name of a great historical figure but which is far removed from his character and purpose. But this analogy is limited. When all is said, we cannot ignore the oppression and suppression that Marxism has practiced with enthusiasm in our own century. Much of this can find a ready home in the theory of conflict and revolution that is central to Marx's own philosophy. With Marx there is no Sermon on the Mount, so to speak, to take him off the hook. His moral fervor tended to be superficial and selective.

What of Marx's critique of religion? Again we need a balanced assessment. It is only a fool or a fanatic who would say that Marx has nothing to teach the religious believer. It is not surprising that he should have become something of an inspiration to many in our day grappling with the harsh realities of poverty and economic oppression. In this sphere Marx can surely perform an invaluable service if only by way of a reminder. He can remind Christians of past errors, for the Christian religion and its central institutions, notably the church, have all too easily been used as a support for unjust systems of government. He can remind them of the social and political dimension to evil, driving home the crucial role that property and money have in our world and of the associated idolatry in our society. He can remind them of the needs of the third and fourth world and of the extent to which the West ignores them in the rat race to increase its luxuries. Above all he can remind them of the judgment of God in history and of his humble, sacrificial identification with the poor and the helpless. Perhaps it was no accident that Marx was reared in an intellectual tradition which cherished but often ignored the prophetic fervor of giants like Amos and Isaiah. For all this Christians can be grateful. There is no need for an alarmed, reactionary response on their part; there is much in Marx that will search and detail religious believers and send them back to their roots.

Despite all these important considerations, the ultimate verdict on Marx must be negative. His account of religion, interesting and illuminating as it is in certain respects, is quite inadequate. For one thing his rather uncritical acceptance of the views of Strauss and Bauer has been challenged by subsequent New Testament research. The Gospels cannot be dismissed as myth. Nor can we detect in the traditions of the New Testament the development of a story which begins with a mere preacher or prophet and progresses through evolutionary stages to a divine figure. This is at the least a highly contested theory about the origins of New Testament Christology. It cannot, of course, be said that no New Testament scholar would take up a position analogous or close to that of Strauss and Bauer; to claim that would be to claim too much. What can be said is that such a position would be highly contested and for good reasons.

A more important point, however, is this. Rather than Marxism showing Christianity to be an illusion, if anything the relation may be the reverse of this. The history of the Christian religion is an excellent test case for the truth of Marx's economic determinism. Consider it after this fashion. The Christian religion has existed for two thousand years. It has spread from one type of society to another; it has survived from one epoch to another. If Marx is correct, it ought to have been transformed completely. Yet this is not what has happened. Despite changes in its character, it is still recognizably the same thing. It is still the same religion, whether it be in cosmopolitan Rome or Charlemagne's empire, with its thinly veneered barbarism, or industrialized Europe or Polynesia or Labrador or Sri Lanka.

Within these societies it has played an active role. It has not been a mere epiphenomenon determined by the economic factors at work. Despite failure to live out to the full its social responsibility, it has stood out heroically at times against oppression and injustice. Its record is mixed, but it is far from entirely negative as witnessed by the prophets, by some of the radical reformation groups, and by the campaign to abolish slavery. Marx could perhaps ignore this; we cannot. To attend to it is to eat away at the foundations of Marx's central philosophical convictions. These considerations added to the continued existence of the church despite determined Marxist opposition within many Communist countries are telling objections to Marxist theory.

THE DILEMMA OF LIBERATION THEOLOGY

In the light of all this extensive criticism it should come as no surprise therefore that I am thoroughly sceptical of those liberation theologians who claim that Christianity can be blended with Marxism. What are we to say, then, about the current fashion to draw on Marxist philosophy to interpret the Christian faith in the modern world? Are those who propose this stupid? How is this fascinating anomaly to be explained?

There are various explanations available. Some who talk this way are very skillfully juggling with words. They take elements of Marxism and combine them with elements of Christianity without coming to terms with the comprehensive and total character of both world faiths. This is not in itself reprehensible. The Christian faith does have enormous capacity to absorb fruitful elements of alien systems, and to some extent that is inevitable in any period of history. Thus Aquinas absorbed much of Aristotle, and Barth has absorbed substantial elements of Kant and Kierkegaard. Neither is worse the wear because of it. But we must not be misled by this kind of partial synthesis; it does nothing to reconcile the fundamental antithesis between Marxism and Christianity.

The most satisfactory explanation of the attempted rapprochement between Christianity and Marxism is that it is a sophisticated variation of this general strategy. As such it cannot be dismissed as a mere playing with words, for it is too well constructed to be open to such criticism. It consists in the critical use of the Marxist analysis of society to understand the dynamics of society and throw light on its general economic character. This is joined to two subsidiary components: first, a sharp distinction is made between this element in Marxism and the rest of Marxism, e.g., its atheism and its ontological materialism; secondly, a sharp distinction is made between true Marxism and contemporary communism as found, say, in the Soviet Union, for the latter is taken as a radical departure from Marx's humanistic and liberal heritage. Rejecting these elements, one is free, so it is said, to draw on Marxist economic theory to analyze society. This position was suitably expressed by Fidel Castro:

> Nobody could love all men and be anti-Marxist in the social meaning of the term . . . to be Christian and Marxist in economy, in politics and in all these things, without entering the field of philosophy, which is never debated among us.[7]

Those who embrace this interesting position face a major dilemma at this point. On the one hand, if they remain true to Marx's economic views their use of

[7]Quoted in Shaw, *Dissuaders*, pp. 50–51.

Marx is nothing unique or special. Marx's strictly economic views as enshrined in his theory of value were entirely orthodox, for he took over the views of the classical economists of his day and made them his own. So those who draw on these views are not really using anything unique to Marx; they are just using the outdated and inadequate economic orthodoxy of the nineteenth century. On the other hand, if they go beyond Marx's economic views, they are doing much more than drawing on Marxist economics as an intellectual tool in analyzing society. They will then be resorting to Marxist wider philosophical commitments and should confess this clearly.

In either case it is difficult to see how we can carve Marxism into these separable elements and embrace this piece or that piece and leave the rest. Marxism is to some extent an evolving theory, but its constituent elements—its economic determinism, its materialism, its atheism—cannot be reconciled with the central tenets of the classical Christian tradition. At this point the real problem is less with Marxists, for few of them fail to see the yawning abyss which separates Christianity and Marxism. The problem is with religious idealists who are reluctant to face facts. It may seem strange that philosophers, who are so often accused of having their heads in the clouds, should have to say this. Nevertheless it must be done, it is part of the philosopher's duty to truth.

Chapter Twenty
Philosophy And Commitment

I began this book by seeking to understand and disarm some of the suspicions religious believers often have of philosophers of religion. I noted that in some cases suspicion gave way to outright hostility. My main objection to that hostility was that it ignored the fact that philosophers raise crucially important questions about religion which no one who is interested in the truth of religion can avoid. This in itself, I suggested, is enough to justify the place of philosophy of religion within both theology and philosophy.

Initially such a claim must be taken on faith. In the last analysis, it can be vindicated only by exploring the questions philosophers raise and then making up one's own mind about what has been offered. At this stage I certainly hope that the reader has not been disappointed. I will be entirely satisfied if I have shown that the philosopher of religion has a valuable service to render to the modern academy both within and without religion.

The service rendered should be neither underestimated nor exaggerated. The role of the philosopher of religion is a modest one, as we can see when we review the central tasks which we have taken upon ourselves. One of these tasks is to become as clear as possible about religion and what it claims. This involves focusing on a particular religious tradition or family of traditions and seeking to determine the meaning of some of its central concepts and the nature of its creedal discourse. A second task is to examine a religious tradition to see if it is clear, coherent, and internally consistent. A third and vital job for the philosopher is to examine arguments for and against religious belief. This in turn leads into deeper questions about the nature of reason and whether it can legitimately be applied to fundamental religious assertions. A fourth task is to unearth and examine the assumptions which inevitably find their way into religion. A fifth and final task is to explore the relation between religion and other areas of life. To some extent this kind of laundry list of tasks is artificial. No formal account of the discipline can capture the internal relations between the issues discussed nor do justice to the loose ends which will always elude precise description. Yet it can reduce the chaos and keep us modest as we see the demands laid upon us.

THE DEMANDS OF PHILOSOPHY OF RELIGION

It will not have escaped the notice of the attentive reader, however, that there is a price to be paid for all of this. Philosophy of religion does not leave everything as it is. It leads us to see things differently. Some things, formerly obscure, have now become much clearer to us. Yet other matters we felt we understood now invite questions which we scarce know how to answer. Moreover, we realize decisions are inevitable. Critical choices about significant issues have to be made not just because it is psychologically difficult always to sit on the fence but because our action or inaction in life presupposes underlying beliefs about the nature of ultimate reality. Sooner or later we shall vote with our feet as to how we shall live, and our votes will reflect what we believe about the world, about God, and about ourselves. Philosophy of religion does not necessarily make these choices any easier. If anything, it makes them more difficult, for it changes us as persons. It develops within us internal standards which can be very difficult to attain. We begin to desire at heart to be rational in our beliefs and decisions; we want to be truly critical rather than just believe what comes easiest to us.

The development of critical standards of our own can be a passion which threatens to absorb us completely; it can also be a very painful process. We are often by nature intellectually lazy, so it is easy to drift through life and not subject our beliefs and commitments to critical scrutiny. In philosophy of religion we inevitably come across ideas and arguments which both perplex and shock us. It is far from easy to come to terms with them. Moreover, as R. G. Collingwood pointed out, people are liable to blow up in your face when you challenge their basic assumptions and beliefs.[1] Clearly this applies very acutely in philosophy of religion where one has to examine some of the most significant convictions which have ever been held. Also, alas, it is extremely difficult to reach agreement on these matters. Thoroughly intelligent people reach radically opposing positions, and there seems to be no generally accepted way of relieving the deadlock. Hence a fair degree of boldness, if not of self-confidence and courage, is needed to bring one to take up and defend a position of one's own with sufficient sensitivity and maturity.

---

[1] R. G. Collingwood, *An Essay on Metaphysics* (Oxford: Clarendon Press, 1940), p. 31.

Until such a point is reached one can find the demands of philosophy quite exasperating. It can easily induce deep melancholy and moods where one looks upon all other questions and interests as trivial and worthless. It can also make one something of a nuisance to one's friends!

It must also be recognized that philosophy can generate enormous internal upheaval. As is well known, Hume found himself so beset with sceptical difficulties about common-sense beliefs that he had to take to playing backgammon with his friends to get relief. Descartes, who found himself totally bewildered by the conflict of opinions, made a virtue of this situation by transforming doubt into a method for arriving at the truth. Even then, however, he was very careful to live by the conventional moral and religious wisdom of his day until he could reach the certainty he desired. Every student who takes philosophy seriously can readily empathize with such experiences and policies.

Whatever the price we pay, there can be no return to a state of naive innocence where we abandon the quest for truth. The development of critical standards is intrinsically valuable. It is important that our beliefs should be true beliefs rather than that they simply give us emotional satisfaction or make other people happy. Hence once we begin, the best policy is to continue and follow wherever the evidence leads.

It has sometimes been asked whether such a policy is really compatible with religious commitment. There seems to be a conflict of duty here. On the one hand, as a rational person, one is called to seek the truth, to be committed only to true beliefs, and to be ready to change one's beliefs in the light of the evidence. On the other hand, as a religious person, one is called upon to believe in God, to be committed to God absolutely, and to continue to believe in God come what may. How can these sets of commitments ever be reconciled? Can one really be a student of philosophy and a religious believer at the same time?

It is important to realize that this is a normative rather than a historical question. It cannot be answered by identifying particular historical examples, say, Aquinas, Descartes, Locke, Berkeley, or Butler, and pointing out that they were devout religious believers. The issue is whether they were *consistent* in being both philosophers and believers. This is not something that historical study alone can settle. Yet the mere fact that some of the greatest philosophers have also been deeply committed religious believers should make us pause before reaching a verdict on this issue. Part of our difficulty is that it is far from easy to determine exactly what the dilemma is. Let us explore this by means of an imaginary dialogue.

RELIGIOUS CERTITUDE

Is the problem here that religious believers are too certain in their beliefs? Well, let us agree that religious believers generally seem to be very certain about what they believe. In paradigm examples, say, of saints and martyrs, they are so certain that they are prepared to die for what they believe. They will not recant but will consider it a privilege to suffer and go to the stake. They will be tenacious to the end.

I can see nothing reprehensible in this. I do not see that there is any philosophical veto to prevent a religious believer from being certain about what he or she believes. Often people admire such a state and may even covet it for themselves. But, it will be said, such certainty involves a degree of commitment which is not warranted by the evidence. There may be some evidence for religious belief, but it can never amount to anything sufficient to license such assurance. At best the available evidence calls for great caution and for tentative commitment.

This objection cannot be met by saying that the level of our certainty is not something under our direct control. This is in fact true; the measure of certainty we have about any particular belief is something that develops automatically. Thus my certainty that $2 + 2 = 4$ or that I have two legs is not something that I create at will. It comes automatically when I review these propositions in my mind. Equally with our doubts. If I am doubtful about this or that proposition, this doubt is something that simply arises as I look at the proposition and consider the evidence for and against it. The critic can agree to all this. What is at issue here is whether we should seek indirectly to change the level of certainty that arises within us. Thus, says the critic, we should try to suppress religious certainty by, say, avoiding the company of saints, staying clear of religious assembly, reading atheistic tracts, or whatever else we happen to find effective. This way we reduce our degree of assent to the appropriate level.

The short reply to our critic is that religious belief is not as unfounded as is assumed by the objection under review. I have sought to show that a cumulative case can be made out which justifies religious belief;[2] therefore it is unnecessary to set about suppressing any certainty which may arise therefrom. How certain one may become will probably depend on the measure of one's religious experience. If one has had something like a mystical experience, then it is highly likely that one will be very certain indeed; equally, if one has experienced what is generally known as the inner testimony of the Holy Spirit. In this experience a person has a deep sense of God's love for herself or himself as an individual. It appears to one that God loves one unconditionally and completely; as a result one looks upon God as a child looks upon a loving father or mother. So long as such experiences as these can be supported by supplementary considerations as I set them out above, then the believer has every right to be certain. I have argued that they can be so supported, hence the believer's certainty is secure.

CERTITUDE AND REASONS

Alas, it will be argued, this is not enough. To satisfy the quest for rationality it is not enough that good reasons can be produced for religious belief. What is crucial is that the believer be aware of those reasons and actually allow his measure of certainty to arise out of those reasons. Once we see this then only a limited few will be

---

[2] See chap. 9.

able to claim the certainty that is appropriate. Only the sophisticated philosopher who has gone over the evidence will be able to claim this coveted prize. The vast majority of simple believers will be deprived of their assurance.

This objection ignores two factors which blunt its edge. First, it assumes that the evidence for religious belief is some kind of esoteric evidence which is worked out by an expert philosopher. This in fact is not the case. Much of the evidence for religious belief is available to the simple believer. The data which constitute the evidence, such as religious experience, general considerations about human nature, general features of the universe, and so forth, are not the products of philosophical discussion. Thus the role of the philosopher is much more modest; he or she seeks to clarify the data and lay bare the nature of the arguments. In the end one must weigh them for oneself and see what happens. To be sure, this does not fully take care of the objection, for some of the data, in particular, considerations related to divine revelation, do depend on expert knowledge. Thus the appeal to the biblical records as embodying divine revelation depends in part on historical judgment about the reliability of the reports about Christ. Hence we need a second and supplementary argument to take this into account.

That second argument is this. The objection in hand sets up conditions of rationality and certainty which we do not normally apply outside religion. Thus we are often very certain about many beliefs which depend on relying on authorities in this or that field of inquiry. We do not normally make it a condition of certainty that we ourselves have gone through all the evidence, made sure that the evidence will stand, and then established that the conclusions really do follow from the evidence. That way we would have to reinvent the wheel every new generation.

It is the case, surely, that many of our beliefs have initially to be taken on trust. We believe things because we read them in books or hear them on television or are told them by our teachers, and so forth. This goes for science as much as for history, geography, beliefs of common sense, and politics. We find ourselves willy-nilly initiated into whole networks of beliefs and come to varying degrees of certainty about them. The idea of starting on our own from scratch and building up our beliefs one upon another in some Cartesian fashion is just absurd. Only philosophers overly impressed by a particular model of belief, as Descartes was by geometry, can take such a theory of belief and certainty seriously. In our normal lives we operate very differently. We take things on trust, test out authorities as best we can, work some things out for ourselves, and generally leave the level of doubt and certainty to take care of itself.

An example will make this clear. Most of the people one meets in the West are liberal democrats. If asked they might say that they were certain that this was the worst form of government except any other, as Churchill put it. Yet when called upon to justify such an assertion they would find it very difficult to satisfy our critic. They would in few cases be able to define or give a clear account of the central concepts involved, or to give a satisfactory outline of the fundamental claims of their system of government, much less to establish it as the most rational way to run a society. The best we might hope for is a rather vague account of what it involves, some reasons for supporting it, and an ultimate appeal to a long tradition of thought which has sought to articulate and defend the tradition as a whole. It would be insensitive to look for more and inappropriate to forbid the level of certainty we normally encounter.

The case is similar in religion. Either religious believers are brought up in the faith and have never known a time when we have not been certain; or they are converted into the faith and as a result of that experience they become certain. Either way they are initiated into a tradition where they take much on trust from those who teach and inform them. Some things they can test out for themselves, but there are limits to what can be done on their own. We all depend to a great degree on the labors of others, for there is a limit to the time that can be given to test out our beliefs. This is not an invitation to intellectual sloth. If the tradition is a healthy one, there will be those within it who will give themselves to testing out its claims. Hence the quest for truth will still go on even though not everyone will participate in this quest first-hand. Thus in most religious traditions there is an enormous scholarly industry, which is funded and supported by the traditions themselves.

TENACITY IN RELIGION

Well and good, the critic may say, but what about the kind of tenacity we see in religion? How can this quest for truth be reconciled to the requirement to give up one's beliefs in the light of contrary evidence? Do not believers characteristically pray that God will strengthen their faith, and do they not say that they should trust in God come what may? Hence religious belief seems to be tenacious and unconditional in a way other beliefs are not.

Before we address this question directly it is important to be very clear on the exact point of the objection. The claim here is not that religious believers hold to their beliefs regardless of the evidence. Some of course do, but this applies to all beliefs rather than just religious beliefs; there will always be those in all areas of life who believe what they have been taught and do not seem to care about evidence. But it need not be the case in religion; there is nothing which makes it a necessary condition of being a religious believer that one believes regardless of the evidence. So this is not the kind of tenacity in mind here.

Nor is it supposed that there is some specific piece of agreed evidence which in itself should lead believers to abandon their faith. The critic is not pointing, say, to the existence of evil and claiming that believers should abandon their theism. If that were the case, then it would have to be argued through in detail in its own right. What is in mind here is a general feature of religious assent which is not easy to describe but which emerges clearly when believers speak of seeking divine aid to keep on believing come what may.

It should be noted immediately that the idea of believing or trusting God come what may is an ambiguous one. It can mean trusting in God no matter what happens or trusting in God no matter what the evidence. The former captures the fact that believers do not normally give up their faith simply because they face trials of one sort or another. Thus they hope that they would not yield and give up their faith were they to suffer severe persecution or were they to face the full measure of pain that human beings presently can endure. Certainly believers in such circumstances hope that they will continue to trust in God come what may. But this is different from continuing to trust in God no matter what the evidence. Many Christians have held, for example, that if Christ is not risen, their faith is in vain and it would be pointless to continue in the faith. Therefore were it shown that Christ had never lived or that he had not been crucified or that he had not been raised from the dead, any idea of trusting in the God who raised Christ from the dead would be incoherent. So there is a clear sense in which religious believers do not keep on believing come what may. Contrary evidence cannot be ignored and is not normally ignored as if it does not matter.

These considerations go a long way in meeting the objection under review. Yet they do not quite fully address the fact that religious believers are peculiarly tenacious in their faith. To understand why this is entirely rational we need to recognize that there are many situations where we normally consider it proper to be tenacious and not abandon our beliefs too quickly. In other words, the critic of religious belief has built up an account of tenacity which is much too brief and simplistic.

We can agree that we ought to abandon many of our beliefs very readily. In fact we will do so automatically. Suppose I believe that Murphy the new librarian is Irish (I automatically take someone with that name to be Irish). Then I meet a friend who says he is an Australian. When I ask for evidence, my friend tells me that he has seen Murphy's passport. Immediately I change my mind. I do not hold tenaciously to my former belief. It is simply a matter of reviewing the evidence and assenting automatically to the new belief. It is like that with many of our beliefs. However, it is not always like this. There are situations where we are and should be much more tenacious. Let us explore these cases in some detail. We shall find that every example we look at throws light on tenacity in religion.

VINDICATING TENACITY

Take first of all those situations where our emotions are liable to smother our beliefs. Here, as C. S. Lewis pointed out, the battle is between faith and reason on one side and emotion and imagination on the other. Lewis explains this and applies it to religious belief as follows:

> A man knows, on perfectly good evidence, that a pretty girl of his acquaintance is a liar and can't keep a secret and ought not to be trusted, but when he finds himself with her his mind loses its faith in that bit of knowledge and he starts thinking, "Perhaps she'll be different this time," and once more makes a fool of himself and tells her something he ought not to have told her. His

senses and emotions have destroyed his faith in what he really knows to be true. Or take a boy learning to swim. His reason knows perfectly well that an unsupported human body will not necessarily sink in water: he has seen dozens of people float and swim. But the whole question is whether he will be able to go on believing this when the instructor takes away his hand and leaves him unsupported in the water—or whether he will suddenly cease to believe it and get in a fright and go down?

Now just the same thing happens about Christianity. I am not asking anyone to accept Christianity if his best reasoning tells him that the weight of the evidence is against it. That is not the point at which Faith comes in. But supposing a man's reason once decides that the weight of the evidence is for it. I can tell that man what is going to happen to him in the next few weeks. There will come a moment when the news is bad, or he is in trouble, or is living among a lot of other people who don't believe it, and all at once his emotions will rise up and just carry out a sort of blitz on his belief. Or else there will come a moment when he wants a woman, or wants to tell a lie, or feels very pleased with himself, or sees a chance of making a little money in some way that's not perfectly fair: some moment, in fact, at which it would be very convenient if Christianity were not true. And once again his wishes and desires will carry out a blitz. I am not talking of moments at which any real new reasons against Christianity turn up. Those have to be faced and that is a different matter. I am talking about moments when a mere mood rises up against it.[3]

A second type of situation where tenacity is very important can be illustrated in this way. Suppose you are a historian and you have been working for years doing research on the origins of the First World War. You have developed an account which you believe best explains the outbreak of war in 1914. You publish a paper or write a book to articulate and defend your position. Suppose now that another historian reads your theory and in response to it points out that your view collapses because it does not square with some evidence that has just recently come to light. What do you do? Do you immediately abandon your position? Surely not. You examine the new evidence, seek to ascertain how cogent it is, and see how far you can account for it within the terms and contours of your own view. You are naturally and quite rightly tenacious. First, you have the faith that your theory is good enough to cope with the new data. You noticed that in the past you had similar problems with known data but could readily cope with them; hence you have some grounds for hope of success once again. Secondly, if you fail to be tenacious, then neither your position nor the new evidence will receive the critical testing it must have if it is to carry conviction. Where there is no decisive proof or disproof, then there is no substitute for carefully considered judgment. Such judgment needs time to evaluate all the evidence sensitively, and you are unlikely to do any evaluating if you abandon your theory at the first sign of trouble. A measure of tenacity is therefore extremely important.

That is certainly so in the case of religious belief. Thus the Christian creed is a complex vision which ranges over a wide field, and there is no quick and fool-proof way to decide if it can cope with this or that objection which may arise in the

[3] C. S. Lewis, *Christian Behaviour* (London: Geoffrey Bles, 1943), pp. 55-56.

multiple contexts in which it must be expressed. It is understandable therefore if believers are tenacious. Objections may have arisen because of inadequate evidence in the first place, or because of an inadequate reading of the tradition, or because of a hasty judgment on the relation between the data on which the objection is based and the relevant part of the tradition against which the objection is made. Without patience and tenacity judgments about these crucial matters would not be made with sufficient thoroughness. To be sure, some believers will abuse their rights by using the required patience as an excuse to believe their creed regardless of the evidence. Thankfully, however, we can generally identify such extreme fideism without too much difficulty, so this need not worry us too much. Besides, the problem is not confined to religious contexts, as we know only too well both in academic and in everyday circles.

A third type of example where tenacity is understandable can be seen in those situations where there are significant gains to be had by continuing to believe as opposed to abandoning oneself to unbelief. Thus imagine that you belong to an army unit fighting a just war, where there are very significant forces ranged against you. Your commander gathers your unit together and tells you that victory is possible. When you look at the evidence you cannot believe this. Yet if you do not believe it there will be no motivation to fight. And you know that if you surrender you will be shot immediately, for in this case you are up against a ferocious enemy who kills all adversaries and takes no prisoners. Hence on the slim chance of winning, you set about reflecting on past victories won against enormous odds in the hope that this will inspire your faith and motivate you to fight and help you to survive. Once your faith is formed, you take steps to hold on to your faith despite the evidence against it. In such circumstances it would surely be an insensitive critic who would say that it was irrational to be tenacious. The stakes are too high for you to be indifferent and careless about what you believe.

The converse of this also applies. If it is acceptable to be tenacious and suppress doubt in cases where much is to be gained, it is equally unacceptable to be tenacious and suppress doubt where much is to be lost. William Clifford supplies a splendid example of the latter.

> A shipowner was about to send to sea an emigrant ship. He knew that she was old, and not over-built at the first; that she had seen many seas and climes, and often needed repairs. Doubts had been suggested to him that possibly she was not seaworthy. These doubts preyed upon his mind, and made him unhappy. He thought that perhaps he ought to have her thoroughly overhauled and refitted, even though this should put him to great expense. Before the ship sailed, however, he succeeded in overcoming these melancholy reflections. He said to himself that she had gone safely through so many voyages and weathered so many storms that it was idle to suppose she would not come safely home from this trip also. He would put his trust in Providence, which could hardly fail to protect all these unhappy families that were leaving their fatherland to seek for better times elsewhere. He would dismiss from his mind all ungenerous suspicions about the honesty of builders and contractors. In such ways he acquired a sincere and comfortable conviction that his vessel was thoroughly safe and seaworthy; he watched her departure with a light

heart, and benevolent wishes for the success of the exiles in their strange new home that was to be; and he got his insurance-money when she went down in mid-ocean and told no tales.[4]

Great care needs to be exercised in applying the lessons of these examples to religious belief. Some have argued that the consequences of belief and disbelief are so momentous that any steps should be taken in order to ensure that one acquires religious belief. This surely goes much too far, for it would turn religious belief quite literally into make believe and would cut the fragile threads between belief and evidence. Yet religious faith may be indirectly related to ultimate human destiny. This is the least that must be said on this difficult and controversial topic. Therefore it is entirely rational for religious believers not to abandon themselves to unbelief at the first sign of intellectual difficulty. The issue here is not whether one takes certain steps to gain any religious beliefs; the issue is whether one continues to believe despite the evidence. If we allow that considerations about gains and losses have a bearing on the rationality of tenacity in cases of nonreligious belief, and we clearly do, then good reason must be given why such considerations should not apply in the case of religious belief.

A fourth consideration which has a direct bearing on the rationality of tenacity stems from the fact that changes in our beliefs may have very significant consequences for our attitudes to other people. Take, for example, the common-sense belief in free will. Suppose you hold this belief and believe that it is incompatible with determinism. Your belief is not just an abstract, theoretical conviction; it has deep repercussions for your attitudes towards, and dealings with, other people. Suppose now you meet a sophisticated determinist who begins to persuade you that hard determinism has much more in its favor than you previously recognized. Indeed you feel very tempted to convert to the determinist position. Yet you tread very warily because you find the moral consequences quite drastic. If you really switch from free will to determinism, there will have to be a major overhaul in your attitudes and dealings with others. In fact, there will have to be a major re-evaluation of the conception you have of your own person and your past action. Part of the reason why you hesitate is that you are not sure how far such consequences should be taken into account in the evaluation of the determinist option. In any case, you are surely correct to think twice about embracing a theory which has such significant implications. Yet your tenacity is not some kind of blind adherence to what you want to believe. You will have reason to believe in free will when you think about it, and determinism has by no means been shown to be wholly unassailable.

There are obvious parallels here to religious belief. Religious belief does make a difference to what we hold to be morally valuable and to the kind of person we become in life. Hence it is natu al for there to be tenacity in adhering to a tradition of thought and action which has nourished and sustained us through perplexity and crisis and which has provided significant moral guidelines for living. Indeed it should

---

[4]William Clifford, *Lectures and Essays,* vol. II, ed. F. Pollock (London: Macmillan, 1879), pp. 177–78.

surprise us if people changed their religion as readily as they changed their shirts. Such hasty conversions are rightly regarded as superficial and fleeting; they show little of the profundity and complexity of genuine religious commitment.

TENACITY AND TRUST

Of all the relevant examples which throw light on tenacity in religion, none is more important than the fifth and last one we shall consider. This is because the heart of religious commitment, at least in the Judaic-Christian tradition, is trust in a Divine Person rather than mere adherence to a set of propositions. To see the full significance of this for tenacity, let us look at a nonreligious example.

Suppose you have a friend whom you know and love dearly. One day you get a telephone call which informs you that your friend has been arrested for a dreadful crime. You are naturally shocked and insist that your friend just could not do that sort of thing. When you talk to the police, you can understand why he has been arrested; there is evidence against him which cannot be denied. You talk to your friend and get his side of the story. He totally denies the charge. Yet he cannot prove that he did not commit the crime, nor can he explain away the evidence. He simply protests that although it does point to him, he is still totally innocent. You may well be tempted to become agnostic about his guilt or innocence in such a situation; yet it is entirely understandable if you resist such temptation and retain the belief that he is innocent. You may even remain in this state should your friend be taken to court and found guilty.

What is significant in this case is the role that personal loyalty plays in tenacity. Change of belief is not just a matter of weighing up evidence, although that is very important and can never be ignored. Change in belief can be seen here as disloyalty to a dear and trusted friend. Hence tenacity is to be expected. It is simply the expression of personal loyalty, a virtue which can only be made manifest in difficult and trying circumstances.

Belief in God in the Christian tradition is akin to such personal loyalty. Given what God is said to have done in Christ, the believer trusts in God unconditionally. God's love and care has known no limits; therefore it evokes a deep sense of loyalty in the believer. To abandon one's faith, therefore, is not just a matter of revising one's beliefs. It is also giving up one's trust in one's heavenly Father. There are dimensions to belief and unbelief in this context which make tenacity entirely rational. If abandoning belief involves lack of trust, then this is bound to influence one's response to contrary evidence. One will be more likely to say, for example, that God remains hidden and to stay a believer than to say that he does not exist and to convert *immediately* to agnosticism or atheism.

It is not at all easy to do full justice to the way the believer may view the situation compared to the outsider. What is fundamentally involved is that loss of faith is seen as a failure to endure and remain loyal to God. J. R. Lucas speaks eloquently of this in the following passage.

It is an age of doubt. And it seems to me that doubt is the form in which many Christians in the present age are called upon to share in the sufferings of mankind after the example of our Lord. And the reason why so many Christians are unable to believe is just this: that doubt is the Cross that Christians of today are called to bear. It is likely then that those Christians whom Christ is calling to share in his sufferings, are going to be called not in the way they had expected, not to some spectacular life or heroism or death of martyrdom, but to the secret agony of indecision, the silent torture of separation. It was as much in the Garden as on the Cross that Christ showed us what was in store for us, and showed that he was at one even with modern, intellectual, sceptical man: and any Christian who is serious in his professed willingness to participate in the passion of our Lord, must be prepared to go to Gethsemane as well as Golgotha, and to be called not to martyrdom but to wrestle with unknown doubts and strange horrors in the dark night of the soul.[5]

Lucas's suggestive remarks bring out the complexity of religious commitment. There is a tenacity here which we do not usually find elsewhere. Indeed we find that believers seek divine aid so that they may not lose their faith. This is entirely sensible in the circumstances, for grace is said to be available to cope with every trial and tribulation. Thus believers ask God to sustain them when they are tempted to allow their emotions to smother their belief, or when they are going through those wilderness wanderings during which the heavens seem to be like brass and God seems to have forsaken them. So no wonder they are tenacious. The situation becomes even more understandable when we remember that it takes time to test out religious beliefs, especially so when there may be critical gains and losses at stake and when change of belief will have significant moral consequences.

CONCLUSION

Yet it must be repeated that this is not a situation where belief can be held regardless of the evidence. Just as trust in a friend does not hang in midair but is related to a network of considerations which established that trust in the first place, so trust in God has its foundations in those considerations which first brought one to faith. For Christians faith is a gift of God nurtured by hearing God's word in its manifold operations but most especially in Christ. Should that word be eroded by counterevidence, then faith will simply dissolve. Thus should the believer come to see that his or her religious experience is illusory, or that Christ never lived, or that the biblical writers were thoroughly deceptive in their intentions, or that the concept of God is really incoherent, or that the free-will defense is a complete failure, or that religion is only truly understood by Marx, the believer's faith would quite rightly be eroded. Praying wou d be well-nigh impossible, for one might no longer believe in God and seeking to produce belief by indirect means would be pious make believe. Tenacity would be dishonest and reprehensible. So nothing I have

[5] J. R. Lucas, "Doubt: A Sermon," in *Freedom and Grace* (London: SPCK, 1976), pp. 121–22.

said should be construed as supporting such a stance. My aim has been the more modest one of making logical sense of the kind of tenacity which we do typically find in religion and defending it against philosophical objection. I see no reason therefore why a person cannot be a keen student of philosophy of religion and a committed religious believer. Philosophy and faith are not necessarily rivals who must constantly be at war with each other. They can be mutually enriching friends.

For Further Reading

Numerous suggestions for further reading can be found in the footnotes to individual chapters. The following are some general works and collections of significant articles.

CAHN, STEPHEN M., and SHATZ, DAVID, eds., *Contemporary Philosophy of Religion*. New York: Oxford University Press, 1982. An advanced collection of papers.

DAVIES, BRIAN, *An Introduction to the Philosophy of Religion*. New York: Oxford University Press, 1982. A short readable introduction.

FLEW, ANTONY, *God and Philosophy*. London: Hutchinson, 1966. A vigorous presentation of the sceptical case.

FLEW, ANTONY, and MACINTYRE, ALASDAIR, eds., *New Essays in Philosophical Theology*. London: SCM; New York: Macmillan, 1955. A very valuable set of essays which have been very influential.

FERRÉ, FREDERICK, KOCKELMANS, JOSEPH J., SMITH, JOHN E., *The Challenge of Religion: Contemporary Readings in Philosophy of Religion*. New York: The Seabury Press, 1982. A collection of articles generally sympathetic to the claims of religion.

HICK, JOHN, ed., *The Existence of God*. New York: Macmillan, 1964. Provides useful sources for the evaluation of the theistic arguments.

————, *Faith and the Philosophers*. New York: St. Martin's Press, 1966. A collection of papers read at a conference at Princeton Theological Seminary by philosophers and theologians.

_____, *Classical and Contemporary Readings in the Philosophy of Religion,* 2nd ed. Englewood Cliffs, N.J.: Prentice-Hall, Inc., 1970. A comprehensive volume of readings.

_____, *Philosophy of Religion,* 3rd ed. Englewood Cliffs, N.J.: Prentice-Hall, Inc., 1983. A short readable introduction.

MACKIE, J. L., *The Miracle of Theism: Arguments For and Against the Existence of God.* Oxford: Clarendon Press, 1982. A comprehensive analysis and rebuttal of the arguments for the existence of God.

MITCHELL, BASIL, ed., *Faith and Logic: Oxford Essays in Philosophical Theology.* London: George Allen and Unwin, 1957. A set of influential essays by a group of Oxford philosophers.

_____, *The Philosophy of Religion.* (Oxford Readings in Philosophy). London: Oxford University Press, 1971. A very valuable collection of papers.

NIELSEN, KAI, *An Introduction to the Philosophy of Religion.* London: Macmillan, 1982. Concentrates on problems of religious language.

OWEN, HUW PARRI, *Christian Theism: A Study in Basic Principles.* Edinburgh: T. & T. Clark, 1984. Concentrates on philosophical aspects of central Christian doctrines.

PENELHUM, TERENCE, *Religion and Rationality: An Introduction to the Philosophy of Religion.* New York: Random House, Inc., 1971. A comprehensive introduction to the philosophy of religion.

ROWE, WILLIAM L., *Philosophy of Religion. An Introduction.* Belmont, California: Wadsworth Publishing Company, Inc., 1978. A valuable introduction.

STEWART, DAVID, *Exploring the Philosophy of Religion.* Englewood Cliffs, N.J.: Prentice-Hall, 1980. Readings from classical and contemporary sources.

SWINBURNE, RICHARD, *The Existence of God.* Oxford: Clarendon Press, 1979. A recent rigorous presentation of the case for theism.

Index